AMAZON HACKS

AMAZON HACKS

Paul Bausch

Beijing · Cambridge · Farnham · Köln · Paris · Sebastopol · Taipei · Tokyo

Amazon Hacks
by Paul Bausch

Printed in the United States of America.

Published by O'Reilly & Associates, Inc., 1005 Gravenstein Highway North, Sebastopol, CA 95472.

O'Reilly & Associates books may be purchased for educational, business, or sales promotional use. Online editions are also available for most titles (*safari.oreilly.com*). For more information, contact our corporate/institutional sales department: (800) 998-9938 or *corporate@oreilly.com*.

Editor:	Rael Dornfest	**Production Editor:**	Emily Quill
Series Editor:	Rael Dornfest	**Cover Designer:**	Hanna Dyer
Executive Editor:	Dale Dougherty	**Interior Designer:**	David Futato

Printing History:

August 2003: First Edition.

ISBN: 0-596-00542-3

[C]

Contents

Credits

About the Author

Paul Bausch is an accomplished Web Application Developer, and is a cocreator of the popular weblog software Blogger (*http://www.blogger.com/*). He cowrote *We Blog: Publishing Online with Weblogs* (John Wiley & Sons), and posts thoughts and photos almost daily to his personal weblog onfocus (*http://www.onfocus.com/*).

Contributors

The following people contributed their hacks, writing, and inspiration to this book:

- Tim Allwine is a Senior Software Engineer at O'Reilly & Associates. He develops software for the Market Research group, various spidering tools that collect data from disparate sites (including Amazon.com), and is involved in the development of web services at O'Reilly.
- Jeff Barr handles web services evangelism and developer relations for Amazon.com. In his spare time he collects RSS newsfeeds at *www.syndic8.com*. He's happily married and the father of five, including a second-generation hacker.
- Erik Benson is the Technical Program Manager of Personalized Merchandising at Amazon.com. He runs allconsuming.net (*http://www.allconsuming.net/*) and has a weblog at erikbenson.com (*http://www.erikbenson.com/*).
- Duke Bhuphaibool studied Fine Arts in preparation for the grueling rigors of Amazon.com web development. He, his lovely wife, and their five rambunctious golden retrievers enjoy daily tea in the shade of their home, Plum Cottage. Duke is currently trying to figure out the difference between a bamboo flute and a back scratcher.

- Bruce Bracken works as a Lead Web Development Engineer in the Search & Browse group at Amazon.com. After collegiate studies in English and Computer Science, he joined the ranks of Amazon.com to further his exploration of search and browse technologies. He co-founded the JavaScript advisory group to help standardize JavaScript use on Amazon.com. Bruce also took eighth place in a Mellow Yellow drinking contest when he was seven.
- James Crowley turned to web development after failing in the high-risk, low-reward field of medieval manuscript study. After completing graduate school he decided that he would much prefer the task of helping people find what they want to buy on the Internet. He is happily married and the proud owner of a lot of books.
- Joanna Daneman is a baby boomer, grew up in Pennsylvania, and attended the University of Michigan. She works in the biotech field and lives in Delaware. Her hobbies are reading, listening to and playing music, and knitting. She also happens to be an Amazon Top Reviewer.
- Rael Dornfest (*http://www.raelity.org*) assesses, experiments, programs, writes, and edits for O'Reilly & Associates. He has edited, coauthored, and contributed to various O'Reilly books. He is program chair for the O'Reilly Emerging Technology Conference. In his copious free time, Rael develops bits and bobs of freeware, including the Blosxom weblog application (*http://www.blosxom.com*), and maintains his raelity bytes weblog.
- Cyrus Durgin is an Information Security Engineer and software developer at Amazon.com. He spends his spare time house-hunting in Seattle with his sweetie.
- Alf Eaton (*http://www.pmbrowser.info*)
- Kevin Hemenway (*http://www.disobey.org*), coauthor of *Mac OS X Hacks*, columnist for MacTech, and better known as Morbus Iff, is the creator of disobey.com, which bills itself as "content for the discontented." Publisher and developer of more home cooking than you could ever imagine, he gets sleepy whenever he drinks merely one cup of coffee.
- Adam Kalsey (*http://kalsey.com*)
- Jonathan Leblang is VP of Web Services at Alexa Internet (*http://www.alexa.com*) and is working on integrating Alexa's web information into the Amazon platform. Prior to Alexa, he was at Amazon for three and a half years, where he launched Wish List, Honor System, and many other site features. Before joining Alexa, Jonathan was one of Amazon.com's first customers and a beta tester of the Amazon.com web site, where he found the infamous "negative quantity" bug (you could order a nega-

tive number of books, and Amazon would owe you money). He lives in Menlo Park, CA.

- Chris McGarel has been a Senior Software Engineer with Cape Clear (*http://capescience.capeclear.com/*) for three years. Prior to that, he worked as a Technical Consultant in Java and web technologies with Cap Gemini Ernst & Young. Chris is also a guitarist and composer, holding a postgraduate diploma in Music Technology from Queen's University in his native Belfast, Northern Ireland.
- Myk Melez has been working with Mozilla since 1999, when he started using it as a DHTML application platform. In 2000 he wrote ForumZilla (*http://forumzilla.mozdev.org/*), a weblog reader built with XUL and other Mozilla application framework technologies, and since 2001 he has worked as a web application developer for mozilla.org (*http://www.mozilla.org/*).
- Nelson Minar likes hacking stuff on the Internet, particularly distributed and decentralized systems. He is a software engineer at Google.
- Sean Nolan founded Software Poetry (*http://www.softwarepoetry.com/*), and was the Chief Technical Officer for drugstore.com, where he was the fifth employee and led the design and implementation of their award-winning e-commerce systems. While at drugstore.com, Sean was honored as one of the nation's Premier 100 IT Leaders for 2001 by Computerworld magazine.
- Reid Philpot lives and works in London, England. He runs Exploding Fist (*http://www.explodingfist.com/*), a popular, award-winning weblog that focuses on new media and technology.
- Mark Pilgrim (*http://diveintomark.org*) is the author of *Dive Into Python*, a free Python book for experienced programmers, and *Dive Into Accessibility*, a free book on web accessibility techniques. He works for Mass-Light, a Washington, DC–based training and web development company where, unsurprisingly, he does training and web development. But he lives outside Raleigh, NC, because it's warmer.
- Jim Roche has worked as a Software Test Engineer for Amazon.com for four years. Since initially joining the Auctions team, he has worked in some degree with most of the software teams in the company. His dog, Maxine, holds court on the seventh floor of the company headquarters, where she makes sure that no one is loitering unnecessarily or wasting food.
- Scott Windsor is a code monkey for Amazon.com in Seattle, WA. In his spare time he collects odd PEZ dispensers and tries to take over the world.

- Dan Wood is chief architect of Watson (*http://www.karelia.com/watson*).
- David Yarbrough is a Senior Systems Engineer at Amazon.com in Seattle, WA.
- Michael Yoon (*http://michael.yoon.org*) has worked in the software industry since 1995, most recently at ArsDigita Corporation (now part of Red Hat). He has a BA in English.

Acknowledgments

To my wife, Shawnde, thanks for all of the love, feedback, and support, and for reminding me to step away from the computer once in a while.

I'd like to thank everyone who generously contributed their hacks, ideas, time, thoughts, and code—with a special thanks to Jeff Barr at Amazon for contributing all of these in abundance. Thanks to Colin, Rob, and everyone at Amazon who provided insider tips and tricks. And thanks to Amazon itself—this book wouldn't exist without the Amazon API, the door they've opened for developers.

For going through the code and double-checking the technical details, thanks to Todd Larason.

Thanks to Tim O'Reilly for making it possible for me to work on this project. And thanks to everyone at O'Reilly who made this book a reality.

And thanks to Rael—a consummate hacker—for the inspiration, guidance, and help every step of the way.

Foreword

Building groundbreaking technology is at the core of the Amazon.com mission. This focus on technology brought us to Amazon, gets us up in the morning, and occasionally keeps us here late at night. And we're not alone. From the edgy garage band selling its first album through the Associates program to the Fortune 500 retailer watching its e-commerce division grow with Amazon Services to the scrappy entrepreneur building a business from the ground up on Marketplace, Amazon.com has become much more than a web site. In fact, we see such abundant activity and opportunity for growth on the Amazon.com platform that we consider it more an ecosystem than a web site.

This Amazon.com ecosystem is creating opportunities not just for online shoppers, but for so many different individuals and businesses of all shapes and sizes that this book comes at an ideal time. There are tools and tips in this book that appeal to a wide variety of audiences: online shoppers, web site owners, sellers of products, and software developers. We hope that *Amazon Hacks* will spur innovation and help people get the most from the ecosystem we all create collectively every day. We've seen the other O'Reilly & Associates Hacks Series books fly off Amazon's virtual shelves by the thousands, know first-hand how far they can reach—to more than 220 countries and counting—and can't wait to see how this book will help people use the ecosystem to surprise us.

Amazon Hacks is much more than a guide for getting the most out of Amazon.com as it is today—it is a call to all true hackers out there to innovate on the platform. Please keep in mind that some of these hacks will continue to evolve. You can always find the current ingredients for any serious software development—the Amazon.com API—at *http://www.amazon.com/webservices*.

The ingenious applications that developers have built in the last year using the rich content and features is just the tip of the iceberg of what is to come. The more innovative technologists working within the Amazon.com ecosystem and APIs—the very participation this book helps drive—the closer we will get to the ever-elusive "Day 2" of the Internet.

By lowering the barriers to entry and experimentation on top of the Amazon platform, we invite true hackers to extend and enhance the platform for all to enjoy—including us!

—Amazon.com Technology Team
June 30, 2003
Seattle, WA

Preface

When Amazon.com opened its virtual doors on July 16, 1995, it was just one among several online booksellers. As Amazon embraced the technology to categorize and display millions of books in one space, people embraced the ability to search for and purchase books in a new way. The experience of building a successful business based on an open system like the Web has influenced Amazon throughout its history.

Amazon has consistently pushed the technology envelope in their quest to provide a satisfying, personalized experience for their customers. What started as a human-edited list of product recommendations has morphed into a sophisticated computer-generated recommendation engine that tailors product choices for tens of millions of individuals by analyzing their purchase history and the patterns of other Amazon customers. As the Web evolved into a two-way space for discussion and community, Amazon developed features that let anyone post information and advice about products. They embraced the marketing power of other web sites by giving site owners a portion of sales they sent to Amazon. They opened their billing system and catalog to third parties and turned their web site into a marketplace, connecting buyers and sellers.

With this history of opening their technology to others, it shouldn't have been a surprise when on July 16, 2002, Amazon released a free Web Services interface that gave developers programmatic access to Amazon's vast collection of product and customer data. With this interface, Amazon combined their core features of recommendations, affiliate marketing, and marketplace commerce into a single technology *platform* that can be used to build applications and businesses.

Why Amazon Hacks?

The term *hacking* has a bad reputation in the press. They use it to refer to someone who breaks into systems or wreaks havoc with computers as their weapon. Among people who write code, though, the term *hack* refers to a "quick-n-dirty" solution to a problem, or a clever way to get something done. And the term *hacker* is taken very much as a compliment, referring to someone as being *creative*, having the technical chops to get things done. The Hacks Series is an attempt to reclaim the word, document the (good) ways people are hacking, and pass the hacker ethic of creative participation on to the uninitiated. Seeing how others approach systems and problems is often the quickest way to learn about a new technology.

Amazon Hacks is not intended to be merely an exhaustive explanation of Amazon's features. Instead, it's intended to highlight some lesser-known features, show some tricks for working with Amazon efficiently, and document ways to access Amazon programmatically. Developers are already creating new features for Amazon through the Amazon API, and it is this book's intent to convey some of their creativity and excitement, inspiring the hacker in you.

How This Book Is Organized

To become an Amazon power user, you'll have to learn about all the core features and how they relate to one another. The hacks are loosely organized by topic within each chapter, and the book itself is divided into several chapters by core feature:

Chapter 1, *Browsing and Searching*
: The ability to find a product among the millions available is a fundamental feature of Amazon. The search box on Amazon's home page is only one way to navigate the catalog. This chapter starts simple, by showing you how to find any product's Amazon Standard Item Number (ASIN); moves on to ways of fine-tuning search results and browsing categories; and ends with integrating Amazon searches into your web browser.

Chapter 2, *Controlling Your Information*
: From the moment you sign into your Amazon account to the moment you close your browser window, Amazon is collecting information to personalize your experience with the site. This chapter's hacks show ways to access, control, and fine-tune that information.

Chapter 3, *Participating in the Amazon Community*
By allowing customers to communicate directly with each other, Amazon has become one of the largest community sites on the Web. This chapter describes ways to participate in the Amazon community, shows how you can integrate Amazon community features into your own web site, and demonstrates some ways to work with those features programmatically.

Chapter 4, *Selling Through Amazon*
Amazon has opened its billing, inventory, and marketing infrastructure to anyone who wants to sell through their site. They've gone from a single-vendor commerce site to a space where entrepreneurs can build businesses. This chapter focuses on how you can make money by efficiently using the sales systems Amazon has in place.

Chapter 5, *Associates Program*
You can earn money by linking to Amazon from your web site. Amazon's affiliate program has spawned a cottage industry of niche sales sites, and has become a way for independent web site owners to earn some money for their efforts. The hacks in this chapter focus on the ways you can integrate an existing web site with Amazon, and maximize your referral fees in the process.

Chapter 6, *Amazon Web Services*
Amazon is extending its presence from a commerce platform to an information and technology platform. Answering developers' calls for programmatic access to its data, Amazon has released a programming interface that allows other applications to integrate with Amazon. The hacks in this chapter range from tips and code snippets to get you started with the API to more developed examples of application integration.

How to Use This Book

You can read this book from cover to cover if you like, but for the most part, each hack stands on its own. So feel free to browse, flipping around to whatever sections interest you most. If you're a programming "newbie," you might want to try some of the easier hacks first, and then tackle the more extensive ones as you get more confident.

Conventions Used in This Book

The following is a list of the typographical conventions used in this book:

Italic
: Used to indicate new terms, URLs, filenames, file extensions, directories, commands and options, and program names, and to highlight comments in examples. For example, a path in the filesystem will appear as */Developer/Applications*.

`Constant width`
: Used to show code examples, the contents of files, or the output from commands.

`Constant width bold`
: Used for emphasis and user input in code.

`Constant width italic`
: Used in examples and tables to show text that should be replaced with user-supplied values.

Color
: The second color is used to indicate a cross reference within the text.

↵ A carriage return (↵) at the end of a line of code is used to denote an unnatural line break; that is, you should not enter these as two lines of code, but as one continuous line. Multiple lines are used in these cases due to page-width constraints.

You should pay special attention to notes set apart from the text with the following icons:

This is a tip, suggestion, or general note. It contains useful supplementary information about the topic at hand.

This is a warning or note of caution.

The thermometer icons, found next to each hack, indicate the relative complexity of the hack:

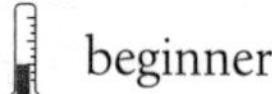

beginner moderate expert

How to Contact Us

We have tested and verified the information in this book to the best of our ability, but you may find that features have changed (or even that we have made mistakes!). As a reader of this book, you can help us to improve future editions by sending us your feedback. Please let us know about any errors, inaccuracies, bugs, misleading or confusing statements, and typos that you find anywhere in this book.

Please also let us know what we can do to make this book more useful to you. We take your comments seriously and will try to incorporate reasonable suggestions into future editions. You can write to us at:

O'Reilly & Associates, Inc.
1005 Gravenstein Hwy N.
Sebastopol, CA 95472
(800) 998-9938 (in the U.S. or Canada)
(707) 829-0515 (international/local)
(707) 829-0104 (fax)

To ask technical questions or to comment on the book, send email to:

bookquestions@oreilly.com

The web site for *Amazon Hacks* lists examples, errata, and plans for future editions. You can find this page at:

http://www.oreilly.com/catalog/amazonhks/

For more information about this book and others, see the O'Reilly web site:

http://www.oreilly.com

Got a Hack?

To explore Hacks books online or to contribute a hack for future titles, visit:

http://hacks.oreilly.com

CHAPTER ONE

Browsing and Searching

Hacks 1–12

Using Amazon.com is easy. Even novice web users with a bit of time and curiosity can find exactly what they're looking for and complete a transaction fairly effortlessly. Beneath this user-friendly exterior, though, is a powerful application that helps people discover information, voice opinions, participate in a community, and sell things.

First and foremost, Amazon.com is a web *application*—not to be confused with simple, flat, static pages. In reality, each "page" at Amazon is generated right when you request it, personalized for your viewing pleasure and particular interests. Amazon can track which products you've viewed and display a list of similar or related products. Or it can include an item from your Wish List on another item's product detail page. When browsing the site, most of the factors that make the experience unique are hidden from view. But the nature of the Web—which for the most part consists of simple, text-based pages addressed by URL—exposes some of these factors, and allows you to play with the settings embedded in URLs and pages to exert some minor control over the application and the pages it cooks up and serves you.

Amazon Product Pages

The core activities at Amazon.com are browsing, searching, and purchasing products. If you've spent any time at Amazon.com, then you know it has millions of products in dozens of categories beyond the books for which it is primarily known. Thinking of the site in terms of individual pages is overwhelming; thinking in terms of page *templates* is much more manageable. A template is like a document shell that can be used over and over again to display information. The shell is filled with whatever information is requested at the time. In these terms, Amazon has only a handful of templates, including search results, category home pages, and product detail pages. Looking at the structure instead of the information makes it much easier to understand how Amazon operates.

Every Amazon page offers *information* for your perusal, and *actions* you can perform. Information includes book titles, prices, customer reviews—anything that adds to your knowledge of products and helps you make a buying decision. Actions include adding a product to your cart or Wish List, posting a review, rating an item, making a purchase—anything that explicitly provides Amazon.com with input or a directive.

You can think of a product detail page as the *home page* of a particular item at Amazon. It's the workhorse of Amazon.com, and studying what's available there provides insight into almost all of the site's features. Figure 1-1 shows a typical product detail page, this one for *Google Hacks*, a sibling of the book you're reading.

Figure 1-1. Amazon detail page

What you'll see first on any product detail page is an image of the product (if available) and quick product details:

Product Name or Title

The most important product detail, of course, is what the item is called. A book might have extra information, like its subtitle or series, in its title. An electronic gadget might include a manufacturer's model number.

Author(s)

Books list all of the authors, and sometimes editors and illustrators. Other products may list the manufacturer in place of the author. CDs include the artist.

Prices: List price, Amazon price, third-party sellers lowest price

Prices shown include the manufacturer's list price, the Amazon.com price, and the lowest third-party price **[in "Understanding Amazon's Sales Programs" in Chapter 4]**.

Availability

This is an estimate of how soon Amazon can ship the product. In some cases, Amazon can't ship the product at all because it's out of print.

Edition, if a book

This refers to the binding of a book, usually *Hardcover* or *Paperback*. Other editions include *School & Library Binding*, *Large Print*, *Leather Bound*, *Audiobook*, etc.

Beyond learning more about the product, there are several actions you can take from a product detail page:

Add to Cart, Wish List, or Registry

Just like a real-world shopping cart, you can add items into a holding area and buy them as a group later—minus the wobbly wheel. And unlike a real store, you can pick up your cart where you left off last time. Wish Lists **[Hack #18]** and registries also hold items, but you have the option of making them public so other people can buy things for you.

Start the process of selling your item

From the product detail page you can start the process of listing your used version of that item for sale on Amazon **[Hack #49]**.

More Buying: Pickup Now, Used & New

You can also find and order the product from third parties—anyone from other Amazon customers to other bookstores **[in "Understanding Amazon's Sales Programs" in Chapter 4]**.

Write an online review

Hate a certain product? Love it? Want to warn others or recommend something else? You can start voicing your opinion **[Hack #27]** from the detail page for that product.

Even further down the page, you'll find more product information:

Media Type

This is the format the product is in: paperback, CD, DVD, etc. You may find additional information such as the number of pages in the book or the item's dimensions.

Manufacturer/Publisher
: This is the name of the company that produced the item.

ASIN
: An ASIN is a unique ID for every product, and being able to find this ID **[Hack #1]** is key for many of the hacks in this book.

Average Customer Rating
: As people write reviews, they also give the item a rating of 1–5 stars. The average rating is how the group feels about the product **[Hack #32]**.

Sales Rank
: This is the sales position relative to other items at Amazon.com. An item with a sales rank of 1 is the best-selling item on Amazon. An item with a sales rank of 1,822,605 is a bit further down the line. With sales rank, lower is better.

Top five similar items
: Customers who bought the item you're looking at also purchased similar items, and Amazon lists the most popular related items. You'll also find information that other customers have left about an item.

Customer Buying Advice
: Along the lines of similar purchased items, this is advice from other customers **[Hack #40]** about other products that may be better than or go well with the product you're looking at.

Where the item is uniquely popular (if available)
: If a product is particularly popular in a certain geographic location or at an organization, Amazon will list that information **[Hack #44]**.

Editorial, Spotlight, and Customer Reviews
: Highlighted editorial reviews are from professional journals or Amazon's in-house editors. Customer reviews are from other Amazon customers. Reviews rated favorably by other customers become spotlight reviews.

Top three user-created How-Tos
: Also known as "So You'd Like To...", these are guides **[Hack #37]** to any topic written by other Amazon.com customers. If you'd like to learn how to make a martini or "chill out" properly, you'll probably find a guide for it at Amazon. If a guide contains the product you're looking at, it might show up as one of the top three on the product detail page.

Top three Listmania! lists the item is on
: Similar to guides, these are lists of books **[Hack #41]** created by Amazon customers.

Browsing/Searching by similar subjects
: This is a list of categories **[Hack #8]** and keywords that the product is categorized under.

All of this information can tell you as much about Amazon.com as it can about the product you're viewing. You can see that Amazon believes in providing lots of data, making actions readily available, connecting users with each other, and providing several paths to more products.

Find a Product's ASIN

Many hacks and features depend on knowing a product's Amazon ASIN; here are a few ways to track it down.

ASIN stands for Amazon Standard Item Number, and every product Amazon sells has one. It's a number that's unique to Amazon, and it is at the center of the Amazon universe. Many pages and features rely on the ASIN, so the first skill needed in tweaking Amazon is the ability to hunt down and gather ASINs.

Finding the ASIN for a book is easy because it's the same as the ISBN. ISBN stands for International Standard Book Number, and is a unique numerical ID given to every book published since 1972. The key word is *standard*, because the ISBN allows the book to be identified across varied systems. Libraries, publishers, bookstores, and anyone who handles books use ISBNs to identify them. Not only does each book have a unique ISBN, but each edition of the book has its own ISBN. That way there's never confusion between the hardback and paperback versions of a book.

So where is this magical ISBN number? Turn this book around, look at the back cover, and find the UPC barcode on the back. Usually printed just above the UPC is "ISBN" followed by 10 digits, as in Figure 1-2.

Figure 1-2. UPC symbol with ISBN highlighted

You can also usually find the ISBN printed somewhere on the copyright page at the front of the book. Sometimes the digits are separated by dashes, but only the numbers are important. This book's ISBN is 0-596-00542-3.

Finding ASINs for other products, such as DVDs, CDs, or even toys, isn't quite as straightforward. Amazon doesn't use any standard method of identification for other products, so each ASIN is unique to Amazon. A quick way to find the ASIN is to search for the item on Amazon and go to its product detail page. The ASIN will be printed on the page, as shown in Figure 1-3.

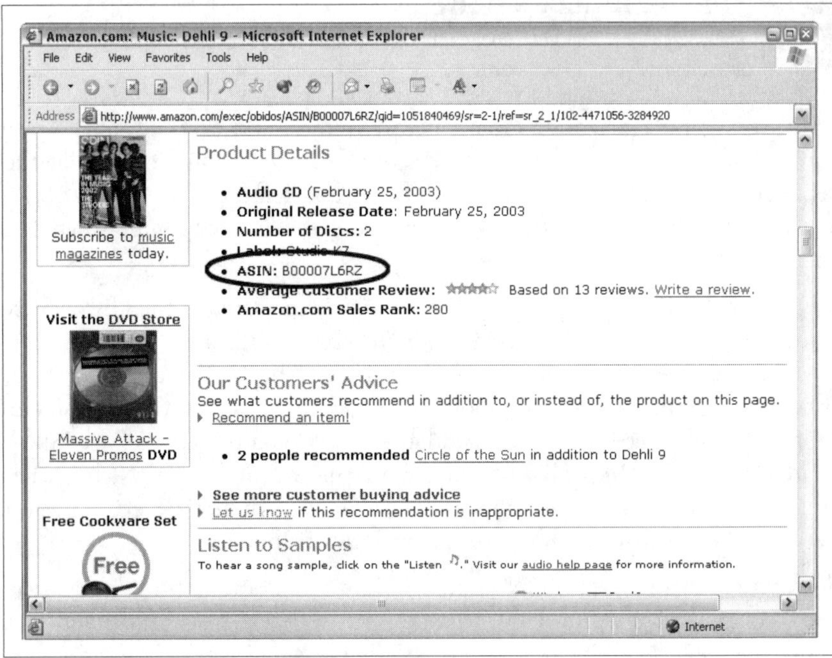

Figure 1-3. ASIN listed in Amazon Product Details

If the ASIN can't be found anywhere on the page, you can always find it in the URL. Examine the address of any product detail page, and you'll likely find a series of 10 letters and numbers separated from other sections of the URL by slashes. They're often preceded by *ASIN*, as in Figure 1-4.

Figure 1-4. Amazon Product Detail URL

#2 Find a CD's ASIN with the UPC

Instead of searching by Title or Artist, you can find an ASIN for a CD by using the UPC.

Almost every product has a UPC (Universal Price Code). Amazon doesn't offer product searches by UPC through their main web site, but they do offer it for music products through their Web Services.

Following is a simple bit of JavaScript code that brings up a CD's product detail page based on a UPC.

To run this script you'll just need a developer's token **[in "What You Need" in Chapter 6]** and Internet Explorer for Windows.

The Code

Save this piece of HTML as a text file on your computer. Name it something appropriate (*cd_asin.html* will do nicely).

```
<html>

<head>

<title>Find a CD's ASIN</title>

<script language="JavaScript">

function getDetailPage(upc) {

    var xmlhttp = new ActiveXObject("Msxml2.XMLHTTP");

    xmlhttp.Open("GET", "http://xml.amazon.com/onca/xml2?t=webservices-↵
20&dev-t=insert developer'stoken&UpcSearch="+upc+"&mode=music&type=lite↵
&f=xml", false);
    xmlhttp.Send( );
    var response = xmlhttp.responseXML;
    if (response.selectSingleNode("/ProductInfo/ErrorMsg")) {
        alert(response.selectSingleNode("/ProductInfo/ErrorMsg").text);
    } else {
        var asin = response.selectSingleNode("/ProductInfo/Details/Asin")↵
.text;
        document.location = "http://amazon.com/o/ASIN/" + asin;
    }
}

</script>

</head>
```

```
<body>

<form>
    <input name="upc" type="text" size="25">
    <input type="button" value="Go"
    onClick="getDetailPage(document.forms[0].upc.value);">
</form>

</body>

</html>
```

Running the Hack

Point your browser at the HTML page, *cd_asin.html*, enter a UPC code into the form, and click the Go button. If a match is found, you'll be taken to that CD's product detail page where you can jot down the ASIN.

#3 Jump to a Product Using Its ASIN

Once you have a product's ASIN, you can jump straight to its product detail page.

Having a product's ASIN means you're never more than one click away from its product detail page. The easiest path to the page is to put the ASIN in any Amazon search box, as seen in Figure 1-5.

Rather than displaying a list of search results for you to choose from, you'll be taken directly to the product's detail page.

You can also skip the searching altogether and just type in the URL. Once you're familiar with the URL pattern, you can plug in any ASIN and get the page you're looking for. Either of these URLs will take you to the product detail page for the corresponding ASIN:

```
http://www.amazon.com/exec/obidos/ASIN/insert ASIN here
http://www.amazon.com/exec/obidos/tg/detail/-/insert ASIN here/
```

It is Amazon's prerogative to change their URL syntax at any point. Amazon.com is a constantly evolving application, and its interfaces change from time to time. You can always find the latest information about linking to Amazon through their Associates site (*http://www.amazon.com/associates/*).

If these URLs aren't bringing up a product detail page, you may have an item that isn't in Amazon's catalog. Chances are good that a book is in the catalog of at least one of Amazon's properties; it just may not be available at Amazon.com. Try changing the base URL to *amazon.co.uk* for books from

Figure 1-5. Searching by ASIN

the UK, or *amazon.ca* for books from Canada. Amazon's international sites all follow the same URL conventions:

```
http://www.amazon.co.uk/exec/obidos/ASIN/insert ASIN here/
http://www.amazon.ca/exec/obidos/tg/detail/-/insert ASIN here/
```

#4 Create Shorter URLs

Shortening a long Amazon URL is just a matter of knowing where to put the ASIN.

If you've ever tried to send a link to an Amazon product detail page to your friends via email, you know what a hassle those long Amazon URLs can be. Most email programs wrap the text at 72 characters and end up breaking the URL, often making it unusable. Next time, instead of copying and pasting the URL exactly as you see it, try cropping it a bit so the lines won't wrap. Here's what a URL copied directly from Amazon looks like:

```
http://www.amazon.com/exec/obidos/ASIN/0596004478/qid%3D1049157816/↵
sr%3D11-1/ref%3Dsr%5F11%5F1/104-2773718-4336742
```

For those of you keeping score at home, that's 114 characters! The core piece we're looking to dig out and preserve, the ASIN **[Hack #1]**, is the only bit really needed to target the right product page. Everything after the 10-digit ASIN is garbage—session tracking and other bits and bobs used by Amazon—when we just want to link to the page. So we can instantly make a shorter link by removing the excess baggage:

```
http://www.amazon.com/exec/obidos/ASIN/0596004478/
```

That's much better. We're down to 50 characters, well within the non-wrap zone of most email clients. But if you really want to push the character-limit envelope, there's a little-known way (contributed by Cyrus Durgin at Amazon) to shorten the URL even further. You can replace `exec/obidos` simply with `o`, as in:

```
http://amazon.com/o/ASIN/0596004478
```

That brings us down to 35 characters. (OK, so maybe taking out the `www.` was cheating, but 39 is still impressive.) Now the URL is suitable for email, instant messages, or even writing out long-hand!

#5 Link Directly to Product Images

Just as product detail URLs follow a certain pattern, image URLs are just as predictable.

Just as every page has a URL, so too does every product image. Finding the URL is fairly easy in most browsers. In Internet Explorer on Windows, right-click the image and choose Properties. Once you have the image URL, you can bring it up in the browser by placing it in the address bar. Some browsers—Safari for Mac OS X, for instance—make this a single step via the Open Image in New Window context-menu item.

Amazon image URLs are just as dynamic as Amazon pages. By understanding the image URL pattern, you can find images for products based on their ASIN and customize from there.

For instance, the following standard image URL brings up a standard product image, the *Google Hacks* book cover in Figure 1-6:

```
http://images.amazon.com/images/P/0596004478.01._PE30_PI_SCMZZZZZZZ_.jpg
```

If you're getting good at spotting ASINs **[Hack #1]**, you'll see this product's ASIN in the URL. By changing it, you can find the image for other products (see Figure 1-7):

```
http://images.amazon.com/images/P/0596004613.01._PE30_PI_SCMZZZZZZZ_.jpg
```

Keep in mind that you can link to an image of any product that Amazon sells, as long as you have the ASIN. The following URL shows an iPod MP3 player from Amazon's *Electronics* catalog (see Figure 1-8):

```
http://images.amazon.com/images/P/B00006FDRB.01._PE30_PI_SCMZZZZZZZ_.jpg
```

Figure 1-6. Google Hacks product image

Figure 1-7. Linux Server Hacks product image

Figure 1-8. iPod product image

These images have something else in common: a *30% off* graphic in the lower-right corner. With closer examination of the URLs, you can see what might be affecting the graphic. The section `PE30` corresponds with the discount amount. What happens if we change this value?

```
http://images.amazon.com/images/P/0596004605.01._PE50_PI_SCMZZZZZZZ_.jpg
```

The `PE50` changes the discount to 50%, as seen in Figure 1-9.

Figure 1-9. Mac OS X Hacks product image, with 50% Discount

Just because you *can* change the discount information on the image doesn't mean you *should*. Giving false information about products will only upset potential customers and potentially Amazon.

What if you didn't want a discount at all? Take out the discount designation for a discount-free image like that shown in Figure 1-10:

```
http://images.amazon.com/images/P/0596004605.01._SCMZZZZZZZ_.jpg
```

Figure 1-10. Mac OS X Hacks image with no discount

Different sizes of images are also predictable and can be requested with a URL. The portion of the URL with all those ZZZ's specifies its size. The codes and their associated sizes are listed in Table 1-1.

Table 1-1. Image codes and their associated images sizes

Image code	Image size
THUMBZZZ	40 x 60 pixels, very small
MZZZZZZZ	93 x 140 pixels, standard size
LZZZZZZZ	317 x 475 pixels, very large

The actual pixel size will vary by item, but these are good approximations for books.

By looking at the URLs for different products, you may even pick up other variable style codes. Throwing a TT in the mix (as Duke Bhuphaibool at Amazon suggested) tilts the product image, shown in Figure 1-11:

```
http://images.amazon.com/images/P/0596004478.01.20TTZZZZ.jpg
```

Figure 1-11. Google Hacks image, tilted

And TR sets it straight again:

```
http://images.amazon.com/images/P/0596004478.01.20TRZZZZ.jpg
```

Most product images on Amazon are JPEG files, but there is a way to force the GIF format:

```
http://images.amazon.com/images/P/0596004478.01._FMgif_ZZZZZZZZZ_.gif
```

Unfortunately, you're stuck with the medium size. There isn't a way to request a larger GIF.

#6 Switch to a Text-Only Amazon

Make the Amazon.com web site leaner and meaner by taking away the images.

Now that you know some of the secrets behind Amazon image URLs, you can make those images go away! Why in the world would anyone want to do that? Well, if you're one of those unfortunate souls who still use a modem to connect to the Web, eliminating images can mean a big boost in speed. It's also handy if you're scraping Amazon with a script. Fewer images means less HTML and fewer bytes transferred.

There are two methods for going all-text. The first involves a little URL customization. Adding a /t/ after any product ID **[Hack #1]**, Wish List ID **[Hack #18]**, or List ID **[Hack #41]** gives you the text-only version of the page:

```
http://amazon.com/o/ASIN/0596004478/t/
```

From there, any links you follow will be in text-only mode. If you'd rather start from the home page, you can use this URL, also with the trailing /t/:

```
http://www.amazon.com/exec/obidos/subst/home/home.html/t/
```

Or, to go extremely minimalist, you could use the version intended for Pocket PCs in a standard browser, as shown in Figure 1-12:

```
http://www.amazon.com/pocketpc/
```

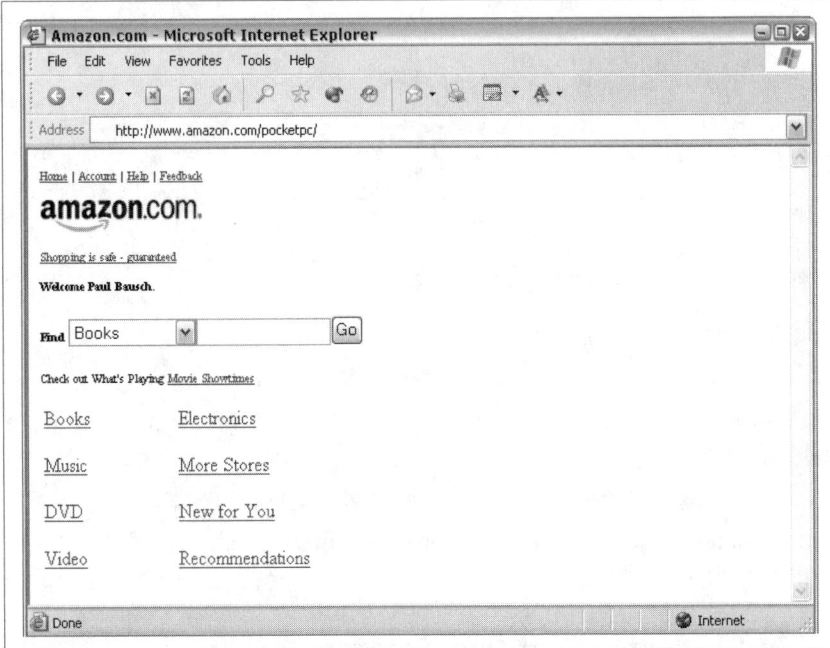

Figure 1-12. Amazon PocketPC version in a standard web browser

#7 Take Amazon Anywhere

Amazon.com is just as on-the-move as you are, and you can access Amazon on your cell phone or PDA if you know where to look.

"Amazon Anywhere" refers to Amazon's system of providing service to alternate devices. Amazon wants their service to be available to any device that connects to the Internet. Beyond the standard web interface written with HTML, they offer their site in a variety of other formats for different devices like cell phones and PDAs. You can find a detailed description at *http://www.amazon.com/anywhere*.

The URL to visit Amazon.com via a mobile device is often already available via your cell/service provider's site. If you'd like to visit these directly, though, you can key in one of these URLs:

- Cell phones: *http://amazon.com/phone*
- PDAs: *http://amazon.com/pocketpc* or *http://amazon.com/mypalm*

If you don't have a WAP phone and you'd just like to get a sense of how the alternate site works, try a web-based WAP emulator. Yospace (*http://www.yospace.com/spedemo.html*) has a good emulator that can impersonate quite a few specific phones. Figure 1-13 shows how Amazon Anywhere appears on the Sony T68i emulator (and the T68i phone itself).

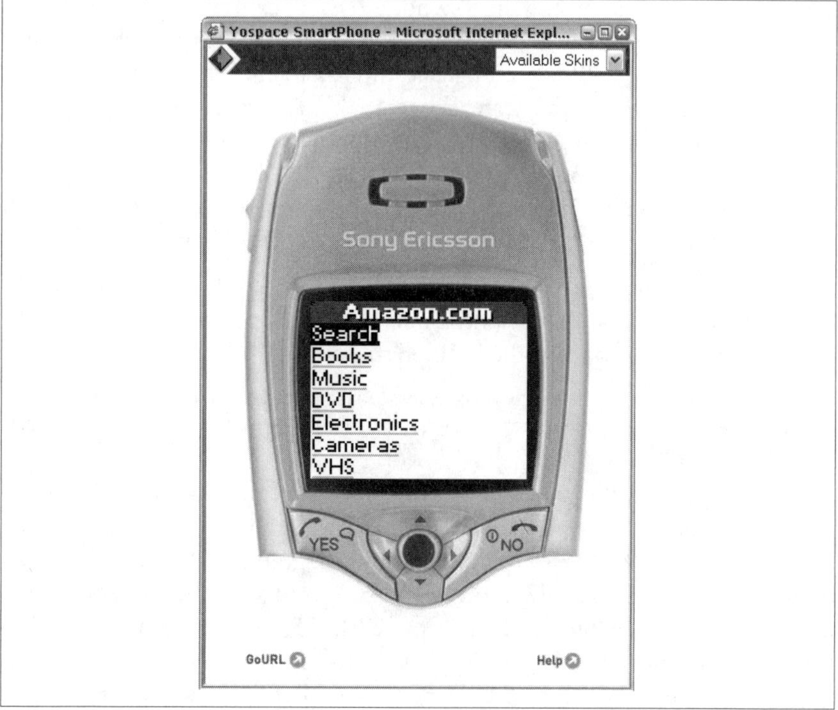

Figure 1-13. Yospace SmartPhone WAP emulator

Though it's a very simple interface, most of Amazon's features are present even in this lo-fi version. You can browse, search for, and buy products; you can also find product information, average customer review ratings, and purchase circles **[Hack #44]**. You also have access to all of Amazon's product lines including cell phones—which means you can buy your next cell from your current cell phone.

#8 Browse and Search Categories with Browse Nodes

Use browse node IDs to find books based on categories.

Just as Amazon has alphanumeric IDs for every item they sell, they also have ID numbers representing each subject area to which items belong. Once you know the browse node IDs for subject areas you're interested in, you can bypass the standard search forms and perform narrow, specialized searches from a URL.

Finding Browse Node IDs

The first trick is finding the browse node IDs. They're not quite as easy to come by as ASINs because they don't appear in URLs as frequently. They also don't seem to follow any logical pattern, so there's no way to guess. Instead you can browse the "category tree" that Amazon has made available through their Associates program. You don't have to be an associate to browse the tree, however; you can reach it at *http://associates.amazon.com/exec/panama/associates/resources/build-links/amazon-recommends/browse-bestsellers.html*.

Once at this page you'll see a list of the highest product category levels: Baby, Books, Camera, Cell Phones, and so on. Click Books and you'll start to see browse node codes in the URL; in this case:

```
http://associates.amazon.com/exec/panama/associates/resources/build-links/↵
amazon-recommends/browse-bestsellers.html/086-9645301-8693838?t=&node=1000↵
&mode=browse-books
```

The only section we're concerned with is the `node=` and its value. The node here is 1000 and represents all books. On this page the categories are refined further under books: Arts & Photography, Biographies & Memoirs, Business & Investing, etc. Click on the entry "Science Fiction & Fantasy." Once again you'll see a new node value in the URL, 25. You can continue to drill this way and find IDs. As you do so, you'll soon find yourself a few levels deep, for example, All Products → Books → Subjects → Science Fiction & Fantasy → Fantasy → Magic & Wizards. Checking the URL, the node ID in this case is 16205.

Browse node IDs are constantly in flux. As product hierarchies change and evolve, the browse nodes evolve along with them. Remember that browse node IDs are temporary guides, not permanent markers. It's a good idea to frequently check to make sure any browse node IDs you're using are still being used by Amazon.

Not all browse node IDs are available through this interface, but it's a good place to start looking for them.

Perform a Keyword Search Within a Browse Node

If you'd like to limit a search to a narrowly defined category, you can do so through the URL if you know the browse node. As with finding product detail pages, it's just a matter of knowing the proper URL patterns (supplied by Bruce Bracken and James Crowley at Amazon) and filling in values in the proper places. Using our previous example, we can perform a search for "merlin" inside of browse node 16205, "Magic & Wizards." The URL is:

```
http://amazon.com/exec/obidos/search-handle-url/index=books↵
&field-keywords=merlin&field-browse=16205
```

Instead of finding all products across every category with the keyword "merlin", this URL shows us only those books within a specific category.

You can also search for multiple keywords by separating them with punctuation. The pipe symbol (|) means "or," and a comma (,) means "and." So if you wanted to find every book within "Magic & Wizards" that contains either "king" or "merlin", separate the terms in the URL like so:

```
http://amazon.com/exec/obidos/search-handle-url/index=books↵
&field-keywords=merlin|king&field-browse=16205
```

If you'd like to find every book that has both terms:

```
http://amazon.com/exec/obidos/search-handle-url/index=books↵
&field-keywords=merlin,king&field-browse=16205
```

Both the "or" and "and" operators also work if you want to browse with multiple browse node codes. Say you want to list books that contain the keyword "merlin" in both the "Magic & Wizards" (16205) category or "Epic Fantasy" (16197) category. You would combine them with the pipe:

```
http://amazon.com/exec/obidos/search-handle-url/index=books↵
&field-keywords=merlin&field-browse=16205|16197
```

If you want to find books that are specifically listed in both of those subject areas, you would use the "and" operation with a comma:

```
http://amazon.com/exec/obidos/search-handle-url/index=books↵
&field-keywords=merlin&field-browse=16205,16197
```

Find Every Item Within a Browse Node

Instead of narrowing down your search results, suppose you'd like to see *every* product within a specific category. The URL is the same as the keyword search; you just replace the keyword with a dash (-) followed by any string of characters. So the following URL would return every book within the "Magic & Wizards" category:

```
http://amazon.com/exec/obidos/search-handle-url/index=books↵
&field-keywords=-junk&field-browse=16205
```

Sort Your Browse Node Search Results

By default, the search results for any of the URLs above are returned in the order of "featured items"—those items Amazon most wants you to know about. You could always re-sort your results with the drop-down menu Amazon provides, as shown in Figure 1-14.

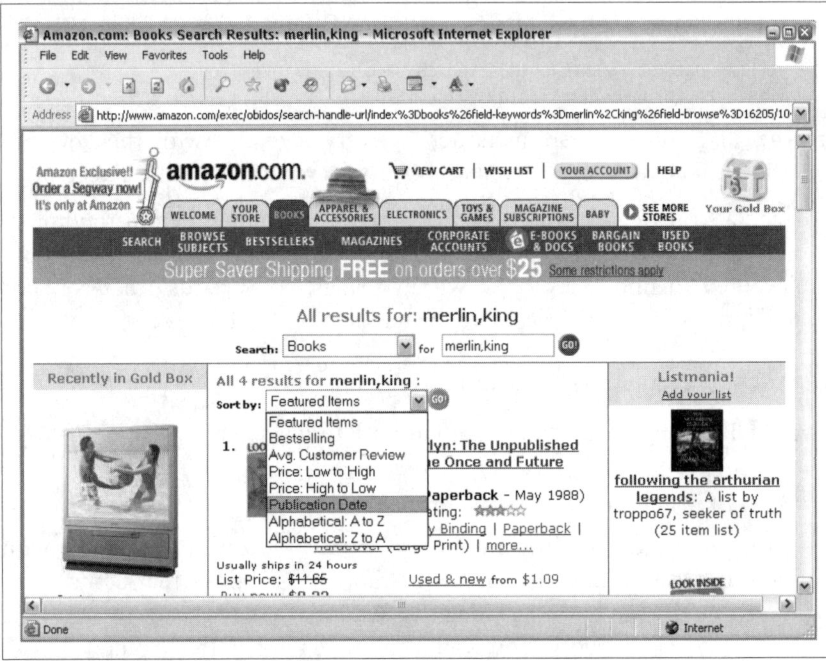

Figure 1-14. Sorting Amazon search results

But you can save yourself a step by sorting results in your initial request. The rank variable allows you to specify the sort. The values available for books are summarized in Table 1-2.

Table 1-2. Specifying sort order using the rank URL variable

Rank value	Sort order
pmrank	Featured Items
salesrank	Best-Selling
reviewrank	Average Customer Review
pricerank	Price (Low to High)
-pricerank	Price (High to Low)
daterank	Publication Date
titlerank	Alphabetical (A-Z)
-titlerank	Alphabetical (Z-A)

All you need to do is append the sort method to the end of the URL. To get every item from within the "Magic & Wizards" browse node, sorted by publication date, use the following URL:

```
http://amazon.com/exec/obidos/search-handle-url/index=books↵
&field-keywords=-junk&field-browse=16205&rank=daterank
```

Each variable/value pair in a URL is separated by ampersands (&). If you're experiencing problems when you add a new variable, make sure it's separated from the previous variable/value pair with an &.

#9 Power-Search for Books

Fine-tune your book searches with the Advanced Search form and Power Search queries.

The search form on the lefthand side of the Amazon home page is the most widely used way to find items. A couple of keywords can get you surprisingly close to what you're looking for. But if you'd like to do more sophisticated searches, you'll have to use the Advanced Search form or learn Amazon's Power Search syntax.

Advanced Search

Amazon offers an Advanced Book Search form on their web site at *http://amazon.com/exec/obidos/ats-query-page*. This form allows you to search for a specific title, author, subject, ISBN, or publisher. And you can narrow your search by format, reader age, language, or publication date.

The query in Figure 1-15 will return all books by O'Reilly with the word "Mac" in the title.

Power Search

Beyond Advanced Search, there's a way to perform even more finely tuned searches of the product database: Power Search. A Power Search uses a special query syntax to define what you're looking for. The syntax consists of field/value pairs that are put together with connecting words like "or" or "and." To perform the same query, we'd include the `publisher` and `title` fields with the appropriate values:

```
publisher:O'Reilly and title:Mac
```

To run the search, paste this into the Power Search form at the bottom of the Advanced Search page at *http://amazon.com/exec/obidos/ats-query-page#powersearch*.

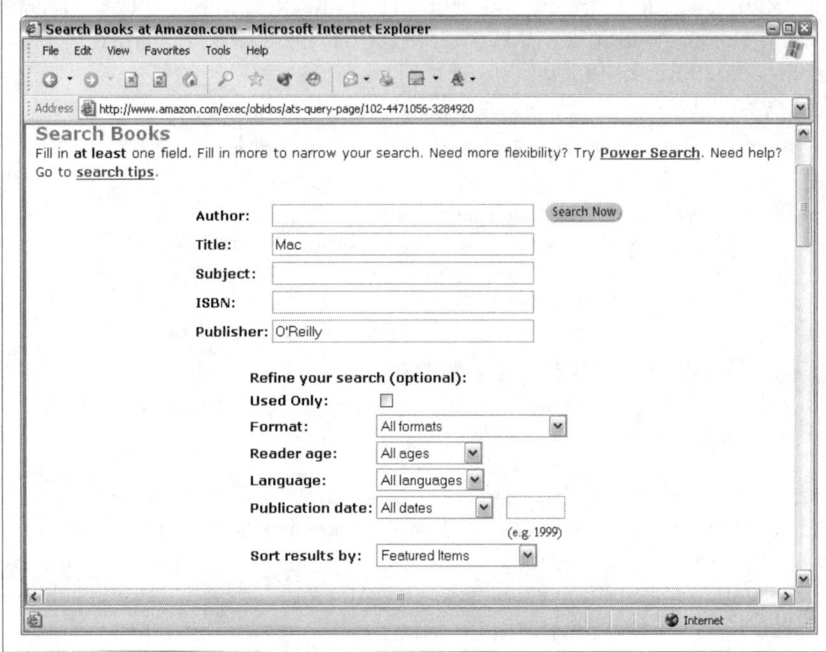

Figure 1-15. Amazon Advanced Search page

There are several fields available to help narrow your search:

```
asin
author
author-exact
author-begins
isbn
keywords
keywords-begin
language
pubdate - [before, during, after] date
publisher
subject
subject-words-begin
subject-begins
title
title-words-begin
title-begins
```

With all of these options, you can see how queries could quickly become very specific. Let's say we wanted to find not only O'Reilly's books with the subject "Mac," but also all O'Reilly books where the title starts with "Mac":

```
publisher:O'Reilly and (subject:Mac or title-begins:Mac)
```

Grouping sections of the queries with parentheses and specifying "and" or "or" allows you to do much more than is possible through the standard Advanced Search form. Just having access to the keywords field is a big advantage. Let's say you're interested in more than just the books *about* Macs that O'Reilly publishes—you're interested in any book remotely related to Macs. That's a perfect use for keywords:

```
publisher:O'Reilly and keywords:Mac
```

Or, just to show how specific you can get, here's another query:

```
publisher:O'Reilly and keywords:Mac and pubdate:before 2003 and not ↵
title-begins:Mac and not subject:Mac
```

If you're getting the hang of Power Searches, you'll see that this query searches for all O'Reilly books with the keyword "Mac" published before 2003, where the title doesn't actually start with "Mac" and the book isn't directly about the subject "Mac".

Power Search URLs

Once again, you can bypass the form altogether. Make sure your Power Search query is URL encoded [Hack #92] and then you can add it into a standard search URL by adding the prefix power%01:

```
http://www.amazon.com/exec/obidos/search-handle-url/ix=books↵
&fqp=power%01publisher%3AO%27Reilly%20and%20keywords%3AMac&sz=100
```

You may notice some other variables in this URL. Specifically, sz can be useful to play with: it lets you specify the size of the result set. The default is 10, but if you want more to be returned in a single page, increase it to something larger (in this case, 100).

#10 Search Amazon from the IE Address Bar

A fast way to search Amazon via your Windows Internet Explorer address bar.

The Internet Explorer address bar is usually where you enter a URL to browse to a web site. This hack adds the ability to do Amazon searches from the same place. Instead of visiting the site, finding the search form, typing your query, and hitting the button, you can simply type amzn [*search term*] to get the same results.

Setting It Up

This is extremely simple to set up, and just requires adding an entry to your Windows registry. Instead of mucking around with a registry editor, you can put the required settings into a *.reg* file. Once there, it's just a matter of double-clicking to install. Here are the steps:

1. Close any open Internet Explorer windows.
2. Open up Notepad (Start → Programs → Accessories → Notepad) and add the following code:

```
Windows Registry Editor Version 5.00

[HKEY_CURRENT_USER\Software\Microsoft\Internet Explorer\SearchUrl\amzn]

@="http://www.amazon.com/exec/obidos/external-search/↵
mode=blended&keyword=%s"
```

3. Save the file as *AmazonSearch.reg* on your desktop.
4. Double-click the file and confirm that you want to add the information to your registry.

Restart Internet Explorer, and your Amazon search shortcut should be available.

Running the Hack

Once installed, it's just a matter of typing amzn in your address bar followed by your search term, as shown in Figure 1-16. It works the same way as entering a URL. Just hit Enter or click the Go button.

Figure 1-16. Searching Amazon from the IE address bar

Hacking the Hack

Once you know this method of adding searches to your address bar, you can create your own specialized searches. The key pieces of the registry file are the key name (amzn in this hack), the search URL, and the term you're searching for (represented by %s in the registry file). By altering these values, you can create entirely different searches. You just need some knowledge of Amazon search URLs and some imagination.

If you want to create an address bar search for ASINs, the steps are the same as those above with a few modifications:

1. Alter the prefix name in *AmazonSearch.reg*. Instead of using the key name `amzn`, create a new title that you'll remember (`asin`).
2. Change the URL. You know the URL template for jumping directly to a book if you have the ASIN **[Hack #3]**.
3. Place the `%s` in the proper position in the URL. This variable represents everything entered after the title.
4. Save the file as *ASINSearch.reg* and double-click.

The new registry file should look something like this:

```
Windows Registry Editor Version 5.00

[HKEY_CURRENT_USER\Software\Microsoft\Internet Explorer\SearchUrl\asin]

@="http://www.amazon.com/exec/obidos/ASIN/%s/"
```

After restarting Internet Explorer, you'll have a new search option in the address bar (see Figure 1-17).

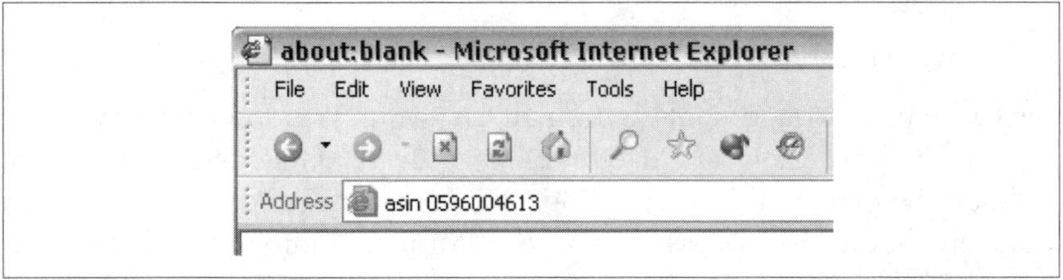

Figure 1-17. Searching Amazon using the ASIN

—*David Yarbrough*

#11 Search Amazon from Any Web Page in IE

Searching Amazon from any web page can be as simple as highlighting and clicking with an Internet Explorer context menu.

If searching Amazon from your address bar **[Hack #10]** isn't your style, you may find it helps to have context. Imagine this: you're reading an article on your favorite news web site about the latest tech trend: *overclocking*. It sounds like something you'd like to try, and you wonder if there are any books on the subject. You highlight the word, right-click, choose "Search Amazon" from the menu, and a new window opens with your answer. You can make this happen with a little JavaScript and a new registry entry.

The Code

First, the JavaScript. This bit of code will open a new browser window and plug the highlighted text into a URL. This code needs to be in a file somewhere on your computer where it can be accessed from the browser, and won't be deleted in a fit of spring cleaning. You could even create a new folder for it, *c:\scripts*. If you have another location in mind, be sure to change any references to *c:\scripts* in the following code.

Create a file called *AmazonSearch.html* and add this code:

```
<script language="JavaScript">
var searchURL = new String("http://www.amazon.com/exec/obidos/↵
external-search/mode=blended&keyword=");

var w = window.external.menuArguments;
var d = w.document;
var s = d.selection;
var r = s.createRange( );
var term = new String(r.text);

window.open(searchURL + term);
</script>
```

Save it in the *c:\scripts* directory.

Next you need to add some information to your Windows registry to let Internet Explorer know where to find *AmazonSearch.html*, and when exactly it should be executed. You could open up a registry editor and add values manually, but it's just as easy to put the information into a *.reg* file and add it by double-clicking. Create a new file called *AmazonContext.reg* and add the following code:

```
Windows Registry Editor Version 5.00

[HKEY_CURRENT_USER\Software\Microsoft\Internet Explorer\MenuExt\↵
Search Amazon]

@="c:\\scripts\\AmazonSearch.html""contexts"=dword:00000010
```

Backslashes, like those in filesystem paths, need to be escaped as double-slashes (\\) in registry entry files.

Save the file on your desktop, double-click it, and confirm that you want to add the new registry information. This setting adds a right-click menu entry called "Search Amazon" that will appear whenever text is highlighted. It also points to the JavaScript file and will execute it when the highlighted entry is clicked.

Running the Hack

Be sure to shut down all running copies of Internet Explorer. Once restarted, try browsing to any web page with text. Highlight any word and click your right mouse button. You should see the new entry as shown in Figure 1-18.

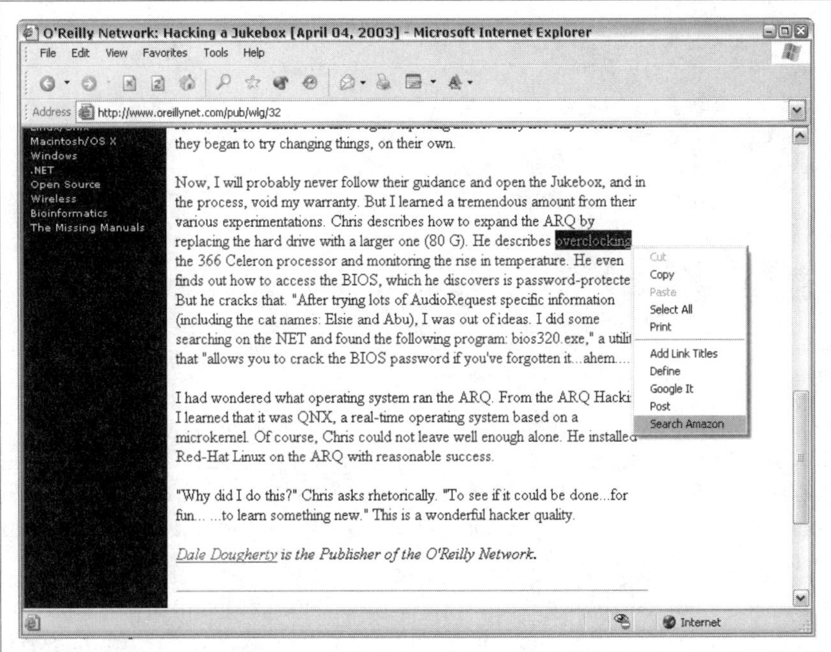

Figure 1-18. Search Amazon context entry

Click "Search Amazon" to open a new window with your search results for that term as shown in Figure 1-19.

#12 Add an Amazon Sidebar Search to Mozilla

Mozilla's built-in search engine sidebar provides a unique way to organize search results from several sources. Using Amazon's API you can add Amazon as a source with a few quick steps.

The Amazon Web Services API has opened up a direct door to Amazon's catalog. Developers can now search and browse Amazon programmatically, and reformat search results in any way they see fit.

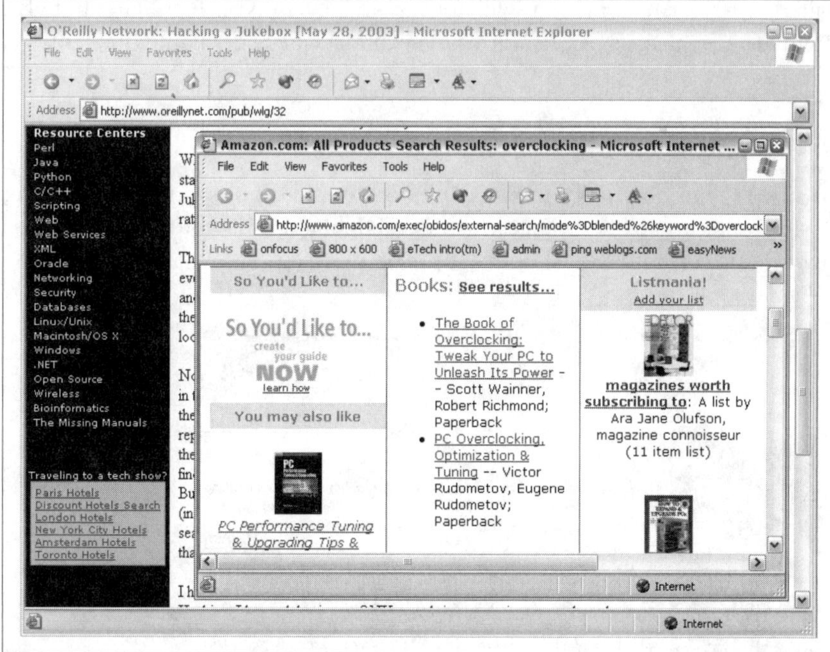

Figure 1-19. Amazon Search Results window

Mozilla (*http://www.mozilla.org*) is an alternative web browser that has been designed from the ground up to be an application platform for working with the Web. Mozilla's sidebar offers a way to search several different search engines. For example, Mozilla comes with Google and dmoz.org installed in the sidebar, as you see in Figure 1-20.

With one search field, you can search these sites individually or mix the results from both at the same time—all the while keeping the results separate from the main browser window. It's a new way to search that removes the problem of paging back and forth between search results, or trying to keep track of several open windows.

The Mozilla-Search plug-in interface allows you to add your own entry to the list of search engines available. Although Google and dmoz.org are there when you install Mozilla, that doesn't mean your search engine selection can't grow. It just takes some understanding of both Amazon and Mozilla to get them talking to each other. Once you set up this hack, you'll have an entry for Amazon in your list of available search engines.

Figure 1-20. Mozilla sidebar search engine selection

The Code

There are two pieces to setting up the sidebar. One file resides locally and tells Mozilla how to search Amazon. The other file resides on a public server and formats the search results for Mozilla.

The local file uses the Mozilla-Search plug-in definition format. Create a file called *amazon.src* and add the following code:

```
# Amazon Search for Mozilla
#
# Adds Amazon.com as an option to Mozilla's
# sidebar search.
#
# Creation:  May 2003

<search
 name="Amazon.com"
 description="Search for products at Amazon.com"
 method="GET"
 action="http://xml.amazon.com/onca/xml3"
 queryEncoding="utf-8"
 queryCharset="utf-8"
>
```

```
<input name="BlendedSearch" user>
<input name="dev-t" value="insert developer tag">
<input name="t" value="insert associate tag">
<input name="type" value="lite">
<input name="f" value="http://example.com/amazon_search.xsl">

<interpret
 browserResultType="result"
 charset="UTF-8"
 resultListStart="<ul>"
 resultListEnd="</ul>"
 resultItemStart="<li>"
 priceStart = "<b>"
 priceEnd = "</b>"
>

</search>
```

This code creates a new search option for Amazon.com in Mozilla's sidebar. It defines the URL to use for searching, as well as any querystring attributes. The `<interpret>` tag performs some pattern matching in the resulting HTML page so Mozilla knows how to format the results for the sidebar. This code tells Mozilla to start treating the file as search results when it sees `<ul>`, and stop when it sees `</ul>`. The code uses `<li>` to determine when something is an individual search result.

The action URL in this case performs a search at Amazon's Web Services, which returns XML. In the querystring, defined by `<input name="f">`, a file on your server is specified to turn that XML into HTML.

The transformation from Amazon's XML to the HTML necessary for the Mozilla search is handled by an XSL file. Add the following code to a file called *amazon_search.xsl*:

```
<?xml version="1.0" encoding="ISO-8859-1" ?>
<xsl:stylesheet xmlns:xsl="http://www.w3.org/1999/XSL/↵
Transform" version="1.0">
<xsl:output indent="yes" media-type="text/html"/>
<xsl:template match="/">
<html>
<head>
<title>Search Results</title>
</head>
<body>
<font face="verdana" size="2">
    <img src="http://g-images.amazon.com/images/G/01/associates/navbar2000/↵
logo-no-border(1).gif"/>
    <h2>Search Results</h2>
    <ul>
    <xsl:apply-templates select="//ProductInfo/Details"/>
    </ul>
```

```
</font>
</body>
</html>
</xsl:template>

<xsl:template match="ProductInfo/Details">
    <li>
        <a><xsl:attribute name="href">http://www.amazon.com/o/ASIN/<xsl:↵
value-of select="Asin"/>/ref=nosim</xsl:attribute>
        <xsl:value-of select="ProductName"/><br/>
        </a>[<xsl:value-of select="Catalog"/>] -
        <b><xsl:value-of select="OurPrice"/></b>
   </li>
</xsl:template>

</xsl:stylesheet>
```

This stylesheet produces a simple HTML page of search results. Note that the XSL has the `<ul>` and `<li>` elements that Mozilla is expecting for the search defined in *amazon.src*.

Running the Hack

You have two files now, and each needs to go to a specific place to set up this hack. The plug-in definition file, *amazon.src*, needs to be placed in the *searchplugins* directory of your Mozilla installation. On Windows, the default directory is *C:\Program Files\mozilla.org\Mozilla\searchplugins*. Once the file's in place, you should have "Amazon" as an option in your list of search engines.

The XSL file, *amazon_search.xsl*, should be uploaded to a publicly available web server. Once uploaded, find the URL and make sure the `<input name="f">` value is set to that URL in *amazon.src*.

With those two files in place, your Amazon sidebar search should be ready for action! Just bring up the sidebar by hitting F9 in Mozilla. You should see a list of search engines. Make sure Amazon.com is checked, type in a search term, and click Search. You should see a list of results in the sidebar that you can click to bring up in the main browser window, as in Figure 1-21.

The search results stay persistent in your sidebar, so you can click from result to result without having to navigate back and forth between pages on the site. And now that Amazon is a search engine option, you can do other fun things such as search Amazon and Google at the same time. This allows you to browse, view, and sort the search results from both sites in one place.

If you really want to go the extra mile to integrate, you can create an icon to represent Amazon results. Mozilla looks for a 16×16 pixel image in the

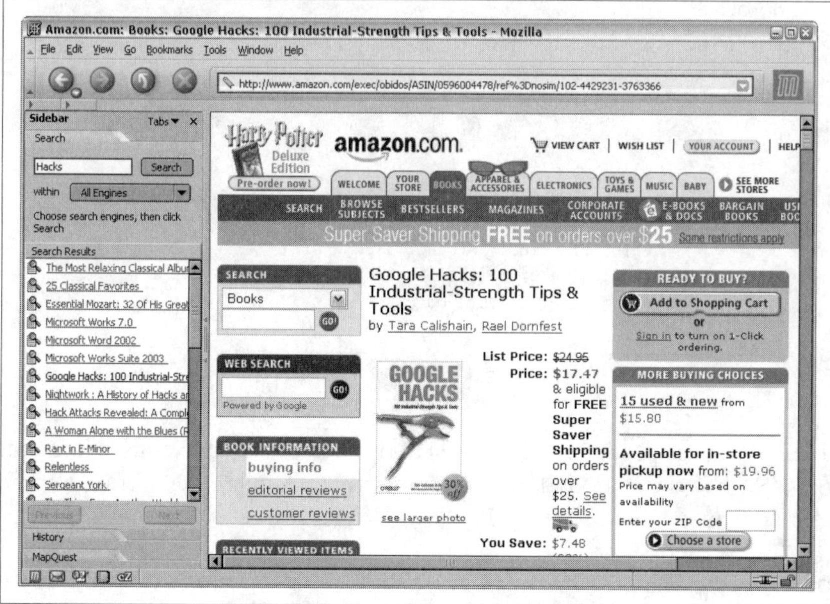

Figure 1-21. Mozilla Amazon sidebar search

searchplugins directory with the same base name as the search definition file. In this example, a file named *amazon.gif* would be displayed in the sidebar with any Amazon search result.

Controlling Your Information

Hacks 13–26

This chapter describes all the ways information flows into Amazon, and how that information can be fine-tuned and controlled. It also offers tips for working with your account at Amazon while maintaining your privacy and security.

Understand Identity at Amazon

Amazon user accounts provide a consistent, personalized experience. Understanding how, when, and why you should log in and out of your Amazon account will help you control that experience.

The general perception of identity on the Web was summed up well in a famous cartoon from the *New Yorker*: a dog in front of a computer turns to another dog and says, "On the Internet, nobody knows you're a dog." If every web request were completely anonymous, though, features like 1-Click buying, personalized recommendations, or wish lists would be impossible. At the very least, personalized web applications like Amazon need to know you're the same dog each time you visit.

Create an Account

Like most web applications, Amazon's answer to the Web's inherent anonymity is user accounts. By identifying yourself with an email address and password, Amazon is able to save your information for subsequent visits.

Exactly what information does Amazon collect, save, and associate with your account? Anything you explicitly type into a form will be saved. That includes your name, billing and shipping information, items you purchase, reviews you add, wish list items, and items you've seen. This may sound like an Orwellian disaster waiting to happen, but in exchange for this information, Amazon provides a unique, customized buying experience. If you were to stop by your corner store on a regular basis, the person behind the counter would eventually get to know your tastes and offer help and recommendations based on your buying patterns. Amazon does the same thing—for tens of millions of people. Some of the features available to registered users include:

- Personalized Product Recommendations [Hack #14]
- 1-Click Buying [Hack #15]
- Persistent shopping carts
- Wish Lists [Hack #18]

If you're visiting Amazon for the first time, you'll see "New customer? Start here" toward the top of the front page. Enter your email address, choose the "No, I am a new customer" radio button, and click the "Sign in..." button. From there you can enter a password and create your account.

Keep in mind that having an account comes with some responsibility. It's a good idea to make your password something difficult to guess. As Amazon states in their conditions of use (*http://www.amazon.com/o/tg/browse/-/508088/*): "...you are responsible for maintaining the confidentiality of your account and password and for restricting access to your computer, and you agree to accept responsibility for all activities that occur under your account or password."

To be able to control how you use your Amazon account, it's important to understand exactly how Amazon uniquely identifies you when you visit.

Understanding Login Status

Anytime you visit Amazon, they start a *session* that allows them to identify an individual browsing their site across pages. Even if you've never been to Amazon before, have no account information, and are completely anonymous, Amazon will know that you are the same person as you click from page A to page B though a *session ID*. Most Amazon URLs contain the session ID. For example, typing in the home page URL, *http://www.amazon.com*, will take you to a URL that looks something like this:

```
http://www.amazon.com/exec/obidos/subst/home/home.html/102-4471056-3284920
```

The 17-digit string of numbers at the end of the URL is your session ID. As you click links from the home page, you'll notice that all of them contain this set of numbers that is unique to your visit.

A session allows you to add items to a shopping cart, continue shopping, return to your specific cart with your items, and check out. A session lasts only as long as your browser window is open. But what if you'd like to add items to a cart, close your browser, leave for a few days, and return to shopping where you left off on a completely different computer? That's what an Amazon account provides.

When you have an account, Amazon sets a data file on your computer (a *cookie*) that uniquely identifies your browser. If the cookie exists when your Amazon session starts, Amazon can bring up your account information and recognize the fact that this session belongs to your account. However, even though the identifying cookie may exist on your computer, it's still not enough to access some account information.

Amazon requires a specific login with your password to access certain areas of the site. To add personal information, change preferences, or view and change orders, Amazon requires you to sign in by supplying your email address and password. You'll be prompted to sign in, as shown in Figure 2-1, anytime it's necessary.

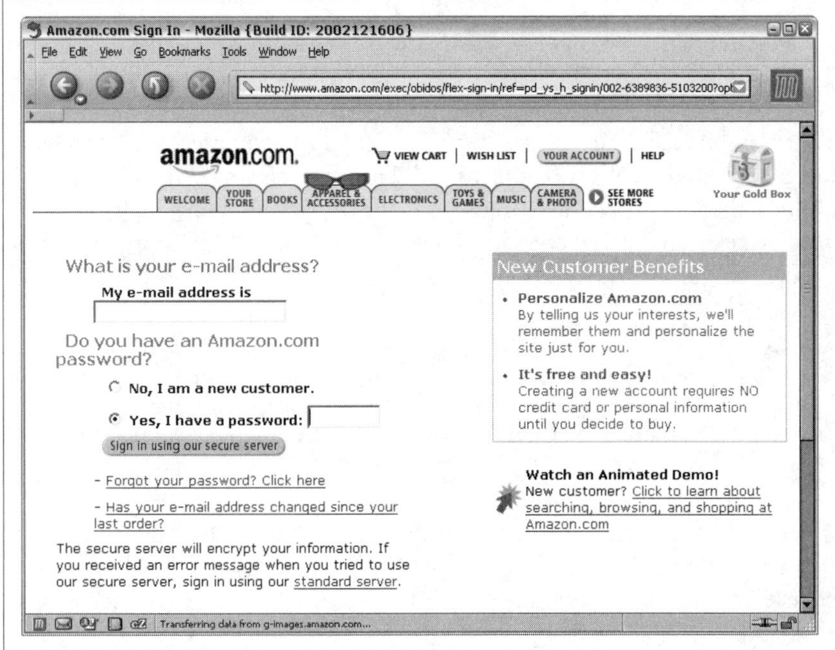

Figure 2-1. Amazon Sign In page

Signing in takes place over a secure connection by default, keeping your password between you and Amazon.

Based on these methods of identification, there are three statuses your Amazon session could be in at any given time:

Logged-Out and Not Recognized
: Your account cookie isn't set, and you haven't logged in. You can still browse and add items to a cart, but you'll need to create an account to actually buy the items—and any items in your cart will be lost when you close your browser.

Logged-Out and Recognized
: Your account cookie is set, but you haven't logged in during the current session. Amazon can offer personalized product recommendations, and you can add items to your wish list and see your shopping cart additions from previous sessions.

Logged-In and Recognized
: You have specifically signed in during the current session with your email address and password. In addition to personalized product recommendations and shopping cart data, you can change personal information, place and update orders, and change preferences.

Signing In and Out

You can change your status from Logged-In/Recognized to completely logged out (and vice versa) at any time. The quickest route to a login form is clicking the Your Store tab from the main navigation menu or from *http://amazon.com/o/tg/stores/your/store-home/-/0/*. On the Your Store page you should see a link at the top that says, "Click here to sign in."

If you're using a public Internet connection or a shared computer, it's a good idea to explicitly sign out when you're done with your Amazon session. Signing out guarantees that a stranger can't walk up to the computer and browse around Amazon with your identity.

If you're signed in and would rather be out, the top of the Your Store page has a link that mentions your name: "Hello, *Your Name*," followed by a chance to log out: "If you're not *Your Name*, click here." Once you've clicked there, you'll be logged out.

If you want to bypass the storefront for changing your status, you can check your login status and sign in or out at any time from the Signing Out page at *http://www.amazon.com/o/tg/browse/-/515722*.

Closing an Account

If you ever decide to stop using Amazon altogether, you can request that your account be closed. You just need to make sure you don't have any current pending orders. You'll lose your wish list, shopping cart, purchase history, and any other information on Amazon. If you're OK with that, send an email from the address associated with your account to *account-close@amazon.com*.

If you've signed up with several different email addresses at Amazon, you can merge your account histories into one. Using one account keeps your experience consistent across sessions. There's no automatic way to merge accounts, but you can contact Amazon Customer Service (*http://amazon.com/o/tg/browse/-/565780/*).

Fine-Tune Your Recommendations

As Amazon gets to know your tastes, it makes recommendations about products you might like. A few quick steps can ensure that your recommendations are on target.

One of the features that makes browsing at Amazon unique is their exceptional ability to personalize the experience. Amazon analyzes your purchase history and makes recommendations of other products you might like based on your unique tastes. You can begin browsing your personal recommendations in Amazon's Your Store section. You can find it by clicking the tab that says "*Your Name* store" from the main menu.

Reactions to recommended products are inevitably polarized, ranging from "that's perfect!" to "that's waaaay off!" The key to getting good recommendations is Amazon having data about what you like, and even if you've never purchased anything there, you can give Amazon plenty of data about your interests.

To reach the fine-tuning features, go to Your Store and choose "Improve Your Recommendations" from the list of links on the lefthand side of the page. This will lead to the appropriately titled Improve Your Recommendations page, shown in Figure 2-2. The following features can be accessed from this page.

Recommendations Wizard

If you're creating an account for the first time, the first thing you'll see is a link that leads to Amazon's Recommendations Wizard. This is a getting-to-know-you process that asks about your favorite subject areas or categories

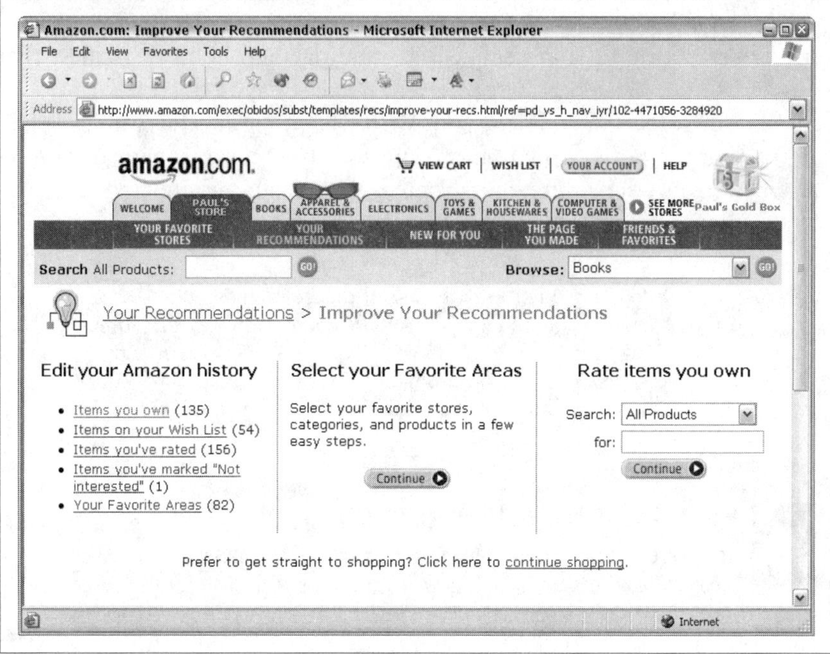

Figure 2-2. Improve Your Recommendations

and some keywords for various departments, and lists some specific products for you to rate. If you're a long-time customer, running through the wizard is a good way to start refining your recommendations. On the Improve Your Recommendations page the wizard is called "Select Your Favorite Areas." Just click Continue under that heading to get started.

Rate Items in Your Amazon History

Your Amazon History is a virtual collection of products associated with your account. It includes products you've purchased, of course, but also items you've rated, items in your wish list, or items you've told Amazon something about in some way. Each item in your Amazon history can have information associated with it that you set:

- The fact that you own it
- A 1–5 star rating
- Whether or not the item should be used to make recommendations
- Or simply, "Not Interested"

Amazon uses all of this information to make your recommendations more accurate. You can start adding this type of data by clicking any of the links under "Edit your Amazon history" (see Figure 2-3).

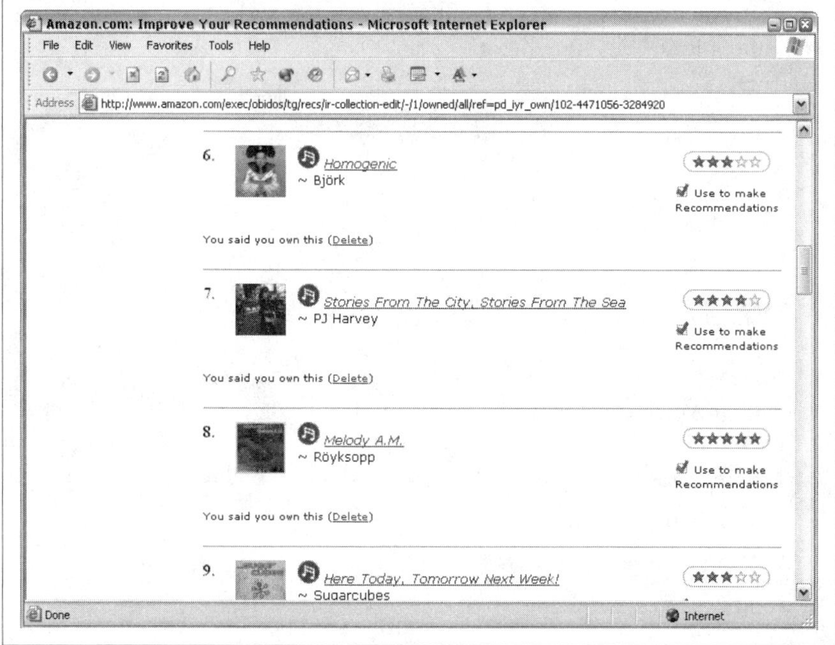

Figure 2-3. Editing personal Amazon history

You can rate an item by clicking the number of stars you'd like to give it. You can also specify whether or not to use the item for recommendations. This is particularly handy to weed out any gift purchases you may have made. Buying children's books for your cousin can throw a wrench into your personal recommendations. This is a way to set the record straight.

Some browsers don't support the 1–5 star interface. Instead, ratings are set with radio buttons. Be sure to click the "Save & Continue" button at the bottom of the page to save your ratings if you don't see the clickable star system.

Add and Rate Items That You Didn't Purchase at Amazon

It's a little-known fact that people actually buy items from stores other than Amazon. If you'd like to use Amazon's recommendation service with these items thrown into the mix, you still can. This is especially helpful when Amazon continually recommends a product that you already own.

From the Improve Your Recommendations page, you can enter a keyword into the form under "Rate items you own," and you'll see a list of search results related to that keyword. Each item has the standard rating options and the ability to mark it as one you own. You can also rate and mark an item as yours from its product detail page. On the lefthand side of the page, you'll find a Rate This Item box (Figure 2-4).

Figure 2-4. Rate This Item box

Now that you've added books that you haven't purchased at Amazon, how can you tell which are which? As you browse your Amazon history (by clicking links under "Edit your Amazon history"), you'll notice a status line under each item that lets you know why it's there. Possible statuses are:

- You said you own this.
- Amazon.com purchase.
- You bought this as a gift.

You can remove any of the items you've explicitly added to your history by clicking "delete" next to this status line.

#15 Enable 1-Click Buying

Zip through the checkout process and indulge the impulse buyer within by setting up push-button buying.

1-Click buying is the impulse buyer's dream—or nightmare, depending upon your point of view. Once activated, you can skip the standard checkout process and buy something by clicking a single button. It takes just a few clicks to set it up.

At the top of every page at Amazon you'll find a consistent set of options in the Amazon Toolbar, shown in Figure 2-5.

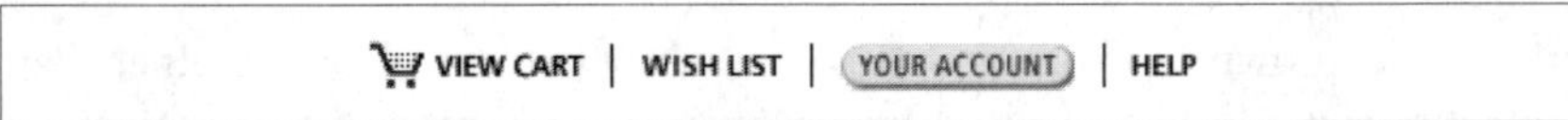

Figure 2-5. Amazon Toolbar

From this toolbar, choose "Your Account" to see your preferences page. In the section titled "Personal Information," choose "View or Change 1-Click Settings." (You'll be asked to sign in if you haven't already.)

Your browser must have cookies enabled if you want to use 1-Click buying.

From this page you'll see your 1-Click status (on or off) in a box at the upper righthand corner of the page. Once you've verified your 1-Click shipping address and payment information, you can enable 1-Click by signing in from any product detail page. Under the "Add to Shopping Cart" button, you'll find "Sign in to turn on 1-Click ordering." Once signed in, you're all set to have products shipped to your house with the click of a button.

There are no price limits on 1-Click buying, so you could find a $9,000 plasma HDTV-ready flat-panel TV on your doorstep with a few careless clicks. But once you've ordered an item with 1-Click, you have 90 minutes to cancel it or add more items. Just click "Your Account" from the top of any page to edit your order.

You can send gifts with 1-Click as well. Just add an address on your 1-Click settings page, click "edit," and be sure that "Include address in your 1-Click drop-down box" is checked. You'll then have the option to choose the target address from a drop-down box before your 1-Click action.

To turn off 1-Click buying for your account, visit your 1-Click settings page and click "Turn 1-Click Off" in the righthand status box.

#16 Set Up a Group Account

Amazon's Corporate Account feature lets a business provide a single point of billing for its employees. You can use this same system to organize the purchases of everyone in your family.

If it came down to it, there's probably someone in your family you could call the Purchase Manager. You can formalize that title on Amazon by setting up a *corporate account* for your family, as Jim Roche at Amazon suggested. Even though they're called corporate accounts, you don't have to be a corporation to start one. Any small business, organization, or family can set one up to let a group of people make purchases with one or two people controlling the billing and shipping information.

Standard Amazon accounts are intended for a single individual. Corporate accounts let you group several standard accounts together to let one of the accounts handle billing and shipping information.

To create a group account, visit the corporate accounts home page, *http://amazon.com/corporate.*

Click "Open a Corporate Account" to begin the process. Once created, you can manage your account on the page you see in Figure 2-6 and invite people to join the account using their email address. Each person will receive an email asking them to confirm their invitations.

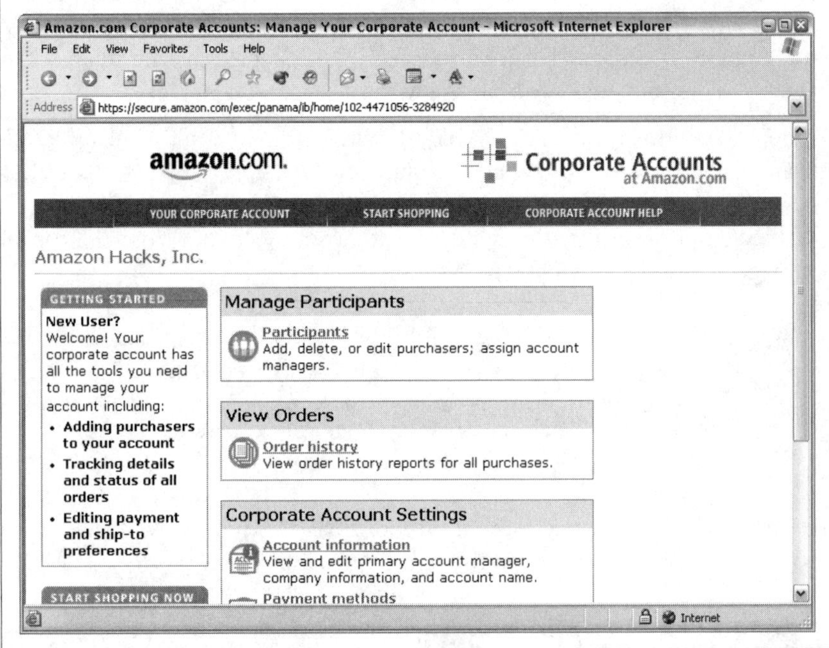

Figure 2-6. Corporate Accounts management page

If the person you invite doesn't already have an account with Amazon using the email address you sent the invitation to, they'll have to create a standard account to join. Another option is to resend the invitation using their Amazon-related email address.

Each person participating in the account is either an Account Manager or an Account Buyer. Managers have certain privileges that buyers don't have. They can:

- Add participants
- Change payment and shipping information
- View the order history
- Assign other account managers

There are even a few actions that you can perform only if you're the founding (or *primary*) account manager:

- Edit the account information (group name and account name)
- Apply for credit with Amazon.com

#17 Create an "About You" Area

By letting other Amazon customers know a little bit about you, you'll add some context and personality to your lists or reviews.

An "About You" page is like a home page for you at Amazon. Any time you add a review, create a Listmania! list [Hack #41], guide [Hack #37], or wish list [Hack #18], it will be accompanied by a link to your About You page. If someone sees something you've contributed to Amazon and wants more information about you, they can visit your page to learn more.

To customize your page, make sure you're logged in [Hack #13], click the Your Store tab from any page, and choose "Your About You Area" from the left-hand side of the page.

Controlling Who Sees What

Click "Edit About You" to add or change information. If it's your first time setting up your page, you'll see a form with a few options you can set:

Name
: This should be your real name. It will be used to personalize Amazon. You can set whether or not other people can see it with your Identity Preferences.

Nickname
: This is a name that will appear instead of your real name in some public spaces. It's also used as your name for any Amazon Chat spaces.

Identity Preferences
: This lets you set whether or not your name is available to other people on your About You page and other nonanonymous contributions to the site. You can set your nickname to override your name for public spaces. Or you can choose to reveal your name only to those people you give the special status Amazon Friend **[Hack #42]**.

Email Preferences
: You can make your email address available to everyone on your About You page, or only to a select few Amazon Friends. With the Amazon Friends option selected, anyone searching for your wish list with your email address will be able to find it.

Description
: This is a spot for your biography. Remember that whatever you write will be available to the public, so make sure you're comfortable with others reading it. Looking at a blank form asking the question "Who Are You?" could invite hours of philosophical introspection. But a few quick facts that will distinguish you from others on the site with the same name is a good place to start.

If you've set up your page before, you won't find all of these settings on one page. Click "Edit E-mail" to change your name, nickname, identity preferences, and email preferences. Click "Edit About You" to change your bio.

Adding a Picture of Yourself

To finish up your About You page, you can add or choose a graphical representation of yourself. This image will appear alongside your name or nickname on your About You page and on any of your Amazon Friends' pages. Click "Edit Image" and you'll find several premade graphics to choose from. They're cartoon-like graphics of people and faces.

To *really* stand out from the crowd, though, you can add a real photograph of yourself. Amazon doesn't host the images, so you'll need to have some web space of your own. Upload an image, copy the full URL, and paste it into the space provided on the "Edit Image" page.

Amazon resizes all About You images to 70 pixels wide by 100 pixels high. Your custom image should be exactly this size to avoid distortion.

#18 Create a Wish List

Amazon's catalog is your oyster! Save those items you want in once place and let everyone know what you really want.

Remember those novelty socks you got as a gift from your aunt on your last birthday? The thought was nice, but if she'd known you would have preferred a *Lord of the Rings* DVD instead, everyone would have been happy. Your aunt would have known she got exactly what you wanted, and you'd think of her fondly as you watched Frodo battle evil. Amazon's Wish List feature lets you set up a list of products you can share. The wish list also stores your address so your aunt won't have to try to remember where you live.

Even though your address is associated with your wish list, people buying gifts won't ever know your exact address. The most they'll see is "Ships to Portland, OR" (or wherever you call home).

Wish lists can be used for more than just accurate presents; they can also help nonprofit organizations. If you visit Amazon's charity page (*http://www.amazon.com/exec/obidos/tg/browse/-/557206/*), you'll find that several organizations like Toys for Tots and Habitat for Humanity have public wish lists of items they need. Buying through their wish list means your donation will make it to the proper address, and you know it's something they've specifically noted they need.

You can create a wish list by clicking the "Add to Wish List" button on any product detail page. It's located on the righthand side of the page under the "Add to Shopping Cart" button. Alternately, you can click "Wish List" from the top of any page. From there you can browse items to add to your wish list.

Once an item is on your wish list, you can set the quantity you'd like ("Desired") and include comments (see Figure 2-7).

You can keep purchased items a surprise by leaving the default "Show" setting at the top of the page at "All items." Or you can choose "Only purchased" from the drop-down menu to see what's been purchased from your list.

You can add more items by browsing Amazon as you normally would, clicking "Add to Wish List" when you spot something you'd like to add. To make changes, you can click the Wish List link from the top of any Amazon page or point your browser to *http://www.amazon.com/wishlist*.

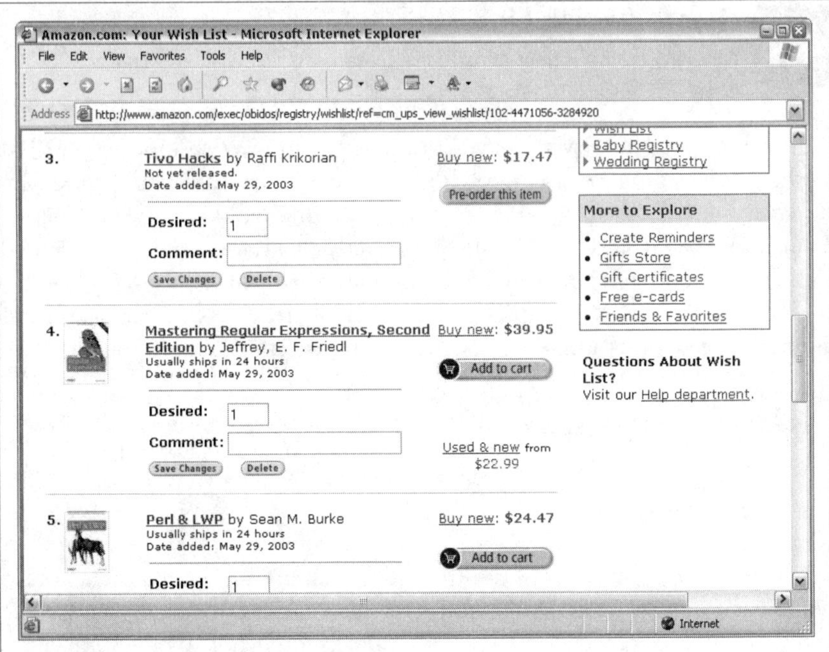

Figure 2-7. Edit Wish List page

Finding Your Wish List ID

Once you have a wish list with some items in it, it's nice to be able to link directly to it. With the public URL in hand, you can post a link to it on your web site or send it to everyone you know via email. This saves people the step of searching for your name or email to find what you're wishing for. And it's good to do everything you can to remove barriers to people buying you stuff!

Every wish list has an internal Wish List ID. You won't find it on any pages at Amazon, but you will find it in your wish list's URL (sometimes). The quickest path to reaching your wish list while guaranteeing that its ID is in the URL is:

1. Click "Wish List" from the navigation menu at the top of any Amazon page. (Sign in if necessary.) Under the title graphic, you'll find "Already have a Wish List? Click here to sign in."
2. Across the top of the page you'll see a navigation trail that says "Friends & Favorites → About You → Your Wish List." Click "About You" to get to your About You page.
3. On the lefthand side of the page in the Browse menu, click the "Wish List" link. It should be at the top of the link list.

You'll find yourself back on your wish list page, but this time you'll see the Wish List ID in the URL. The URL should look something like this:

```
http://www.amazon.com/exec/obidos/registry/3FOF79BIVB2XX/ref=...
```

That bundle of characters after /registry/ is your Wish List ID. Armed with this ID, you can create short links **[Hack #4]** that are suitable for sending via email:

```
http://www.amazon.com/o/registry/insert wish list ID
```

Also, Jonathan Leblang at Amazon noted a URL shortcut for jumping to a wish list if you know the list owner's email address:

```
http://www.amazon.com/o/wishlist/insert email address
```

Because you're always in editing mode when looking at your own wish list, you never quite see it as others do. To see how your list appears to others, note your wish list URL, log out **[Hack #13]**, and go to your list directly for an outsider's perspective.

If you'd rather keep your wish list completely private, you can alter your settings slightly to make sure no one can find it. Browse to your wish list and click the "Edit Info" button under "Your Searchable Options" on the right-hand side of the page. You'll find a form that contains the information associated with your wish list. Simply uncheck the box next to "Keep My Wish List Searchable," update it, and the items on your list will be between you and Amazon.

Recommendations Based on Wish List Items

If you'd like to see product recommendations based on items that are similar to those in your wish list, make sure you're signed in and then click "Your Wish List recommendations" from the top of your wish list page. You can also visit the recommendations page directly at *http://www.amazon.com/o/subst/stores/registry/wishlist/recommendations.html.*

To see recommendations based on *other* people's wish lists, track down their Wish List ID and browse to this URL:

```
http://www.amazon.com/o/tg/cm/wishlist-gifts-detail/-/insert wish list ID/
```

Deleting Your Wish List

If you'd like to remove your wish list for good, you can do so from the "Deleting Your Wish List" page, *http://www.amazon.com/exec/obidos/tg/browse/-/501090/*. Once it's gone, though, it's gone forever!

#19 Add Items to a Wish List Remotely

A simple HTML form allows your visitors to add items you mention to their own wish lists.

If you list items on your own web site and you'd like to let people add them to their Amazon wish lists with the click of a button, you can do this with a simple HTML form.

To set up the form, you need to know a product's ASIN **[Hack #1]** and (optionally) an Amazon associate tag **[in "Make Money by Linking to Amazon" in Chapter 5]**.

```
<form method="POST" ↵
    action="http://www.amazon.com/o/dt/assoc/handle-buy-box=insert ASIN ">
<input type="hidden" name="asin.insert ASIN" value="1">
<input type="hidden" name="tag-value" value="insert associate tag">
<input type="hidden" name="tag_value" value="insert associate tag">
<input type="submit" name="submit.add-to-registry.wishlist"↵
      value="Add to Amazon.com Wish List">
</form>
```

Just fill in the ASIN and affiliate tag in the code and include it on any web page. If someone has the Amazon identity cookie or is logged in, the item will be added directly to their wish list when they click the button. Otherwise, they'll be required to sign in at Amazon before the item is added.

#20 Add Multiple Items to a Wish List at Once

Speed up the process of adding items to your wish list with a bit of scripting.

Creating a wish list with 15–20 products is usually a slow process, adding one or two items while you're browsing. Amazon doesn't offer an interface for adding multiple items to a wish list, but you can build one with a bit of scripting. This PHP script accepts a comma-separated list of ASINs and adds them to your wish list all at once.

What You Need

This script relies on automatic form posts, and there are some external PHP tools to speed up this kind of development. *Snoopy for PHP* is an open source class that handles HTTP requests. You can download a copy from SourceForge (*http://sourceforge.net/projects/snoopy/*) and include it in the same directory as this script.

The Code

This script runs as a web page and presents a simple form for entering ASINs. Once you enter a list of ASINs, this script performs three main actions:

1. With the Snoopy PHP class, it simulates a Sign In form post at Amazon with your email address and password to retrieve a session ID.
2. It then loops through the ASINs.
3. For each ASIN, it uses Snoopy to send a form post with the variables from the remote wish list form **[Hack #19]**.

Because you need to be signed in to add items to your wish list, the key to this script is obtaining a 17-digit Amazon session ID **[Hack #13]** that is associated with your account when you visit the site. Be sure to include your email address and Amazon password in the following code. Your Amazon password will be in the source of the file, so make sure you're the only one with access. You can also insert an associate tag **[in "What You Need" in Chapter 5]** if you have one, to make sure you get a commission on your wish list purchases.

```
<?php
# add_wishlist_items.php
# Adds multiple items to an Amazon Wish List
# Usage: A PHP page called via web browser

$aff_tag = "insert associate tag";

error_reporting(E_ERROR | E_WARNING);

if ($HTTP_POST_VARS) {
   include "Snoopy.class.inc";
   $snoopy = new Snoopy;

   $snoopy->agent = "(compatible; MSIE 4.01; MSN 2.5; AOL 4.0; Windows 98)";
   $submit_url = "https://www.amazon.com/exec/obidos/flex-sign-in-done/";

   $submit_vars["email"] = "insert email address";
   $submit_vars["password"] = "insert Amazon password";

   $submit_vars["method"] = "get";
   $submit_vars["opt"] = "oa";
   $submit_vars["page"] = "recs/instant-recs-sign-in-standard.html";
   $submit_vars["response"] = "tg/recs/recs-post-login-dispatch/-".
                              "/your/pd_ys_fr_ur";
   $submit_vars["action"] = "sign-in";
   $submit_vars["next-page"] = "recs/instant-recs-register-standard.html";

    //submit email and password to start a session
    if($snoopy->submit($submit_url,$submit_vars))
    {
```

```
        while(list($key,$val) = each($snoopy->headers)) {
            if (preg_match("/session-id=(.*?);/i", $val, $ubid)) {
                $session_id = $ubid[1];
            }
        }
    } else {
        echo "error fetching document: ".$snoopy->error."\n";
    }

   $snoopyAdd = new Snoopy;
   $snoopyAdd->agent = "(compatible; MSIE 4.01; MSN 2.5; AOL 4.0; ".
                       "Windows 98)";

   $ASIN_list = split(",",$_POST['txaASINs']);
   $submit_add["tag-value"] = $aff_tag;
   $submit_add["tag_value"] = $aff_tag;
   $submit_add["submit.add-to-registry.wishlist"] = ↵
            "Add to Amazon.com Wish List";
   $cntAdded = 0;
   for($i = 0;$i < count($ASIN_list); $i++) {
        $thisASIN = trim($ASIN_list[$i]);
        $submit_url = "http://www.amazon.com/o/dt/assoc/handle-buy".
                      "-box=".$thisASIN."/".$session_id;
        $submit_add["asin.".$thisASIN] = "1";
        if(!$snoopyAdd->submit($submit_url,$submit_add)) {
            echo "error adding item ".$thisASIN.": ".
                 $snoopyAdd->error."<br>\n";
        } else {
            $cntAdded++;
        }
        unset($submit_add[$thisASIN]);
   }
   echo $cntAdded . " item(s) added to your wishlist!";
} else {
?>
<html>
<head>
    <title>Add Wishlist Items</title>
</head>

<body>
Add a list of ASINs below, separated by commas:
<br>
<form action="add_wishlist_items.php" method="post">
    <textarea cols="35" rows="6" name="txaASINs"></textarea>
    <br><input type="submit" value="Add Items">
</form>
</body>
</html>
<?php } ?>
```

Note the `https://` in the section that signs in to Amazon. As the script gets a session ID, the POST is made over an SSL connection—so you can be sure that using this script is as secure as signing in at Amazon personally.

Running the Hack

Add the code to a file called *add_wishlist_items.php* and upload it to your web server. Bring up the page in your web browser, enter a list of ASINs separated by commas (e.g., 0596004478, 0596004605, 0596004613) and click "Add Items." A page should appear letting you know that three (or however many you entered) items were added to your wish list. Just visit your wish list on Amazon to verify!

#21 Organize Your Wish List by Priority

Amazon provides a few ways to sort your wish list, but missed an important one: sorting by which items you want most.

When I sat down to create my Christmas list in November of 2002, I decided to use my Amazon wish list. I added all the books, CDs, and DVDs that I had been craving to my list. Next, I went to the "Your Wish List" page, where I planned to rank the items on my list. To my surprise, I found that Amazon doesn't allow you to rank your wish list.

Instead, all you can do is sort the list by (a) date added, (b) last updated, or (c) price. Even worse, the default sorting is by date added, and, since the items I wanted the most were the first ones I added, they ended up at the bottom of my list. (Amazon does provide a "Comment" field for each wish list item, so I initially thought I could store my ranks as comments, but Amazon doesn't let you sort by comment either.)

In search of a solution, I took a look at Amazon Web Services (*http://www.amazon.com/webservices*) and found that I could build my own simple application that adds ranking ability for Amazon wish lists.

Ranking Your Wish List

Using the Wish List Ranking application is simple. First, fill out the registration form (*http://www.yoon.org/amazon/register*). The only tricky part is that you have to enter your Wish List ID manually [Hack #18]. The FAQ (*http://www.yoon.org/amazon/faq*) includes instructions on how to find your Wish List ID. Then, as you can see in Figure 2-8, the application fetches your wish list from Amazon.

Figure 2-8. A Wish list pulled from Amazon

As with any third-party service that requires registration, always use a different email and password combination than you use for your Amazon account. It's easy to use the same combination to save space in your memory, but you may be giving away the key to your account.

Click the "Change rankings" link at the top to go to a page where you can rank the items on your list, as shown in Figure 2-9.

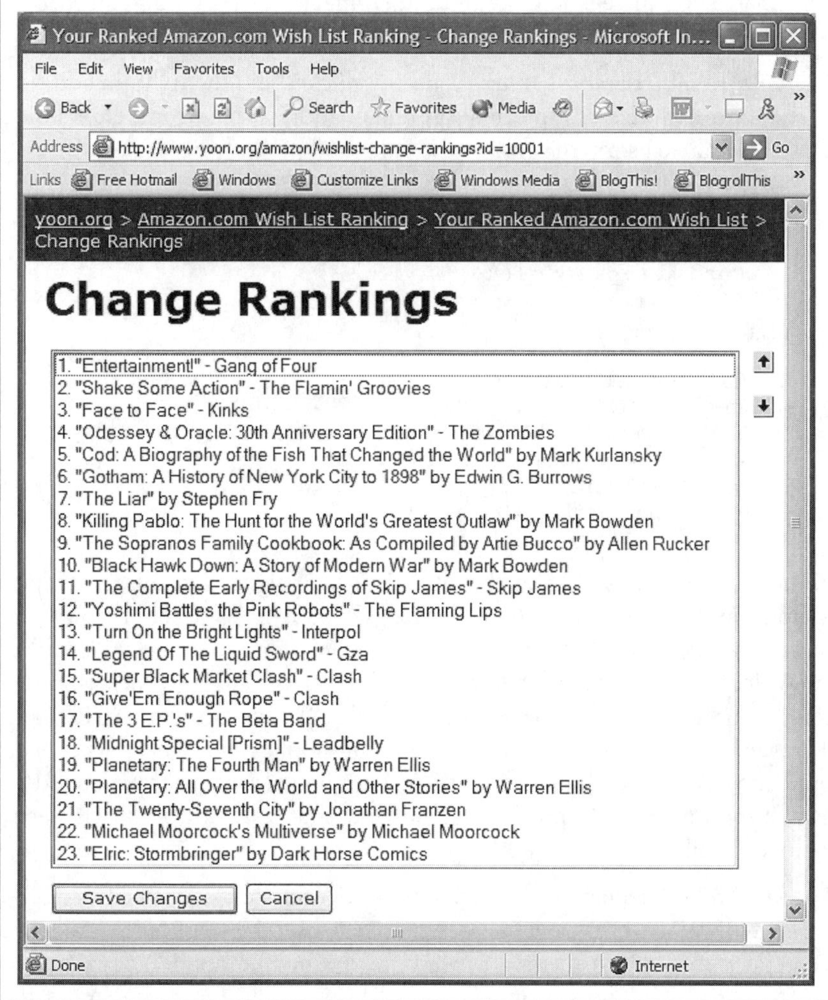

Figure 2-9. Changing the order of items in a wish list

Use the arrows to move your wish list items into the order you want, click the "Save Changes" button, and you're done. Use the "Share your Ranked Wish List with your family and friends" link so that they'll know what you really want.

How It Works

Amazon's Web Services API provides a `WishlistSearchRequest` method, which returns information about each item in a specific wish list. Since each item that Amazon sells has a unique identifier (the ASIN), all I needed to add was a way to store the rank of each ASIN in a given wish list.

A simple MySQL database (*http://www.mysql.com*) did the trick. In addition to standard user account information (email address, password, etc.) stored in a table named users, the core of the data model is just two tables:

```
CREATE TABLE wishlists (
 wishlist_id INTEGER NOT NULL PRIMARY KEY,
 user_id INTEGER NOT NULL REFERENCES users(user_id),
 amazon_wishlist_id VARCHAR(100) NOT NULL,
 UNIQUE (user_id, amazon_wishlist_id)
);

CREATE TABLE wishlist_items (
    item_id INTEGER NOT NULL PRIMARY KEY,
    wishlist_id INTEGER NOT NULL REFERENCES wishlists(wishlist_id)
    asin VARCHAR(100) NOT NULL,
    rank INTEGER NOT NULL,
    UNIQUE (wishlist_id, asin)
);
```

In the `wishlists` table, I store the Wish List ID assigned by Amazon (which is not simply a number) in the `amazon_wishlist_id` column. I don't use `amazon_wishlist_id` as my primary key because doing so would create a minor security hole: if I wanted to prevent you from ranking your wish list, I could search for it on Amazon (the Wish List ID appears in the URL) and then register it with the Wish List Ranking application. Then, when you came to rank your wish list, you'd find that it had already been registered by me. (If the Amazon API provided some kind of access control for wish lists, that would alleviate this issue.)

The `wishlist_items` table is where the ranks of each item, identified by ASIN, are stored. Whenever someone views a wish list, the application calls the `WishlistSearchRequest` method to load the product information of each wish list item (name, authors, price, image URL, etc.) into memory, fetches the rankings from the database, and then re-sorts the Amazon data in rank order.

Handling Deletions and Additions

The Amazon API doesn't provide any way to find out if a wish list has been modified, so we have to use a brute-force method to handle additions and deletions. Fetch the wish list periodically (whenever someone views the ranked version of the list) and then compare it to the rankings stored in our database. Any ASINs that are in the database but not in the list returned by Amazon are deleted from the database, and any ASINs that are in the Amazon search results but not in the database are inserted into the database at the bottom of the list.

Running It Yourself

I wrote this application in PHP (*http://www.php.net*), using the NuSOAP library (*http://dietrich.ganx4.com/nusoap*) to invoke the Amazon Web Services API and the Smarty template engine (*http://smarty.php.net*) to separate presentation from application logic. (Of course, I could have written the application with any number of tools: Java, ASP.NET, Perl, Python, what have you. PHP just happened to be installed by my hosting service.)

If you want to run the application on your own server, download the code (*http://www.yoon.org/amazon/download/amazon-wish-list-ranking-1.0.tar.gz*) and follow the instructions in the INSTALL file.

—*Michael Yoon*

#22 Set Email and Messages Preferences

You can decide how often Amazon contacts you by setting your preferences.

If your primary method of communication on the Internet is email, you can have Amazon send information to your inbox. Amazon sends several different types of email, and you can manage your settings at any time by clicking "Your Account" at the top of any page and scrolling down to the "E-mail Notifications" section. The different types of email are:

Alerts
: Set a keyword for certain product categories at Amazon, and you'll receive an email when new products are available that match your criteria. For example, a "hacks" alert in books would let you know when this book was released. You can add an alert at *https://www.amazon.com/exec/obidos/subst/alerts/signup.html/*.

Delivers
: Choose your favorite product categories at Amazon and receive recommendations, reviews, and interviews by editors from those categories. Figure 2-10 shows the Amazon.com Delivers category selection form.

Available to Order notifications
: If you're browsing around Amazon and spot an item that is out of stock or that Amazon doesn't know the release date for, you can sign up to be alerted when it's available.

New for You
: This is an email version of the site feature "New for You." It lists new products. The web version is available at *http://amazon.com/o/tg/new-for-you/new-for-you/-/main/*.

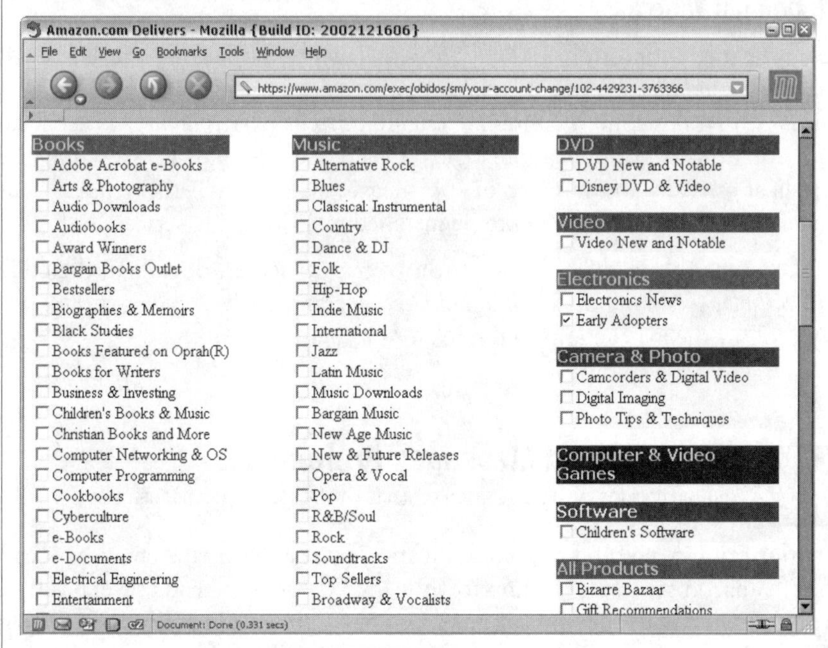

Figure 2-10. Amazon.com delivers category selection

Special Occasion Reminders
: These are email alerts that you specifically set up to remind you **[Hack #24]** of important days.

Weekly Movie Showtimes
: Based on your zip code, Amazon sends an email with movie showtimes **[Hack #23]** for your area. This service is also available on their site.

Get Movie Showtimes

You can use Amazon to plan your evening by finding out when, where, and what movies are playing in your local theaters.

It's Saturday afternoon—time to make plans for the evening. Of course the Web holds all the information you need to figure out what to do. Surprisingly, though, Amazon.com is among the sites that can help you out. One of the lesser-known features Amazon provides is movie showtimes. Figure 2-11 shows the home page of the Movies category (*http://www.amazon.com/movies*). When you provide Amazon with your zip code, you'll see a list of the theaters in your area along with movies and times they're playing.

Figure 2-11. Amazon movie showtimes

The zip code form is an interface for creating a URL that gets the information you want. Typing your zip code and clicking Submit creates a URL like this:

```
http://www.amazon.com/exec/obidos/search-handle-url/?index=showtimes↵
&field-power=zips5:insert zip code&field-date=insert date&item-start=1↵
&item-end=10
```

If you want to tweak the results page so that it displays more than one zip code, it's possible to examine the URL and change some values. The first relevant value is `field-power`. You can set this to a two-part value that's formatted like this:

```
zipsinsert mile radius:insert zip code
```

For example, if you want to find movies playing within five miles of Sebastopol, CA, you could set the field like this:

```
zips5:95472
```

The next value you need to set is `field-date`. It has a straightforward format that includes the year, month, and day: `yyyymmdd`. So if you want to know the movies playing on July 4, 2003, you would set `field-date` to `20030704`.

However, Amazon stores movie times for only seven days beyond the current date, so you can't research the past or predict the distant future.

Now that you know the syntax, you can begin to modify it a bit. Amazon's interface doesn't let you choose multiple zip codes, but you can list movies in several areas by tweaking the URL. Say you wanted to know movies playing within five miles in both Sebastopol, CA and Corvallis, OR. Just set several values in `field-power` with "or":

```
zips5:95472 or zips5:97330
```

The value has to be URL-encoded **[Hack #92]** by converting the spaces to `%20`; once that's done, you can make the full request. Be sure to set the date to the current day, or a few days in the future.

```
http://www.amazon.com/exec/obidos/search-handle-url/?index=showtimes↵
&field-power=zips5:95472%20or%20zips5:97330&field-date=20030704↵
&item-start=1&item-end=10
```

In addition to viewing times on the Web, you can receive local showtimes via email. Visit *http://www.amazon.com/movies-email* to subscribe.

#24 Create an Amazon Event Reminder

Don't miss another birthday or anniversary! Let Amazon remind you of important dates via email with their event reminder service.

Wouldn't it be great to have a personal assistant to remind you of important events that you need to buy gifts for? And wouldn't it be great if this assistant handed you a list of potential gifts? Amazon can remind you of important days and recommend gifts to go along with them using their reminder service.

To add a reminder, click the "Your Store" tab, choose "Friends & Favorites" from the submenu, then click "Add a Reminder" from the lefthand list of links. You'll see the event reminder form (Figure 2-12), where you can fill in all of the details related to the event: the person's name, type of occasion, date, and how long before the event you'd like to be notified. You can even choose several different event times in case you need several reminders.

If you choose to fill in personal information about the gift recipient, Amazon will search for their wish list and make suggestions based on your information.

Finding a list of all your reminders can be a bit tricky. Just follow the path outlined to make your way to the event reminder form. At the top of the

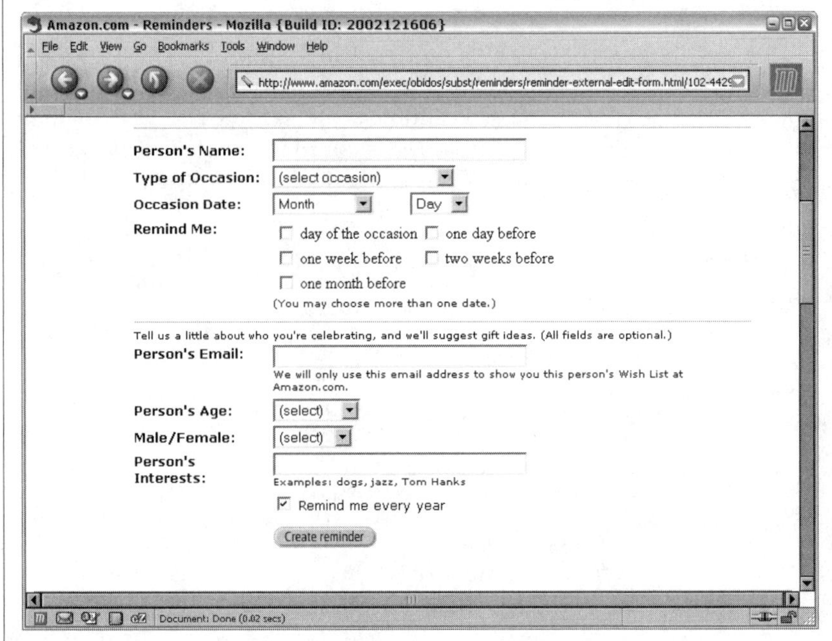

Figure 2-12. Event reminder form

page you'll see a navigation trail that says, "Gift Services → Special Occasion Reminders → Create a Reminder." Click "Special Occasion Reminders" from this list and you'll see the events you have set. From here you can edit or remove them.

If someone has their birth date associated with their wish list, you can automatically add a reminder by clicking "Create a reminder for this date" on the righthand side of their wish list page.

#25 Create Several Birthday Reminders at Once

You probably have dozens of birthdays to track. You can speed up the process of adding Amazon event reminders with a script.

If you have an entire address book of people's birthdays that you'd like to receive reminders about, it could be a long process to enter them one by one into Amazon's event reminder form. Instead, you can speed up the process considerably with some scripting.

This ASP page accepts a text list of names and birth dates and enters them all as Amazon events. This script runs on Windows servers running IIS.

The Code

As with other services that require you to be logged in, the event reminder service requires an Amazon session ID that is tied to your account. This script first logs in as you via SSL and sets the session ID. Then it loops through the birthdays, calling the `AddEvent` subroutine, which sends a form post to Amazon with the event information.

```
<%
' add_reminders.asp
' Turns a supplied list of names and birthdates into Amazon events
' Usage: An ASP page called from any web browser

Const YOUR_EMAIL = "insert email address"
Const AMZN_PASSWORD = "insert Amazon password"
Const WinHttpRequestOption_EnableRedirects = 6

Sub AddEvent(sid,name,e_month,e_day)
    strURL = "https://www.amazon.com/exec/obidos/reminder-edit-done/"
    strURL = strURL & strSessionID
    strPostData = "reminder-id=" & _
                  "&reminder-frequency=on" & _
                  "&sort-by=reminder-date" & _
                  "&customer-email=" & YOUR_EMAIL & _
                  "&occasion-id=3" & _
                  "&smart-send-options-enabled=yes" & _
                  "&time-zone-name=US/Pacific" & _
                  "&7-days-before=no" & _
                  "&recipient-customer-id=" & _
                  "&recipient-name=" & name & _
                  "&recipient-lower-email=" & _
                  "&gift-recipient-customer-id=" & _
                  "&gift-recipient-age-range=00-00" & _
                  "&gift-recipient-gender=" & _
                  "&month=" & e_month & _
                  "&day-of-month=" & e_day & _
                  "&14-days-before=on" & _
                  "&0-days-before=no" & _
                  "&1-days-before=no" & _
                  "&interest1=" & _
                  "&30-days-before=no" & _
                  "&x=63" & _
                  "&y=7"

    Set httppost = Server.CreateObject("Msxml2.SERVERXMLHTTP")
    httppost.Open "POST", strURL, false
    httppost.setRequestHeader "Content-Type",↵
        "application/x-www-form-urlencoded"
    httppost.Send(strPostData)
    If Err.Number <> 0 Then
        'WScript.Echo httppost.Error
    End If
```

```
    strText = httppost.ResponseText
    strHeaders = httppost.GetAllResponseHeaders
    strStatus = httppost.status
    Set httppost = Nothing
End Sub

If Request("txaBirthdays") <> "" Then
    'Start an Amazon Session
    strURL = "https://www.amazon.com/exec/obidos/flex-sign-in-done/"
    strPostData = "email=" & YOUR_EMAIL & _
                  "&password=" & AMZN_PASSWORD & _
                  "&method=get" & _
                  "&opt=an" & _
                  "&cont-page=cm/reminders-signed-in-continue" & _
                  "&cont-type=add-reminder" & _
                  "&response=reminder-add" & _
                  "&response=" & _
                  "stores/gifts/gifts-sign-in-secure.html" & _
                  "&action=sign-in" & _
                  "&next-page=" & _
                  "stores/gifts/gifts-register-secure.html"

    Set httppost = Server.CreateObject("WinHttp.WinHttpRequest.5")
    httppost.Open "POST", strURL, false
    'Turn off redirects
    httppost.Option(WinHttpRequestOption_EnableRedirects) = False
    httppost.setRequestHeader "Content-Type", ↵
"application/x-www-form-urlencoded"
    httppost.setRequestHeader "User-Agent", ↵
"(compatible; MSIE 4.01; MSN 2.5; AOL 4.0; Windows 98)"
    httppost.setRequestHeader "Accept", ↵
"image/gif, image/x-xbitmap, image/jpeg, image/pjpeg, */*"
    httppost.Send strPostData
    If Err.Number <> 0 Then
        response.write httppost.Error
    End If
    strHeaders = httppost.GetAllResponseHeaders
    strStatus = httppost.status
    'response.write "<xmp>" & strStatus & Chr(13) & strHeaders & "</xmp>"

    Set objRegExpr = New regexp
    objRegExpr.Pattern = "session-id=(.*?);"
    objRegExpr.Global = True
    objRegExpr.IgnoreCase = True
    Set objMatches = objRegExpr.Execute(strHeaders)
    If objMatches.Count = 0 Then
        response.write "Amazon session couldn't be started."
        response.end
    Else
        For Each objMatch In objMatches
            strSessionID = objMatch.SubMatches(0)
        Next
    End If
```

```
    Set objMatches = Nothing
    Set objRegExpr = Nothing
    Set httppost = Nothing

    'Loop through the Birthdays
    cntEvent = 0
    arBDays = Split(Request("txaBirthdays"),Chr(13))
    For x = 0 To UBound(arBDays)
        arNameDate = Split(arBDays(x),",")
        strName = arNameDate(0)
        strDate = arNameDate(1)
        arMonthDay = Split(strDate,"/")
        strMonth = arMonthDay(0)
        strDay = arMonthDay(1)
        AddEvent strSessionID, strName, strMonth, strDay
        cntEvent = cntEvent + 1
    Next
    response.write cntEvent & ↵
" events added! Check your email for confirmation."
Else
%>
<html>
<head>
    <title>Add Event Reminders</title>
</head>

<body>
Add a list of birthdays below, one on each line:<br>
Format: [Name], [Birthday mm/dd]
<br>
<form action="add_reminders.asp" method="post">
    <textarea cols="35" rows="6" name="txaBirthdays"></textarea>
<br><input type="submit" value="Add Items">
</form>
</body>
</html>
<% End If %>
```

Running the Hack

Add the code to an ASP file, *add_reminders.asp*. Upload the file to your server and point your browser at it:

```
http://your.server/add_reminders.asp
```

Because your Amazon password is stored in the file, make sure that you're the only one with access to the source code.

You'll see the simple HTML form waiting for birthdays. Add a list of names and dates separated by carriage returns. If you happen to store your birthdays in a spreadsheet or other electronic format, it should be fairly easy to export them in this format. Click "Add Items," and the script should let you know how many events were added at Amazon. Log in and check your events list [Hack #24] to verify that the script worked.

Hacking the Hack

To understand the form variables that are sent in the `AddEvent` subroutine, view the source HTML of Amazon's event reminder [Hack #24] form and take a look at the form fields and their values. By playing with values set in `strPostData`, you could easily turn this script into an anniversary reminder, or change the notification time of the reminders from the default 14 days to any other available value.

Best Practices for Your Amazon Account

Eight steps you can take to personalize, control, and secure your Amazon account.

Your Amazon account does more than just let you purchase items through the Amazon site. It lets you participate in the community and personalize your experience. Here are a few concrete steps you can take right now to protect—and get the most out of—your Amazon account.

Customize email preferences
: Visit the email preferences page [Hack #22] and make sure it's set to a level you're comfortable with. This page also lets you see all of the email options that Amazon offers in a glance.

Customize public identity preferences
: Check the identity section of your About You area [Hack #17] to make sure other Amazon customers can see only what you want them to see.

Use a complex password
: It's always a good idea to use a password that's difficult to guess with any application. Because Amazon stores personal information on their servers, you should take your password seriously. Make your password at least eight characters and a combination of letters and numbers. If you created your account [Hack #13] with a simple password, you can change it anytime at *http://amazon.com/o/self-service-forgot-password-get-email*.

Always log out of public machines
: If you share your computer with others or if you're using a public machine, learn how to log in and out [Hack #13] and make sure you're logged out when you're done.

Don't share your account

Nothing skews product recommendations like several people sharing the same Amazon account. If you share a computer in one household, learn about logging in and log out when you're done. If you're using one account to control billing for several people, you can set up a corporate account **[Hack #16]** instead.

Add a brief biography to your account

Your About You area **[Hack #17]** is your public face to other Amazon customers, and a brief biography is like a quick spoken introduction. It doesn't have to include any specifics but letting others know a bit about you will add some depth to your reviews and contributions.

Run the Recommendations Wizard

When Amazon knows what you like, its recommendations can be startlingly accurate. The Recommendations Wizard **[Hack #14]** is a quick way to point Amazon in the right direction. It also provides an opportunity to remove items (like gift purchases) that may be throwing your recommendations off.

Start a wish list

Even if you don't plan on sharing your wish list **[Hack #18]** with others, it's a good place to stash items you might want to buy in the future. Wish list items are also taken into account when Amazon makes product recommendations.

CHAPTER THREE

Participating in the Amazon Community

Hacks 27–48

Imagine walking into your favorite physical bookstore to browse the aisles. Imagine that you're *encouraged* to leave notes on any book, CD, or DVD letting others know how you feel about it—good or bad. Imagine being able to peer into other people's shopping bags when they have items similar to yours. Or imagine looking at the store's business records to see which books are most popular with people from your area. Amazon provides features that make all of this possible. Browsing the virtual aisles of Amazon is a unique experience because there are opportunities at every turn to connect with other Amazon visitors.

The hacks in this chapter focus on how you can use the community features effectively, integrate them with a remote web site, or combine them in different ways to get a different view of the information.

Community Features

Direct communication involves users speaking to each other in their own words. Amazon's direct community features include:

Reviews
: Reviews are the most direct way to let others know how you feel about any item in Amazon's catalog—in your own words. The review includes a 1–5 star rating that summarizes your opinion at a glance. Each review can also be rated "helpful" or not by anyone reading it. Reviews (positive or negative) that have been rated helpful by other Amazon visitors then bubble up to the top of the list. "Write a Review" **[Hack #27]**.

Listmania! Lists
: You can use lists to rewrite the way items are categorized using your own unique perspective. A bookstore wouldn't normally put a book of Antarctic photography right next to a biography of Antarctic explorer

Ernest Shackleton—and they definitely wouldn't have a GPS navigation system on the same shelf as well. Lists provide a chance to show how seemingly disconnected items actually share a common thread. "Create a Listmania! List" **[Hack #41]**.

Guides
: Lists allow you to attach a few comments to each item. Guides, on the other hand, allow you to attach a few items to your much longer writing. They're free-form tutorials about any topic. If you're an expert wilderness trekker, for example, you could write a guide about picking out and using the perfect GPS navigation system and survival gear—listing those items that helped you along the way. "Create a Guide" **[Hack #37]**.

Amazon Friends
: This feature allows you to find specific Amazon users (including people you know in real life), add them to a list, and keep up with their reviews, lists, guides, and Wish Lists. You can even selectively share your purchase history (and potentially view their history) with some or all of them. "Gather Your Friends on Amazon" **[Hack #42]**.

Product Advice
: You can recommend another product instead of (or in addition to) any given product by entering its ASIN. The recommendations are collected and displayed on product detail pages. "Add Product Advice Remotely" **[Hack #39]**.

Share the Love
: This feature allows you to send additional product discounts on items that you purchase to anyone you know. If someone you sent the discount to purchases one of those items within seven days, you'll receive a credit toward your next purchase. While not specifically available in Amazon's community area, it involves connecting with other Amazon customers. "Share the Love (and Savings!) with Your Friends" **[Hack #36]**.

Aggregated data differs from direct communication in that it's not just individuals giving advice and information—it's looking at how whole groups of people interact with the site. Looking at the big picture like this can show trends, and give you some insight into how your interests fit in (or not) with others at Amazon. This information answers some common questions people have about how other people are using Amazon:

Related Products
: What else are people who bought a particular item buying? When you're looking at a single item, Amazon shows similar items that customers have purchased along with that item.

Purchase Circles

What are people near me—my neighbors, those in my town, at my university—buying? Narrowing down customer purchase patterns to specific geographic areas or organizations, you can see product purchases unique to specific groups of people.

Sales Rank

What are all Amazon customers buying? Each item that has been sold at Amazon has a number that reflects its sales in comparison with other items at Amazon.

Average Ratings

How did the group of people who reviewed this item rate it? By collecting and averaging all of the star ratings from reviews of a product, this feature provides a quick summary of the thoughts of all reviewers.

These features do more than let you know what others on Amazon are up to. All of this data is a gold mine for product vendors, book readers, music fans, authors, and anyone interested in trends across different industries. Everyone from businesses to hobbyist developers are starting to see the value in having the ability to manipulate, integrate, or customize Amazon community data in ways that are unique to their perspectives.

Accessing Community Features

Amazon of course provides access to all of their community features through their web site. As more and more sites integrate closely with Amazon, though, there is more demand to tap into the community via code.

Accessing Through Web Services

The Web Services API (see Chapter 6) offers some access. When accessing an individual product's information through the API, you can find the following community data:

- The three latest reviews
- ASINs of five related items
- Three lists that contain the item

This is fantastic information to have access to. Developers are building tools that work with this data in many creative ways. But when compared with the volume of information that's available on Amazon's site, the community information in the API is only a small window into the larger community. That leaves one route for integration-minded developers: screen scraping.

Accessing Through Screen Scraping

The term *screen scraping* refers to requesting a web page programmatically with a script, and picking through the resulting HTML for the interesting data. Finding the data itself involves writing complex *regular expressions*. Regular expressions are a pattern-matching syntax that can become complicated quickly. For example, here's a regular expression that extracts a list of books from a purchase circle page **[Hack #44]**:

```
<td.*?<b><a.*?-/(.*?)/.*?>(.*?)</a></b>.*?by (.*?)<br>.*?</td>
```

You can see some HTML there, and the expressions are based on where the data is within the HTML and the fact that the data appears in regular patterns. Unfortunately screen scraping is rather brittle; if Amazon changes their design even slightly, this particular regular expression won't work. The expression would have to be changed by hand to sort through the new HTML to find the right pattern of data.

There are several screen-scraping examples in this chapter, and the general methods of accessing a page and parsing its contents will work. But keep in mind that the regular expressions provided could become obsolete at any time as Amazon changes the pages accessed by the scripts.

#27 Write a Review

Everyone has an opinion. You can give other Amazon customers your insights about a product by posting a review.

Anyone with a customer account at Amazon.com can post a public review of products sold on the web site. You can post under your own name, under a handle (nickname), or anonymously as just "a reader from Poughkeepsie."

You can get started reviewing books and other products on Amazon.com by finding the product detail page for the product you want to review. You'll find a link under either Spotlight Reviews or All Customer Reviews that says "Write an Online Review." Click the link and you'll find yourself at the review editor.

Before you write your review, it's a good idea to click the link to "Guidelines for Reviewing." Reviews that don't meet the guidelines are removed from the site. Some rules to keep in mind:

- Keep your review under the maximum length of 1,000 words, though the recommended length is 75–300 words.
- Make the review about the content of the book or product and how *you* feel about it.

- Don't give away the plot! Even if you think the book is terrible, you want others to have the chance to enjoy it.
- Don't include URLs, phone numbers, addresses, or profanity.
- Don't reference other reviewers. The reviews section wasn't meant for conversations. Though it's tempting to speak directly to someone else's review, each review should be able to stand on its own.

Once you understand the rules for posting, you can move to writing your review.

1. Choose your rating. Click the drop-down box "How do you rate this book?" and choose from 1 to 5 stars (1 is the lowest and 5 is the highest). This rating will be posted alongside your review, and will be used to calculate the Average Customer Review rating for the book.
2. Enter a title for your review. You are limited to 60 characters, including spaces. Special symbols can't be used in the title (you might be able to enter them, but they will not show up correctly upon posting).
3. Write your review in the text box. A good way to do this is to create your review using a word processor, then copy and paste the text into the box. This gives you the chance to spellcheck your review and to check for mistakes using all of the word processor's features.

Once you've starting writing your review, don't back out to find more information! If you want to view the original product page for reference, open a second browser window and find the page you want. If you leave your edited review to check another page, you can lose what you've written.

4. Choose your public signature. If you choose the "anonymous" option, your review will show up with "A reader from…" or "A viewer from…", depending on what you review.
5. Enter your city, state, country, or region in the next box.
6. Click "Preview your review."

When you preview, you can see your review as it will look when posted on Amazon.com. Don't like what you see? Click the white "Edit" button to go back to editing mode. From there you can fix the problems and preview again. You can repeat this process as many times as you need to until the review is ready to post. Once you are satisfied, click the yellow "Save" button.

It takes about a week to ten days to see your published review. If you don't see your review after two weeks, contact Community Help (*community-help@amazon.com*) to find out if there is a problem with your review.

If you'd like to save a copy of the review for yourself, highlight the review after editing and copy and paste it into a word processor. Use the title of the book you're reviewing in the filename and save it to a special *reviews* folder. This way you'll have easy access to a local copy of all your work.

In addition to saving a local copy of each review, you can link directly to a page on Amazon in the About You area **[Hack #17]** that shows all of the reviews you've written **[Hack #35]**.

Reviewers who post a lot of reviews and whose reviews are voted "helpful" by other Amazon customers get a privileged status at Amazon called Top Reviewer. Top Reviewers get a "badge" displayed alongside their reviews. There is a badge for reviewers in the Top 1000, Top 500, Top 100, Top 50, Top 10, and #1. The ranking is based on the number of reviews posted and the number of "helpful" votes received from other Amazon customers.

If you want to know more about reviews, you can visit the Review Discussion Board (*http://forums.prosperotechnologies.com/am-custreview*) and talk directly with other reviewers.

—Joanna Daneman

#28 Link Directly to Reviews of a Product

With a little URL hacking, you can link directly to any product's reviews from another web site.

Reviews are one of the most interesting pieces of community information available on Amazon. A positive or negative review rating can have a big impact on an item's sales. Naturally some people are very interested in this information: publishers, authors, other merchants, or fans of a particular book, DVD, or CD.

Each item's product detail page shows a handful of reviews, but if there are dozens—or sometimes hundreds—of reviews, most are tucked away on that item's Customer Reviews page. Once you know the URL format for this page, you can link to it directly with any item's ASIN. And once you have the URL, you can link directly to the page from another web site.

Keep in mind that Amazon URLs change from time to time, but as of this writing you can simply designate the ASIN in this URL:

```
http://amazon.com/o/tg/detail/-/insert ASIN/?vi=customer-reviews
```

There are 10 reviews per page, so if there are more than 10 reviews for the product, you can go directly to other pages by adding page numbers to the URL:

```
http://amazon.com/o/tg/detail/-/insert ASIN/insert page/?vi=customer-reviews
```

So, the following URL would take you to the second page of reviews for *Google Hacks*:

```
http://amazon.com/o/tg/detail/-/0596004478/2/?vi=customer-reviews
```

By default the reviews are ranked by date with the newest first. The simplest way to change the order in which they're returned is to choose a sort method at the site, as shown in Figure 3-1.

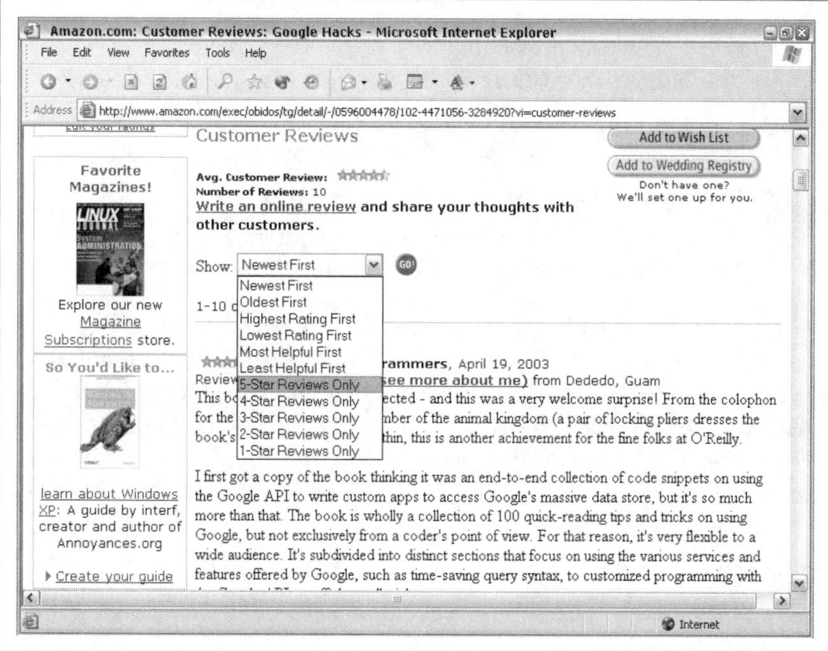

Figure 3-1. Sorting customer reviews

You can also change the sort value in the URL, so you can link directly to a sorted list of reviews. By appending `&show=` to the URL with various values, you can perform the same actions that are available at the site.

For example, if you want to link directly to reviews of *Google Hacks* with the most helpful reviews (as voted by Amazon users) listed first, the following URL would work:

```
http://amazon.com/o/tg/detail/-/0596004478/?vi=customer-reviews&show=-rating
```

Table 3-1 shows the available sorting methods and associated values for the show variable.

Table 3-1. Customer Reviews sort methods

Show variable value	Sort order
-submittime	Newest first
+submittime	Oldest first
-rating	Highest rating
+rating	Lowest rating
-votes	Most helpful
+votes	Least helpful

To view only certain ratings, set show to the number of stars:

```
http://amazon.com/o/tg/detail/-/0596004478/?vi=customer-reviews&show=5
```

This URL will show only 5-star reviews for *Google Hacks*.

#29 Post a Review from a Remote Site

To integrate adding Amazon reviews into a web publishing system or web site, examine the way Amazon posts information and create a remote copy.

Just as hundreds of sites are integrating with Amazon to provide product data and sales, there are many ways to tap into Amazon's community. If you'd like to integrate Amazon's review system into an existing site, you can do so with some simple HTML. By studying the HTML Amazon uses to submit reviews, you can create a generic form that sends reviews to Amazon from any site.

The Code

Create a file called *remote_form.html* containing the following code:

```
<html>
<head>
    <title>Remote Amazon Review</title>
</head>

<body>

<form method="POST" action="http://amazon.com/exec/obidos/preview-review/↵
insert ASIN/104-2773718-4336742">

<!-- Visible Form Fields -->
Rating:<br>
<select name=rating>
```

```
    <option value="" selected>-</option>
    <option value="5">5 stars</option>
    <option value="4">4 stars</option>
    <option value="3">3 stars</option>
    <option value="2">2 stars</option>
    <option value="1">1 star</option>
</select>
<br><br>

Title:<br>
<input type="text" name="summary" value="" size=56 maxlength=60>
<br><br>
Review:<br>
<textarea wrap=virtual name="review" rows=9 cols=65></textarea>
<br><br>
Email:<br>
<input type=text name=email size=35 maxlength=250 value=" ">
<br><br>
Name:<br>
<input type=text name=source size=35 value="">
<br><br>
Show Name:
<input type=radio name="display-email" value="SOURCE" checked><br>
Stay Anonymous:
<input type=radio name="display-email" value="NO">
<br><br>
Location:<br>
<input type="text" name="user-location" value="" size=35 maxlength=120>

<!-- Hidden Form Fields -->
<input type=hidden name=secure-rate-review-next-page value=/exec/obidos/tg/↵
cm/review-thanks>
<input type=hidden name=store.store-name value="books">
<input type=hidden name=detail.this-asin value="insert ASIN">
<input type=hidden name=detail.this-area value="customer-review-form">
<input type=hidden name=product.product-name value="book_display_on_↵
website">
<input type="hidden" name="fp_ts" value="stores/detail/preview-customer-↵
review">
<input type="hidden" name="fe_ts" value="stores/detail">
<input type="hidden" name="priority" value=2500>

<!-- Submit Button -->
<br><br>
<input type="submit" value="Preview your review">
</form>

</body>
</html>
```

By now you're probably getting good at spotting ASINs **[Hack #1]**, and there are two places you need to set the ASIN for the product you're reviewing. One spot is in the `action` attribute of the opening `<form>` tag, and the other is in a hidden form field called `detail.this-asin`.

There are several values possible for the `product.product-name` variable, and this needs to be set depending on the type of product you're reviewing. Here are a few examples of possible values:

- `book_display_on_website` (books)
- `music_display_on_website` (music)
- `classical_display_on_website` (music)
- `ce_display_on_website` (electronics)
- `dvd_display_on_website` (dvd)

If an item you want to review doesn't fall into one of these categories, you can find the value by looking through Amazon's HTML. Bring up the review form, scan for the `product.product-name` field in the HTML, note its value, and include it in your version of the form.

Running the Hack

To add a review, just open *remote_form.html* anywhere, and write your review. Click the submit button to send the information to Amazon. You'll see your review on a preview page where you can double-check your review to make sure it is exactly what you want. Remember, there's no going back once it's submitted. If you want your review to be tied in with your Amazon ID and appear in your About You section **[Hack #17]**, you'll want to be logged into Amazon when you send the review.

#30 Add Pop-up Amazon Reviews to Your Web Site

With a few lines of JavaScript, you can add Amazon customer reviews to your web site.

The Amazon pop-up review service is a simple yet powerful way to integrate your site with Amazon. It allows anyone with a web site to generate dynamic customer reviews without needing to know anything about Amazon's API (see Chapter 6). An independent developer has provided this service to anyone who would like to use it.

All you need to set up the service on your site is a product's ASIN **[Hack #1]**. When a visitor clicks the pop-up review link, the application receives the ASIN, connects to Amazon's API, downloads the specific XML data, and parses through it to build the product page with reviews. The data is then displayed on a stylized web page in a new browser window.

The Code

Displaying the generated code in a pop-up window takes just two easy steps. First, create a new HTML page and paste the following JavaScript between the `<head></head>` tags. This code creates a function called `AmazonLookup` that will control the state of the pop-up window and initiate a link to the remote server.

```
<script type="text/javascript">
    function AmazonLookUp(ASIN) {

      // Set pop-up window properties
      var winoptions = 'toolbar=no,';
      winoptions += 'menubar=no,';
      winoptions += 'location=no,';
      winoptions += 'scrollbars=yes,';
      winoptions += 'resizable=yes,';
      winoptions += 'statusbar=yes,';
      winoptions += 'width=470,';
      winoptions += 'height=500';

//Set the remote service URL, including the ASIN
var URL = "http://www.explodingfist.com/quickreview/index.php?ASIN="+ASIN

//Open a new window with the remote URL
OpenWin = this.open(URL, "Amazon", winoptions);
    }
</script>
```

Running the Hack

To open the pop-up window and establish a connection with the service, you simply invoke the JavaScript function you created above. For example, to generate customer reviews for *The Matrix* on DVD you would insert the following link anywhere in the body of the page. (Note the ASIN inside the single quotes; we are passing it to the service as a parameter.)

```
<a href="javascript:AmazonLookUp('B00000K19E')">The Matrix on DVD</a>
```

It's that simple! As you can see in Figure 3-2, the link will open a new browser window where you can read customer reviews, see product information, and even add *The Matrix* to your Amazon shopping cart.

For further information on this hack, to download the code, or to see a working demo, visit *http://www.explodingfist.com/amazonhack/*.

—*Reid Philpot*

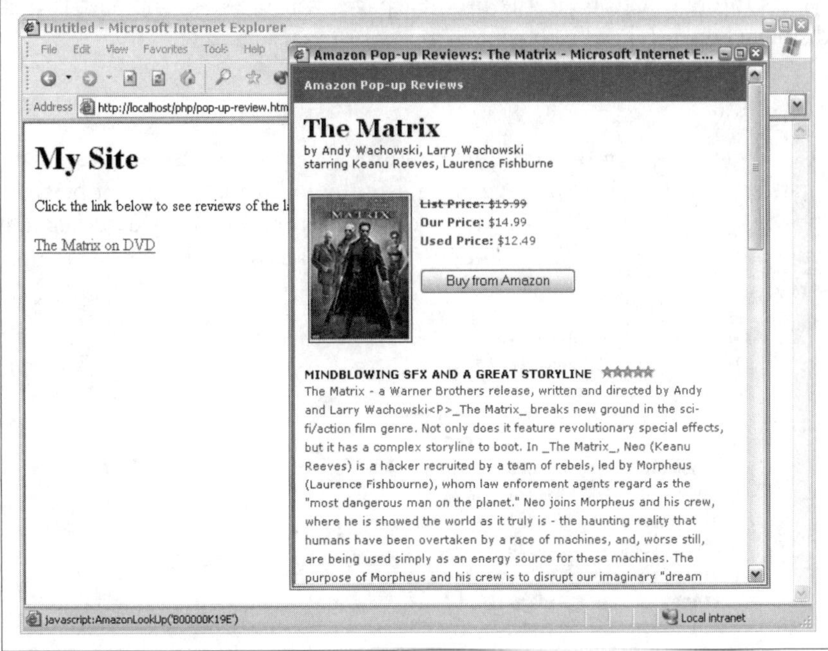

Figure 3-2. Amazon pop-up review

#31 Send an Email Alert if a Review Is Added to a Product

This script keeps an eye on Amazon and notifies you when a new review is posted.

There are obviously some products you care about more than others, and it's good to be aware of how those products are perceived. Reviews give feedback to publishers, authors, and manufacturers, help customers make buying decisions, and help other retailers decide what to stock. If you want to monitor all the reviews for a product or set of products, visiting each product detail page to see if a new review has been added is a tedious task.

Instead, you can use a script to periodically check the number of reviews for a given item, and have it send you an email when a new review is added.

The Code

You'll need two nonstandard Perl modules to run this code: LWP::Simple to make the AWS (Amazon Web Services) request, and XML::Simple to parse the results. The combination provides a simple way to access AWS XML over HTTP with Perl [Hack #80]. Create a file called *review_monitor.pl* with the following code:

```
#!/usr/bin/perl
# review_monitor.pl
#
# Monitors products, sending email when a new review is added
# Usage: perl review_monitor.pl <asin>
use warnings;
use strict;
use LWP::Simple;
use XML::Simple;

# Your Amazon developer's token.
my $dev_token='insert developer token';

# Your Amazon affiliate code.
my $af_code='insert affiliate code';

# Location of sendmail and your email.
my $sendmailpath = 'insert sendmail path';
my $emailAddress = 'insert email address';

# Take the asin from the command-line.
my $asin = shift @ARGV or die "Usage: perl review_monitor.pl <asin>\n";

# Get the number of reviews the last time this script ran.
open (ReviewCountDB, "<reviewCount_$asin.db");
my $lastReviewCount = <ReviewCountDB> || 0;
close(ReviewCountDB); # errors?! bah!

# Assemble the query URL (RESTian).
my $url = "http://xml.amazon.com/onca/xml2?t=$af_code" .
          "&dev-t=$dev_token&type=heavy&f=xml" .
          "&AsinSearch=$asin";

# Grab the content...
my $content = get($url);
die "Could not retrieve $url" unless $content;

# And parse it with XML::Simple.
my $response = XMLin($content);

# Send email if a review has been added
my $currentReviewCount = $response->{Details}->{Reviews}->↵
{TotalCustomerReviews};
my $productName        = $response->{Details}->{ProductName};
if ($currentReviewCount > $lastReviewCount) {
    open (MAIL, "|$sendmailpath -t") || die "Can't open mail program!\n";
    print MAIL "To: $emailAddress\n";
    print MAIL "From: Amazon Review Monitor\n";
```

```
        print MAIL "Subject: A Review Has Been Added!\n\n";
        print MAIL "The total review count for $productName is ↲
    $currentReviewCount.\n";
        close (MAIL);

        # Write the current review count to a file
        open(ReviewCountDB, ">reviewCount_$asin.db");
        print ReviewCountDB $currentReviewCount;
        close(ReviewCountDB);
    }
```

This code performs a standard Web Services ASIN query looking for one bit of data: the total number of customer reviews (`TotalCustomerReviews`). The script saves the number of reviews in a text file *ASIN.db*, and if the number is different than the last time the script was run, it sends an email to let you know.

Be sure to include your local path to *sendmail*, a program that sends email from the server. Most ISPs have *sendmail* installed in some form or another, (often at */usr/bin/sendmail*); check with your local administrator or Internet service provider (ISP) if you're not sure where it's located.

Running the Hack

You can run the code from the command line:

```
perl review_monitor.pl ASIN
```

Ideally, you want to run this script once every so often in the background instead of manually executing this query every day. On Linux you can set it to run as a cron job. Open cron:

```
crontab -e
```

Then hit Enter and add something like the following:

```
0 12 * * 1-5 perl review_monitor.pl ASIN
```

This schedules the script to run Monday through Friday at noon. Be sure to replace *ASIN* with a real ASIN, and add jobs as necessary for all of the items you want to monitor.

On Windows, you can run the script as a *scheduled task*. From the Control Panel, choose Scheduled Tasks, and then Add Scheduled Task. Follow the wizard to set your execution time, and you should be all set for review notifications!

Sort Books by Average Customer Rating

Use customer ratings as a guide to which books you should be looking at.

Average customer ratings are one of those aggregate features where it's not the voice of a single Amazon user giving advice, but rather it's the collective advice of everyone who has written a review. Each review includes a 1–5 star rating, and the average review reflects the group opinion of a book.

Sorting Search Results

You can sort any search results by choosing Avg. Customer Review from the "Sort by:" drop-down menu on any results page (see Figure 3-3). Make the selection and click Go! to reorder the results.

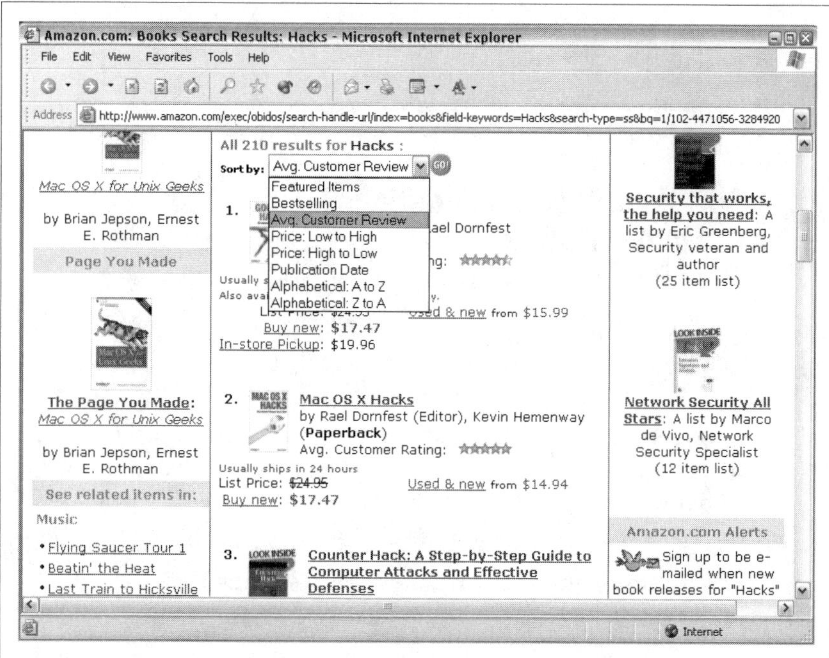

Figure 3-3. Sorting by Average Customer Review

If you're performing power searches via a URL **[Hack #9]**, you can sort by review with the rank variable set to reviewrank:

```
http://www.amazon.com/exec/obidos/search-handle-url/↵
ix=books&fqp=power%01publisher%3AO%27Reilly%20and%20keywords%3AHacks↵
&sz=100&rank=reviewrank
```

If you have a specific set of books that you'd like to sort by review rank, you can use a power search and include each ASIN:

```
http://www.amazon.com/exec/obidos/search-handle-url/ix=books&fqp=↵
power%01isbn%3A0596004478%7C0596004605%7C0596004613&sz=10&rank=reviewrank
```

This query looks for the products 0596004478, 0596004605, and 0596004613 and sorts the results by average customer rating.

As with most sorting-related values, you can specify + or - in front of the value to reverse the results. For example, you can specify `-reviewrank` to sort in reverse order: from lowest to highest customer review.

Sorting Web Services Queries

Web Services XML/HTTP queries **[in "Making Requests" in Chapter 6]** use the same method with the sort variable in the URL.

```
http://xml.amazon.com/onca/xml2?t=insert affiliate tag&dev-t=insert dev ↵
token&type=heavy&f=xml&mode=books&KeywordSearch=Hacks&sort=+reviewrank
```

#33 Sort Your Recommendations by Average Customer Rating

Find the highest rated items among your Amazon product recommendations.

If you've taken the time to fine-tune your recommendations **[Hack #14]**, you know how precise they can be. If you've also looked at the star rating for some of your favorite products, then you know that the rating can be a good indication of quality. Both the Amazon recommendation and the customer rating add important information to a product, and can help you make a decision about whether to buy one item over another.

To get a feel for the products Amazon recommends for you, you can visit your book recommendations at any time at the following URL:

```
http://www.amazon.com/o/tg/stores/recs/instant-recs/-/books/0/
```

In addition to books, you can also find recommendations in other product categories. You can replace `books` in the URL with any of Amazon's catalogs, including `music`, `electronics`, `dvd`, and `photo`.

When you browse to your recommendations, you'll likely find several pages of items. Wouldn't it be great if you could add the customer review dimension by sorting the entire list by its average star rating? This hack does exactly that with a bit of screen scraping.

The Code

Because Amazon doesn't offer sorting by customer rating, this script first gathers all of your Amazon book recommendations into one list. By providing your Amazon account email address and password, the script logs in as you, and then requests the book recommendations page. It continues to request pages in a loop, picking out the details of your product recommendations with regular expressions. Once all the products and details are stored in an array, they can be sorted by star rating and printed out in any order wanted—in this case, the average star rating.

Be sure to replace your email address and password in the proper places below. You'll also need to have write permission in the script's directory so you can store Amazon cookies in a text file, *cookies.lwp*.

```
#!/usr/bin/perl
# get_recommendations.pl
#
# A script to log on to Amazon, retrieve
# recommendations, and sort by highest rating.
# Usage: perl get_recommendations.pl

use warnings;
use strict;
use HTTP::Cookies;
use LWP::UserAgent;

# Amazon email and password.
my $email = 'insert Amazon account email';
my $password = 'insert Amazon account password';

# Amazon login URL for normal users.
my $logurl = "http://www.amazon.com/exec/obidos/flex-sign-in-done/";

# Now login to Amazon.
my $ua = LWP::UserAgent->new;
$ua->agent("(compatible; MSIE 4.01; MSN 2.5; AOL 4.0; Windows 98)");
$ua->cookie_jar( HTTP::Cookies->new('file' => 'cookies.lwp','autosave' ↵
=> 1));
my %headers = ( 'content-type' => "application/x-www-form-urlencoded" );
$ua->post($logurl, [ email       => $email,
          password    => $password,
          method      => 'get',
          opt         => 'oa',
          page        => 'recs/instant-recs-sign-in-standard.html',
          response  => 'tg/recs/recs-post-login-dispatch/-/recs/pd_rw_gw_r',
          'next-page' => 'recs/instant-recs-register-standard.html',
          action      => 'sign-in' ], %headers);

# Set some variables to hold
# our sorted recommendations.
```

```
my (%title_list, %author_list);
my (@asins, @ratings, $done);

# We're logged in, so request the recommendations.
my $recurl = "http://www.amazon.com/exec/obidos/tg/".
             "stores/recs/instant-recs/-/books/0/t";

# Set all Amazon recommendations in
# an array /  title and author in hashes.
until ($done) {

     # send the request for the recommendations
     my $content = $ua->get($recurl)->content;
     #print $content;

     # loop through the HTML looking for matches.
     while ($content =~ m!<td colspan=2 width=100%>.*?detail/-/(.*?)↵
/ref.*?<b>(.*?)</b>.*?by (.*?)\n.*?Average Customer Review&#58;.*?(.*?)↵
out of 5 stars.*?<td colspan=3><hr noshade size=1></td>!mgis) {
         my ($asin,$title,$author,$rating) = ($1||'',$2||'',$3||'',$4||'');
         $title  =~ s!<.+?>!!g;          # drop HTML tags.
         $rating =~ s!\n!!g;             # remove newlines.
         $rating =~ s! !!g;              # remove spaces.
         $title_list{$asin} = $title;    # store the title.
         $author_list{$asin} = $author;  # and the author.
         push (@asins, $asin);           # and the ASINs.
         push (@ratings, $rating);       # and th... OK!
     }

     # see if there are more results... if so continue the loop
     if ($content =~ m!<a href=(.*?instant-recs.*?)>more results.*?</a>!i) {
        $recurl = "http://www.amazon.com$1";# reassign the URL.
     } else { $done = 1; } # nope, we're done.
}

# sort the results by highest star rating and print!
for (reverse sort { $ratings[$a] <=> $ratings[$b] } 0..$#ratings) {
    next unless $asins[$_]; # skip blanks.
    print "$title_list{$asins[$_]}  ($asins[$_])\n" .
          "by $author_list{$asins[$_]} \n" .
          "$ratings[$_] stars.\n\n";
}
```

Running the Hack

Run the hack from the command line and send the results to another file, like this:

```
get_recommendations.pl > top_rated_recommendations.txt
```

The text file *top_rated_recommendations.txt* should be filled with product recommendations, with the highest rated items on top. You can tweak the URL in `$recurl` to look for DVDs, CDs, or other product types by changing `books` to the product line you're interested in.

#34 Scrape Product Reviews

Amazon has made some reviews available through their Web Services API, but most are available only at the Amazon.com web site, requiring a little screen scraping to grab.

Here's an even more powerful way to integrate Amazon reviews with your web site. Unlike linking to reviews [Hack #28] or monitoring reviews for changes [Hack #31], this puts the entire text of Amazon reviews on your web site.

The easiest and most reliable way to access customer reviews programmatically is through the Web Services API. Unfortunately, the API gives only a small window to the larger number of reviews available. An API query for the book *Cluetrain Manifesto*, for example, includes three user reviews. If you visit the review page [Hack #28] for that book, though, you'll find 128 reviews. To dig deeper into the reviews available on Amazon.com and use all of them on your own web site, you'll need to delve deeper into scripting.

The Code

This Perl script, *get_reviews.pl*, builds a URL to the reviews page for a given ASIN, uses regular expressions to find the reviews, and breaks the review into its pieces: rating, title, date, reviewer, and the text of the review.

```
#!/usr/bin/perl
# get_reviews.pl
#
# A script to scrape Amazon, retrieve reviews, and write to a file
# Usage: perl get_reviews.pl <asin>
use strict;
use warnings;
use LWP::Simple;

# Take the asin from the command-line
my $asin = shift @ARGV or die "Usage: perl get_reviews.pl <asin>\n";

# Assemble the URL from the passed asin.
my $url = "http://amazon.com/o/tg/detail/-/$asin/?vi=customer-reviews";

# Set up unescape-HTML rules. Quicker than URI::Escape.
my %unescape = ('&quot;'=>'"', '&amp;'=>'&', ' '=>' ');
my $unescape_re = join '|' => keys %unescape;
```

```
# Request the URL.
my $content = get($url);
die "Could not retrieve $url" unless $content;

#Remove everything before the reviews
$content =~ s!.*?Number of Reviews:!!ms;

# Loop through the HTML looking for matches
while ($content =~ m!<img.*?stars-(†)-0.gif.*?>.*?<b>(.*?)</b>, (.*?)↵
\n.*?Reviewer:\n<b>\n(.*?)</b>.*?</table>\n(.*?)<br>\n<br>!mgis) {

    my($rating,$title,$date,$reviewer,$review) = ↵
($1||'',$2||'',$3||'',$4||'',$5||'');
    $reviewer =~ s!<.+?>!!g;   # drop all HTML tags
    $reviewer =~ s!‹.+?›!!g;   # remove anything in parenthesis
    $reviewer =~ s!\n!!g;      # remove newlines
    $review =~ s!<.+?>!!g;     # drop all HTML tags
    $review =~ s/($unescape_re)/$unescape{$1}/migs; # unescape.

    # Print the results
    print "$title\n" . "$date\n" . "by $reviewer\n" .
          "$rating stars.\n\n" . "$review\n\n";

}
```

Running the Hack

This script can be run from a command line and requires an ASIN. The reviews are too long to read as they scroll past on your screen, so it helps to send the information to a text file (in this case, *reviews.txt*) like so:

```
perl get_reviews.pl asin > reviews.txt
```

#35 Publish Your Amazon Reviews on Your Site

With a little screen scraping, you can gather all the reviews you've posted to Amazon and publish them on your own web site.

If you've contributed reviews to Amazon and also have your own space on the Web, you might want to gather your reviews together and make them available to readers of your site. With your Amazon ID **[Hack #43]** in hand, you can link directly to a page on Amazon that lists all of your reviews:

```
http://www.amazon.com/exec/obidos/tg/cm/member-reviews/-/insert Amazon ID
```

If you want to take it a step further, you can use some regular-expression pattern matching to grab your reviews with one request and format them for your site.

The Code

The following ASP script requires your Amazon ID. Create a file called *my_reviews.asp* and enter the following code:

```
<% Const AmazonID = "insert Amazon ID" %>
<html>
<head>
    <title>My Amazon Reviews</title>
</head>

<body>
<%
strURL = "http://www.amazon.com/exec/obidos/tg/cm/member-reviews/-/" & _
         AmazonID & "/t/"
Set xmlhttp = Server.CreateObject("Msxml2.SERVERXMLHTTP")
xmlhttp.Open "GET", strURL, false
xmlhttp.Send(Now)
strContent = xmlhttp.responseText
Set xmlhttp = Nothing

Set objRegExpr = New regexp
objRegExpr.Pattern = "<a [^>].*detail/-/(.*?)/[^>].*><b>(.*?)</b>[\s\S]*?(\↵
d) out of 5 stars[\s\S]*?<b>(.*?)</b> \n(.*?)\n<br>\n(.*?)\n<br><br>"
objRegExpr.Global = True
objRegExpr.IgnoreCase = True
Set objMatches = objRegExpr.Execute(strContent)
If objMatches.Count = 0 Then
    response.write "No reviews found."
Else
    For Each objMatch In objMatches
        strASIN = objMatch.SubMatches(0)
        strTitle = objMatch.SubMatches(1)
        strRating = objMatch.SubMatches(2)
        strReviewTitle = objMatch.SubMatches(3)
        strReviewDate = objMatch.SubMatches(4)
        strReviewText = objMatch.SubMatches(5)
        response.write "<u>" & strTitle & "</u> - "
        response.write "ASIN: " & strASIN & "<br>"
        response.write "(" & strRating & " stars.) "
        response.write "<b>" & strReviewTitle & "</b>, "
        response.write strReviewDate & "<br>"
        response.write "<blockquote>" & strReviewText & "</blockquote>"
        response.write "<br><br>"
        response.flush
    Next
End If
Set objMatches = Nothing
Set objRegExpr = Nothing
%>
</body>
</html>
```

This code requests the review page from Amazon and finds matches in the HTML for the relevant data. It breaks the review down into its parts (ASIN, title, rating, review title, date, and review text) and formats it for the page.

Running the Hack

Upload the file to a web server running IIS, and request it from your browser. The page should show your Amazon reviews. Screen scraping is a costly process that requires trips to remote servers, so if you're going to make this page public, it's a good idea to use the same method to cache this data in memory **[Hack #94]** as you can with Amazon Web Services responses.

#36 Share the Love (and Savings!) with Your Friends

Amazon's Share the Love program lets you and your friends save money by buying the same products. Here's a way to keep track of who wants what.

Amazon's "Share The Love" feature lets you send a 10% discount to people for the products you've purchased. For example, as you're checking out while purchasing *The Matrix* DVD, you're given the option to send a Share the Love discount via email. If anyone you send the discount to purchases the *The Matrix* DVD within a week, you'll receive a credit (the amount the 10% provides off of the regular price—so the more expensive an item, the bigger the credit).

The problem is, it's hard to know who among your friends is interested in the products you're purchasing. (Not to mention the struggle to remember their email address while you're checking out.)

This script comes to the rescue by gathering product requests from your friends, allowing all of you to share the savings with each other when you purchase products from Amazon. As you check out at Amazon, you can stop by this script to see if any of your friends have requested discounts for the products you're purchasing.

The Code

This PHP script performs two separate actions depending on what variables are passed to it. If someone is adding a product they'd like to receive a discount on, it adds their email address to a text file. (The file is written to the same directory as the script with the name of the ASIN as the title, *ASIN.db*.) If someone is looking for email addresses to send "the love" (discount) to, it displays all of the email addresses saved in the ASIN text file. Create a PHP file called *share_love.php* and add the following code:

```
<?php
// share_love.php
// A Web page that associates ASINs with email addresses
// and then displays them. This helps take advantage of
// Amazon's *Share the Love* discount system.
if ($HTTP_GET_VARS) {
    if ($HTTP_GET_VARS['sub']=="add item") {
        $file=($HTTP_GET_VARS['asin'] . ".db");
        $fp=fopen("$file", "a+");
        fwrite($fp, $HTTP_GET_VARS['email']);
        fclose($fp);
        echo "Asin added!<br><br>";
    } elseif ($HTTP_GET_VARS['sub']=="get addresses") {
        $file=($HTTP_GET_VARS['asin'] . ".db");
        if (file_exists($file)) {
          echo "<h2>Sharing Love</h2>";
          echo "Paste these addresses into Amazon's Share the Love";
          echo " form:<br><br>";
            $fp=fopen("$file", "r");
            $contents = fread ($fp, filesize ($file));
            $a_adds = split("\n", $contents);
            if (count($a_adds) > 1) {
                for($i = 0;$i < count($a_adds)-1; $i++) {
                    echo $a_adds[$i] . ", ";
                }
            } else {
                echo $contents;
            }
        } else {
            echo "<h2>No Love</h2>";
            echo "No email addresses for this ASIN.";
        }
    }
} else {
?>
<html>
<body>
<h2>Add Product</h2>
<form action="share_love.php" method="get">
ASIN:<br><input type="text" name="asin" size="10"><br><br>
Email:<br><input type="text" name="email" size="25"><br><br>
<input type="submit" name="sub" value="add item">
</form>
<br><br>
<h2>Get Addresses</h2>
<form action="share_love.php" method="get">
ASIN:<br><input type="text" name="asin" name="" size="10"><br><br>
<input type="submit" name="sub" value="get addresses">
</form>
</body>
</html>
<?php } ?>
```

Running the Hack

Upload this file to your server and visit the page. Get the ball rolling by entering your email address along with the ASIN of the products you'd like a discount for. Let your friends know about the page, and have them add products as well.

Now that you know who wants what, visit the page again as you're checking out of Amazon to see if anyone has requested discounts for the products you're buying. If they have, copy the list of addresses and paste them into Amazon's Share the Love form.

#37 Create a Guide

Share your expert knowledge with the world by creating a tutorial that shows up on product detail pages.

Have you ever wanted to know how to "Make-Out to the Right Music," or "Be Serious About Your Photographs"? Both of these are titles of guides available on Amazon.com that were written by other Amazon visitors. Anyone can write a guide about any topic.

To get a sense of how guides work, start looking for them on Amazon pages. Amazon links to guides toward the bottom of product detail pages with the heading "So you'd like to..." with the guide titles as you see in Figure 3-4.

So You'd Like To...

- fix someone, or some thing.: by Cammy Diaz, Legal beagle and a cute bookworm
- Living with MS Windows: by Anita Tenenbaum, Assisted living manager
- learn about Windows XP: by interf, creator and author of Annoyances.org

▸ Let us know if any of these guides are inappropriate.

Figure 3-4. Links to guides from a product detail page

A product detail page will link to a guide when that product (or a related product) appears in the guide. Amazon links to only three related guides; if more related guides are available, they're rotated with each page view. You can also find guides with related items on search results pages. The guides themselves are free-form, essay-like writing, like you see in Figure 3-5. The guides contain headlines for different sections and links to products. Each guide must have at least three product references.

Once you're ready to tackle a guide, visit your Friends & Favorites page (*http://www.amazon.com/friends*) and click "Write a So You'd Like to...

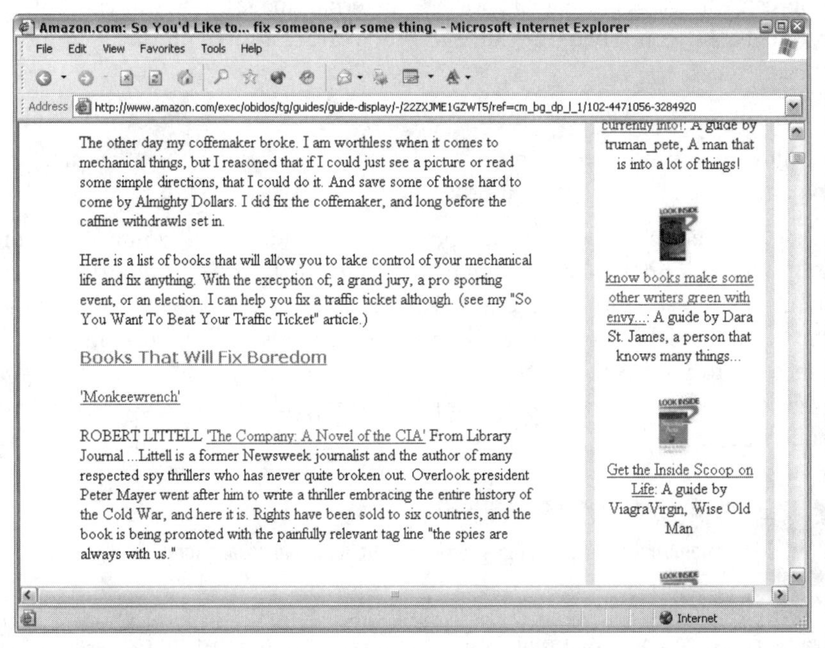

Figure 3-5. An Amazon Guide

guide" in the lefthand column. Alternately, you can visit the guide-creation form directly at *http://www.amazon.com/o/guide-create/*.

The first step is adding a title. Keep in mind that the title will usually immediately follow the words "So you'd like to…", which means it's a good idea to let the sentence flow. "So you'd like to *Good Hiking Advice*" just doesn't flow as well as "So you'd like to *Hike Like an Expert.*" Then you'll need to add your qualifications for writing the guide. Of course they don't have to be professional qualifications, just something that gives the guide reader a bit more context about who you are.

Next, enter the entire text of the guide. Each guide has a 100-word minimum and a 1,500-word maximum. Because it can be fairly long, you might want to compose your guide in a word processor (taking advantage of its spellchecking and other features) and copy the text into the guide form.

HTML isn't allowed in the guides, but you can do some minimal formatting. To create a headline for a section of your guide, you can use this tag:

```
<HEADLINE: "insert headline">
```

You can't link to external sites or add external images, but you can link to products. As mentioned, you have to link to at least three products with this special tag:

```
<ASIN: insert ASIN>
```

At most, you can have 50 product links in a single guide, but if you need to expand you can always start another guide.

Once you've previewed and then posted your guide, it will go into rotation on the product detail pages of items you included. Keep in mind that if an item is extremely popular, there may be several guides vying to be one of the three listed on the product detail page. You can also edit your guide at any time. Go to your About You page (click "Your About You Area" at *http://www.amazon.com/friends*) and you'll see your guides page listed on the left-hand side.

#38 Post a Guide Remotely

Customize the guide-writing experience with a remote posting form.

If you're a guide-writing junkie or thinking about becoming one, you may want to create your own page so you can control the posting experience for yourself. You can add a guide-writing form to your own web site, customize it, and even offer it to your visitors as a convenience.

The Code

This is just standard HTML, so create a file called *remote_guide.html* with the following form:

```
<html>
<body>
<form method=post action="http://amazon.com/exec/obidos/guide-preview/">

<!-- Visible Form Fields -->
Title:<br>
<input type=text name="guide.title" size=50 value=""><br><br>
Qualifications:<br>
<input type=text name="guide.qualifications" size=50 value=""><br><br>
Guide:<br>
<textarea name="guide.text" cols=80 rows=10></textarea><br><br>

<!-- Hidden Form Fields -->
<input type=hidden name="guide.author" value="insert Amazon ID">
<input type=hidden name="guide.format.asin-link" value="<a href=&quot;↵
/exec/obidos/ASIN/%s/102-4471056-3284920&quot;>'%s'</A>">
<input type=hidden name="guide.format.heading-link" value=↵
"<a href=&quot;#guide.heading.%03d&quot;><b class=sans>%s</b></a>">
```

```
<input type="submit" value="Add Guide">
</form>
</body>
</html>
```

The only changes to Amazon's form are the addition of the full URL in the form's `action` attribute, and of your Amazon ID **[Hack #43]** to the `guide.author` hidden field.

Running the Hack

Since the code is standard HTML, you can open *remote_guide.html* in any browser locally, or include the code in any existing web page. Click Add Guide, and you'll be taken to a preview page where you'll be notified of any errors. You can also double-check everything before you approve it. (You'll be required to sign in with your Amazon account at this point, if you're not already signed in.) If others will be posting guides from this form, change the `guide.author` form field type from `hidden` to `text`. This will allow anyone to add a guide if they know their Amazon ID.

#39 Add Product Advice Remotely

Allow your site's visitors to add product buying advice directly to Amazon.

The Customer Advice feature lets you recommend another product in addition to or instead of the current product. You can usually find the form on the product detail page under the heading "What's Your Advice?". If it's not there, you can always find the form on the product's advice page:

```
http://amazon.com/o/tg/detail/-/insert ASIN/?vi=advice
```

The form shown in Figure 3-6 accepts an ASIN and allows you to choose how you're recommending the item.

If you'd like to integrate this feature within a remote site, you can duplicate the form elements with HTML. Keep in mind that your visitors will be able to add advice from your site only if they're registered Amazon users.

The Code

This code takes the key elements from the product advice form at Amazon. Each advice form links to a specific item, and you'll need to include the ASIN for that product where indicated.

```
<html>
<body>
<form action="http://amazon.com/exec/obidos/flex-sign-in/ref=cm_custrec_f_
advice/" method=post>
```

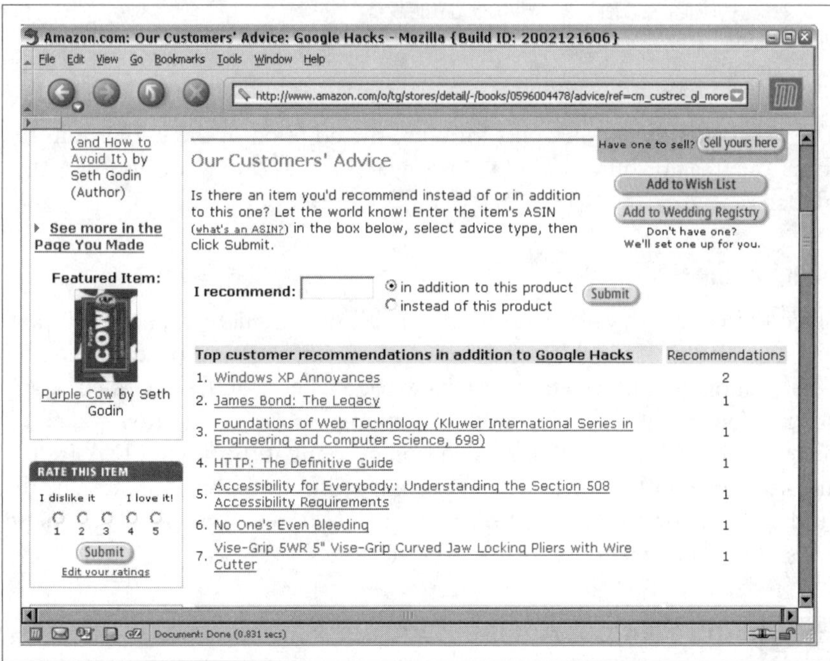

Figure 3-6. Customer Advice form

```
<!-- Visible Form Fields -->
<b>I recommend:</b> <input type=text name="related-asin" size=10><br><br>
<input type=radio name="rating-type" value="customer-accessories" checked>in
addition to this product<br>
<input type=radio name="rating-type" value="customer-recommends">instead of
this product<br><br>

<!-- Hidden Form Fields -->
<input type=hidden name="method" value="GET">
<input type=hidden name="opt" value="n">
<input type=hidden name="cont-page" value="cm/custrec-signed-in-continue">
<input type=hidden name="cont-type" value="cust-rec">
<input type=hidden name="response" value="rate-item">
<input type=hidden name="page" ↵
      value="community/recommend-sign-in-secure.html">
<input type=hidden name="secure-rate-item-next-page"↵
      value="tg/stores/detail/-/books/insert ASIN/advice">
<input type=hidden name="rate-item-next-page"↵
      value="tg/stores/detail/-/books/insert ASIN/advice">
<input type=hidden name="rated-item-id" value="insert ASIN">
<input type=hidden name="rated-item-value" value="+">
<input type=hidden name="creator-customer-id" value="insert Amazon ID">
<input type=hidden name="require-valid-asin" value="true">
```

```
<input type="submit" value="add advice">
</form>
</body>
</html>
```

Running the Hack

Because this is standard HTML, you can add it to any existing web page. If you'd like to take away the user's choice of "in addition to" or "instead of," you can make the visible form fields invisible by changing the field type for the choice you want to use to `hidden`, and removing the alternate choice.

#40 Scrape Customer Advice

Screen scraping can give you access to community features not yet implemented through the API—like customer buying advice.

Customer buying advice isn't available through Amazon's Web Services, so if you'd like to include this information on a remote site, you'll have to get it from Amazon's site through scraping. The first step to this hack is knowing where to find all of the customer advice on one page. The following URL links directly to the advice page for a given ASIN:

```
http://amazon.com/o/tg/detail/-/insert ASIN/?vi=advice
```

The Code

This Perl script, *get_advice.pl*, splits the advice page into two variables based on the headings "in addition to" and "instead of." It then loops through those sections, using regular expressions to match the products' information. The script then formats and prints the information.

```
#!/usr/bin/perl
# get_advice.pl
# A script to scrape Amazon to retrieve customer buying advice
# Usage: perl get_advice.pl <asin>

#Take the asin from the command-line
my $asin =shift @ARGV or die "Usage:perl get_advice.pl <asin>\n";

#Assemble the URL
my $url = "http://amazon.com/o/tg/detail/-/" . $asin .
          "/?vi=advice";

#Set up unescape-HTML rules
my %unescape = ('&quot;'=>'"', '&amp;'=>'&', ' '=>' ');
my $unescape_re = join '|' => keys %unescape;
```

```
use strict;
use LWP::Simple;

#Request the URL
my $content = get($url);
die "Could not retrieve $url" unless $content;

my($inAddition) = (join '', $content) =~ m!in addition to(.*?)<tr>↵
<td colspan=3><br></td></tr>!mis;
my($instead) = (join '', $content) =~ m!recommendations instead of(.*?)</↵
table>!mis;

#Loop through the HTML looking for "in addition" advice
print "-- In Addition To --\n\n";
while ($inAddition =~ m!<td width=10>(.*?)</td>\n<td width=90%>.*?ASIN/(.↵
*?)/.*?">(.*?)</a>.*?</td>.*?<td width=10% align=center>(.*?)</td>!mgis) {
    my($place,$thisAsin,$title,$number) = ($1||'',$2||'',$3||'',$4||'');
    $title =~ s/($unescape_re)/$unescape{$1}/migs; #unescape HTML
    #Print the results
    print $place . " " .
          $title . " (" . $thisAsin . ")\n(" .
          "Recommendations: " . $number . ")" .
          "\n\n";
}

#Loop through the HTML looking for "instead of" advice
print "-- Instead Of --\n\n";
while ($instead =~ m!<td width=10>(.*?)</td>\n<td width=90%>.*?ASIN/(.*?)/.↵
*?">(.*?)</a>.*?</td>.*?<td width=10% align=center>(.*?)</td>!mgis) {
    my($place,$thisAsin,$title,$number) = ($1||'',$2||'',$3||'',$4||'');
    $title =~ s/($unescape_re)/$unescape{$1}/migs; #unescape HTML
    #Print the results
    print $place . " " .
          $title . " (" . $thisAsin . ")\n(" .
          "Recommendations: " . $number . ")" .
          "\n\n";
}
```

Running the Hack

Run this script from the command line, passing it any ASIN:

```
perl get_advice.pl ASIN
```

If the product has long lists of alternate recomendations, send the output to a text file. This example sends all alternate customer product recommendations for *Google Hacks* to a file called *advice.txt*:

```
perl get_advice.pl 0596004478 > advice.txt
```

#41 Create a Listmania! List

Show other Amazon customers your unique way of combining products with a list.

Consciously or unconsciously, we're continually organizing and categorizing the world around us. The way you organize things is often unique to your experience, occupation, personality, and a host of other factors. Amazon's *Listmania!* feature embraces these unique ways of framing the world by allowing you to organize any of their products however you'd like. Once organized, others can see your take on a subject.

Because you can add any product from Amazon's catalog, your list can contain items from more than just one area. A Beatles-related list, for example, may contain books, CDs, DVDs, and even clothes.

As with most Amazon Community features, you'll need to have an Amazon account **[Hack #13]**. To get started, visit the "Create a Listmania List" page (*http://www.amazon.com/exec/obidos/fil-create/*) shown in Figure 3-7 and sign in if necessary.

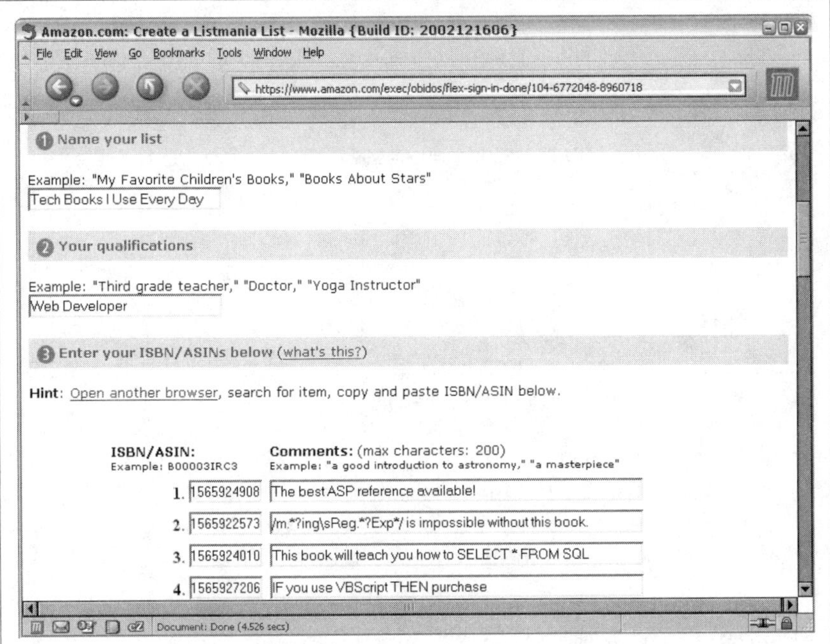

Figure 3-7. Listmania! creation form

The list creation form provides a spot for a title, your qualifications, and a list of up to 25 ASINs **[Hack #1]**.

You can't change the order of your items without copying and pasting ASINs and comments. If you're concerned about the order of your list, be sure to get the items in the proper sequence when you create your list. Comments are easy to edit, but changing the order can be time consuming.

Once you've entered your ASINs, click "Preview" to double-check your list before publishing it. Figure 3-8 shows a typical Listmania! preview page. You can then click "Publish this list" to make your list available to others.

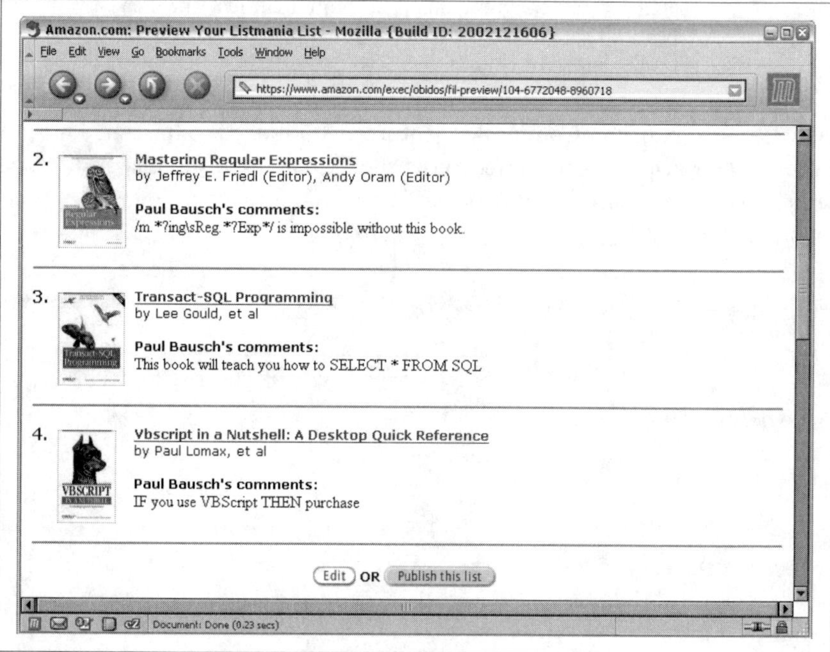

Figure 3-8. Previewing a Listmania! list before publishing

If thinking of your audience as the entire Amazon community is overwhelming, think about using Amazon's Listmania! feature for your own, smaller audiences. You could create a list just for your co-workers, classmates, or any other group you'd like to share your unique view with.

Once you've published a list, it could show up on product detail pages **[in "Amazon Product Pages" in Chapter 1]**. It will also be available on your lists page, which you can access directly with your Amazon ID **[Hack #43]**:

```
http://amazon.com/o/tg/cm/member-fil/-/insert Amazon ID
```

To share your list with a specific group on a web site or via email, you'll need to link to it directly. You can link to any Listmania! list if you know its List ID. Finding the List ID is just a matter of examining URLs.

Visit your lists page and click the title of the list you want to link to. The URL should look something like this:

```
http://www.amazon.com/exec/obidos/tg/listmania/list-browse/-/2RJC5ST5VZDF1/
```

That alphanumeric code at the end of the URL is the List ID for the list you clicked on. Once you have a List ID, you can link to it directly:

```
http://www.amazon.com/exec/obidos/tg/listmania/list-browse/-/insert List ID/
```

You can also access your list programmatically as XML via the Web Services API. A query to access a list as XML looks like this:

```
http://xml.amazon.com/onca/xml3?t=insert affiliate tag&dev-t=insert dev ↵
token&type=heavy&f=xml&ListManiaSearch=insert List ID
```

#42 Gather Your Friends on Amazon

Track your friends' Amazon activities by adding them to your Friends list.

Getting all of your friends together in one place is never an easy task. But if your friends have Amazon accounts, Amazon gives you a chance to make it happen. Adding friends to your Amazon Friends list allows you to see products they've added to their Wish Lists, read their latest product reviews, and potentially see items they've recently purchased.

You can find other users on Amazon and add them to your Friends list. The easiest way to find people is to use the search box in the upper lefthand corner of the Friends & Favorites page at *http://amazon.com/exec/obidos/subst/community/community-home.html*.

The drop-down menu is set to "People" by default. Try typing in the name or email address of someone you know. You'll be surprised at how many people already have Amazon accounts. If you spot someone you'd like to add, click their name, then click "Make Amazon Friend" on the righthand side of their member page.

Another way to add people you know to your Amazon Friends list is to send them an invitation email. Make sure you're logged in, and then visit the invitation page, *http://www.amazon.com/exec/obidos/invite-friends/*.

Separate your friends' email addresses by commas, like so:

```
adam@example.com, beth@example.com, cassie@example.com
```

Click "Add" and you're all set! Your friends will receive an invitation to join Amazon and will be added to your friends list.

There are two statuses for your friends at Amazon. One is "Favorite People" and the other is "Amazon Friend." Favorite People have the ability to see your lists, Wish Lists, and reviews. Amazon Friends can see all of those and selected items from your purchase history.

Amazon defaults to making people Amazon Friends, so be sure you're willing to share purchased items with them. If you'd like to change the access level of your friends at any time, visit the Update Favorite People page at *http://amazon.com/o/customer-link-management.*

#43 Gather Your Friends' Amazon IDs

Linking directly to someone's community activities requires finding their Amazon ID.

Each community user at Amazon is identified with an Amazon ID, an alphanumeric string that represents an Amazon account. The URLs of the community features revolve around these IDs, and to link directly to certain features (and to use some of the hacks in this book!) you'll need to know your own Amazon ID.

Your Amazon ID can be found in almost every community feature URL. Start out at the Friends & Favorites page, *http://amazon.com/exec/obidos/subst/community/community-home.html*. On the lefthand side of the page, click "Your About You Area" and note the URL. The string after `member-glance` is your Amazon ID.

```
http://www.amazon.com/exec/obidos/tg/cm/member-glance/-/Amazon ID
```

Linking Directly to Community Features

Now that you know your ID, you can link directly to any of your community-related activities:

About You Area
: Your Amazon home page that includes a summary of all your community activities, and links to other community areas.

```
http://amazon.com/exec/obidos/tg/cm/member-glance/-/Amazon ID/
```

Favorite People
: A list of people you've added to your Friends list.

```
http://amazon.com/exec/obidos/tg/cm/member-favorites/-/Amazon ID/
```

Reviews
: A list of all the reviews you've contributed to Amazon.

```
http://amazon.com/exec/obidos/tg/cm/member-reviews/-/Amazon ID/
```

Lists

A list of all the Listmania! lists you've published.

http://amazon.com/exec/obidos/tg/cm/member-**fil**/-/*Amazon ID*/

Guides

A list of the guides you've created.

http://amazon.com/exec/obidos/tg/cm/member-**guides**/-/*Amazon ID*/

Linking to your activities is a bit narcissistic, so it'd be nice to have your friends' Amazon IDs to speed up the community deep linking. You know how to access your Favorite People page, and collecting their IDs is a snap with screen scraping.

The Code

This Perl script, *get_friend_IDs.pl*, uses an Amazon ID, grabs the HTML of the Friends list, and finds your friends' Amazon IDs.

```
#!/usr/bin/perl
# get_friend_IDs.pl
# A script to scrape Amazon, retrieve friend IDs, and write to a file
# Usage: perl get_friend_IDs.pl <amazonID>

#Take the asin from the command-line
my $amazonID =shift @ARGV or die "Usage:get_friend_IDs.pl <amazonID>\n";

#Assemble the URL
my $url = "http://amazon.com/exec/obidos/tg/cm/member-favorites/-/" .
          $amazonID . "/";

use strict;
use LWP::Simple;

#Request the URL
my $content = get($url);
die "Could not retrieve $url" unless $content;

my $friends = (join '', $content);

while ($friends =~ m!<b><a href="/exec/obidos/tg/cm/member-glance/-/(.*?)/↵
ref=cm_aya_av.fp_faya/">(.*?)</a></b>!mgis) {
    my($amznID,$name) = ($1||'',$2||'');
    #Print the results
    print $name . " (" .
          $amznID . ")" .
          "\n\n";
}
```

Running the Hack

Run this code from a command line, passing it your Amazon ID:

```
perl get_friend_IDs.pl Amazon ID
```

The script will return all of the users on the Friends page, along with their Amazon IDs in parentheses:

```
User Name (Amazon ID)
```

Get Purchase Circle Products with Screen Scraping

Purchase Circles provide a unique look at sales patterns. You can access them programmatically only with screen scraping.

Amazon's purchase circles are specialized bestseller lists broken down by geography or organization. If you visit the Friends & Favorites page, choose "Purchase Circles" from the drop-down list, and type the name of your city, chances are you'll find what's uniquely popular among your fellow residents. Amazon also lists what's popular at universities and large corporations. If everyone at Microsoft is reading about a certain technology, you may find it in the next version of Windows!

Finding Purchase Circle IDs

In fact, you can link directly to the Microsoft Corporation purchase circle:

```
http://www.amazon.com/exec/obidos/tg/cm/browse-communities/-/211569/
```

The six-digit code at the end of the URL is the Purchase Circle ID for Microsoft. Every purchase circle has a unique ID. You can find IDs by noting them from URLs as you browse circles. The purchase circles home page (*http://www.amazon.com/exec/obidos/subst/community/community.html*) is a good place to start.

Once you know an ID, you can link to it directly using the URL format. You can also write scripts to access the page and retrieve a list of items.

The Code

This script takes a Purchase Circle ID and returns the books listed. Create a file called *get_circle.pl* and add the following code:

```
#!/usr/bin/perl
# get_circle.pl
# A script to scrape Amazon to retrieve purchase circle products
# Usage: perl get_circle.pl <circleID>
```

```
#Take the asin from the command-line
my $circleID =shift @ARGV or die "Usage:perl get_circle.pl <circleID>\n";

#Assemble the URL
my $url = "http://amazon.com/o/tg/cm/browse-communities/-/" .
          $circleID . "/t/";

use strict;
use LWP::Simple;

#Request the URL
my $content = get($url);
die "Could not retrieve $url" unless $content;

my $circle = (join '', $content);

while ($circle =~ m!<title>(.*?)</title>!mgis) {
    print $1 . "\n\n";
}

while ($circle =~ m!<td.*?<b><a.*?-/(.*?)[?/].*?>(.*?)</a></b>.*?by↵
(.*?)<br>.*?</td>!mgis) {
    my($asin,$title,$author) = ($1||'',$2||'',$3||'');
    #Print the results
    print $title . "\n" .
          "by " . $author . "\n" .
          "ASIN: " . $asin .
          "\n\n";
}
```

One thing to note about this code is that it passes the `/t/` URL argument to return a text-only version of the purchase circle page. Text-only pages have less HTML, which means that fewer bytes are flying around and it's generally easier to scrape for information.

Running the Hack

You can run this hack, providing a Purchase Circle ID, from the command line like this:

```
perl get_circle.pl insert purchase circle ID
```

Hacking the Hack

This script returns popular books for a given circle, but there's no reason you can't also get lists of the most popular music or movies for a circle. Add a catalog after the Purchase Circle ID to find what you're looking for. Here are the possible catalogs:

```
music
dvd
```

```
video
toy
ce (electronics)
```

So, for example, to link directly to DVDs that are popular in Sebastopol, CA, find the Purchase Circle ID, and add /dvd/ to the URL:

```
http://amazon.com/exec/obidos/tg/cm/browse-communities/-/216435/dvd/
```

If you'd like to keep it text-only as in the script, the /t/ follows the catalog:

```
http://amazon.com/exec/obidos/tg/cm/browse-communities/-/216435/dvd/t/
```

Find Purchase Circles by Zip Code

Combining two different Web Services can create a new feature.

Finding purchase circles is pretty easy, and with a bit of scraping, you can tie them into geographic data. Amazon doesn't offer the ability to look up purchase circles by U.S. zip code, but using the USPS web site and some simple pattern matching, you can find purchase circles for all cities within a given zip code.

The Code

This PHP script combines two different services with screen scraping. It looks for all of the cities within a particular zip code at the U.S. Postal Service web site. Then it finds matching purchase circles at Amazon and provides links to them. Create *zip_circle.php* with the following code:

```
<?php
$strZip = $_GET['zipcode'];
$zipPage = "";
$indexPage = "";
$cntCity = 0;
$myCity = "";

set_time_limit(60);

//get a certain number of characters
function left($str_in,$num) {
    return ereg_replace("^(.{1,$num})[ .,].*","\\1", $str_in);
}

function findCircle($city) {
    $indexPage = "";
    //Find purchase cirlce brose codes
    $abc = "a,b,c,d,e,f,g,h,i,j,k,l,m,n,o,p,q,r,s,t,u,v,w,x,y,z";
    $a_abc = split(",", $abc);
    $thisLetter = strtolower(substr($city,0,1));
    for($j = 0;$j < count($a_abc)-1; $j++) {
        if ($thisLetter == $a_abc[$j]) {
```

```
            $thisCode = 226120 + ($j + 1);
        }
    }
    $url = "http://www.amazon.com/exec/obidos/tg/cm/browse-communities/-/" .
           $thisCode . "/t/";
    $contents = fopen($url,"r");
    do {
       $data = fread ($contents, 4096);
       if (strlen($data) == 0) {
          break;
       }
       $indexPage .= $data;
   } while(1);
    fclose ($contents);
    $k = 0;
    if (preg_match_all('/i>.*?<a href=/exec/obidos/tg/browse/-/(.*?)/t/↵
.*?>(.*?)</a>.*?<l/s',$indexPage,$cities)) {
      foreach ($cities[2] as $cityName) {
        if (strtolower($city) == strtolower($cityName)) {
          $link = "http://www.amazon.com/exec/obidos/tg/cm/↵
browse-communities/-/";
          $link = $link . $cities[1][$k];
          $link = "<a href=" . $link . ">";
          $link = $link . $cityName . "</a>";
          return $link;
        }
        $k++;
       } // foreach
       return "No purchase circle found for " . $city;
    } //if
} //function

//Get cities associated with zip codes from USPS
$url = "http://www.usps.com/zip4/zip_response.jsp?zipcode=" . $strZip;
$contents = fopen($url,"r");
while (!feof ($contents))
    $zipPage .= fgets($contents, 4096);
fclose ($contents);

if (preg_match_all('/<tr valign="top" bgcolor=".*?">(.*?)</tr>/
s',$zipPage,$cityState)) {
    foreach ($cityState[0] as $cs) {
        $cntCity++;
        if (preg_match_all('/\n\n(.*?)</font></td>\n/',$cs,$c)) {
            foreach ($c[1] as $d) {
                $myCity = $myCity . $d . ", ";
            }
        $myCity = $myCity . Chr(8);
        $myCity = ereg_replace(", ".chr(8), chr(8), $myCity);
        } else {
            echo "city not found.";
        }
    }
```

```
}

echo "<h2>Purchase Circles</h2>";

$a_myCity = split(chr(8), $myCity);
for($i = 0;$i < count($a_myCity)-1; $i++) {
    $thisCity = $a_myCity[$i];
    echo findCircle($thisCity) . "<br>";
}
?>
```

Scraping both the USPS site and Amazon can take some time, so the time limit for the script has been increased to 60 seconds.

This script relies on the fact that certain purchase circle pages have predictable IDs. Armed with the knowledge that every city that starts with A is in Purchase Circle 226121, we can assume that cities that start with *B* will be in Purchase Circle ID *226122*, etc. As cities are found at the USPS site, their first letter is matched up with a Purchase Circle ID, and the page is scraped to find an exact match.

Running the Hack

Upload this script to a web server and access the page providing a zip code in the querystring, like so:

```
http://your.server/zip_circle.php?zipcode=zip code
```

The result should be a list of links to Amazon purchase circles for cities in that code.

#46 Track the Ranks of Books Over Time

Knowing an item's sales rank gives an indication of how it's selling right now. Tracking that rank over time gives an indication of how its sales are changing.

Sales rank is a look at how a particular item is selling in relation to every other item. An item with a sales rank of 1 is the best-selling item at Amazon right now. The lower the number, the better the sales.

One problem with the sales rank number is that it's only a snapshot of the last 24 hours of sales data. There's no indication of the way sales have changed over periods of time for any particular item. Luckily, there's an application that can help out.

Using JungleScan.com

JungleScan (*http://www.junglescan.com*) tracks any item at Amazon and charts the progress of its sales rank over time. The front page includes those items with the biggest changes for the day (both good and bad), much like a stock report.

If you're interested only in certain products rather than general trends, you can add items to your JungleScan profile. Click on "your portfolio" and create an account if you don't already have one.

Once logged in, you need to add items that you'd like to track. The quickest way to add products to your portfolio is to click "track new item" on the top menu. In a new browser window, visit Amazon.com and find the item you're interested in. Browse to its product detail page and copy the URL; then go back to JungleScan and paste in the URL. If the item has a sales rank, you'll have the option to "Save this product into your personal AmazonScan portfolio." Continue adding products until you've assembled a list of those you're interested in. Figure 3-9 shows a JungleScan Portfolio tracking six items.

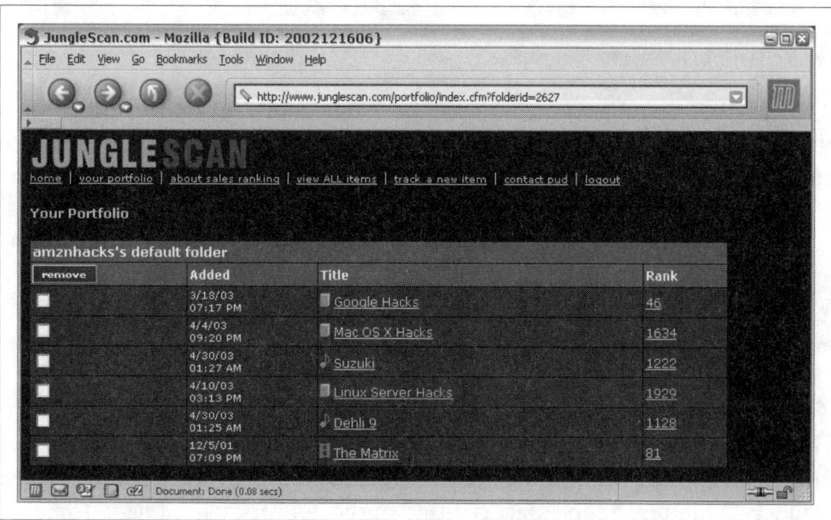

Figure 3-9. JungleScan portfolio page

On the portfolio page, you'll see the time that JungleScan began tracking the item, its title, and its current sales rank. The rank is updated roughly every 24 hours. Clicking the current rank takes you to the product details, as shown for *Google Hacks* in Figure 3-10.

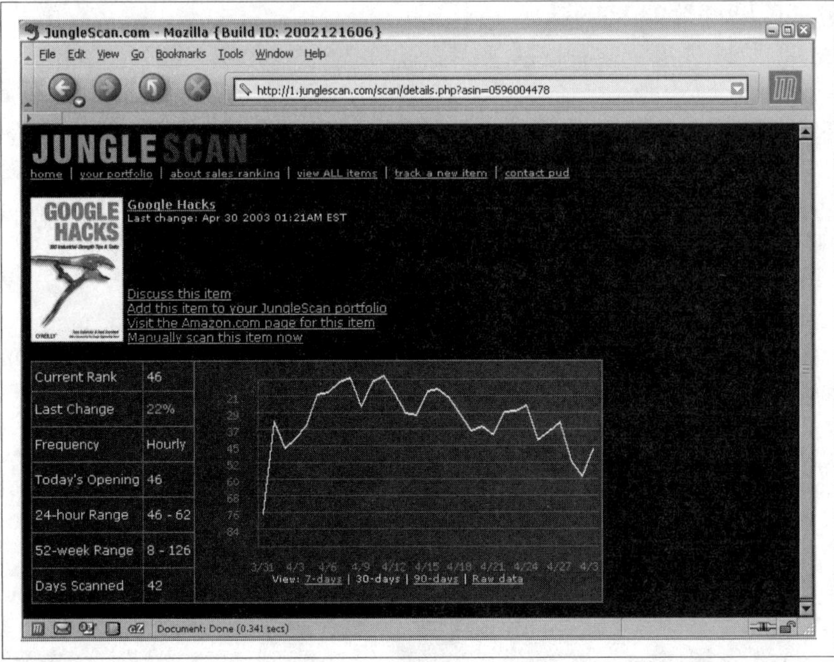

Figure 3-10. JungleScan product details page

The details page provides a look at how the sales rank has changed over time, along with a nifty graph to give a visual sense of its movement. You can adjust the graph to show different time periods, or even zero in on the raw data used to generate the graph.

#47 Group Conversations About Books

You can get insight into loosely connected conversations about books at All Consuming.

Think about all the conversations taking place on the Web at this moment. Unlike spoken conversation, conversations on the Web have a physical presence, a shape that persists over time in the form of digital text, and a visible trail left behind by people participating in the conversation. Trying to figure out what these conversations are about and following them from beginning to end, however, is not as easy as it might seem.

Conversations rarely give indicators allowing you to easily tell what they are about. Creating a script to determine this would require that it be able to interpret the meanings of sentences. To complicate things further, conversations can expand quickly to fill the entire community's consciousness overnight, or may lie dormant for months or years before being picked up again. Tracking and grouping these various bits of conversations has become a great opportunity and challenge for tool developers. All Consuming (*http://allconsuming.net*) is one web site that uses Amazon's friendly Web Services to attempt to track a tiny fraction of these conversations: those about books.

What Makes Grouping Conversations Possible

Tracking and following conversations about books became possible because these conversations had a couple fortunate characteristics.

First of all, books have unique identifiers. They have ISBNs (International Standard Book Numbers) that are recognized by almost everyone, including retailers, libraries, and, most importantly, the people having the conversations. These unique identifiers make it easy to find out when different people are talking about the same book.

Second, Amazon's Web Services make it easy get detailed book information about any ISBN. Even though people might occasionally misspell an author's name, link to a different version of its title, or leave the title or author out altogether, you can still easily figure out what book they're talking about if they link to Amazon or another retailer that has the ISBN in the URL.

Combining these two advantages, it took me just a few days to put together a web site that grouped conversations about the same book together from all over the Web. All Consuming slices and dices these conversations in a couple different ways.

Features at All Consuming

Books mentioned in the last hour
: Every hour, All Consuming visits the recently updated weblogs and looks for links to Amazon, Barnes & Noble, Book Sense, and even to itself. For each link that it finds, it checks to see if it had found that book on that web site before, and if not it saves it as a newly mentioned book. The newly mentioned books from each hour are listed at the top of All Consuming's home page, as you see in Figure 3-11.

Most popular books mentioned this week
: In addition to the standard hourly report, there is also an hourly list of the books mentioned the most this week, giving preference to the most recent. When half a dozen web sites mention the same book on the same day, it will appear near the top of the list so you can instantly see

Figure 3-11. All Consuming home page

when a book is generating buzz in the weblog community. You can also see snippets of the conversation on All Consuming or go directly to the site to see the conversation in context.

Weblogs mentioning this book
In addition to showing the most talked about books on the Web at the moment, there is a way to find out who's been talking about any book in Amazon's catalog. This allows you to visit a grouped conversation about a book even if it hasn't become active enough to make the front page.

Books mentioned by this weblog
Yet another way to slice the data is to display all of the books mentioned by a particular weblog or person. Every weblog has its own page on All Consuming, with a list of books mentioned on the weblog or directly through All Consuming.

If you want, you can also create an account at All Consuming, add books to your Currently Reading list, and then add a line of code to your site **[Hack #48]**.

—Erik Benson

#48 Add a "Currently Reading" List to Your Web Site

With a single line of code, you can give visitors an instant glimpse into what you're reading.

Letting people know what we're reading has always been an efficient way to give them a quick glimpse into our tastes—giving us a chance to appear insightful or silly or witty or dumb at a glance. We mention books we're reading at parties, during interviews, at the dinner table, so it's no surprise that we're also mentioning them in our web sites. Unfortunately, until recently, this required messing around with HTML to get the book's title, author, cover image, and maybe a few comments about the book on your site, and there was no way to find other people who were reading the same book.

Amazon's Web Services make it easy for a programmer to write a script to retrieve information and do all kinds of fun stuff with it, but programmers shouldn't be the only ones to get cool book lists on their sites. All Consuming allows you to maintain a list of books on your site with minimal effort and no programming knowledge at all. You don't even need to know HTML; you just have to cut and paste a couple lines of code into your site, and then you can maintain your list remotely from All Consuming. Also, because All Consuming knows what a lot of different people are reading, it gives you an easy way to find other people who are reading the same books, and instantly includes your comments in the loosely connected conversations around the Web.

Setting Up Your Book List

To set up your Currently Reading list, you first need to create an account at All Consuming (*http://allconsuming.net*). Then, search for the book you're reading and scroll down to the form that lets you add that book to your collection, as shown in Figure 3-12.

The Code

When you're done adding books to your list, go back to the control panel and the code will be right there for you to cut and paste into your site. It'll look something like this (of course, instead of having *erik* in the filename, it'll have your username):

```
<style type="text/css">
<!-
.ac_image {}
.ac_link {}
.ac_image_tag {}
```

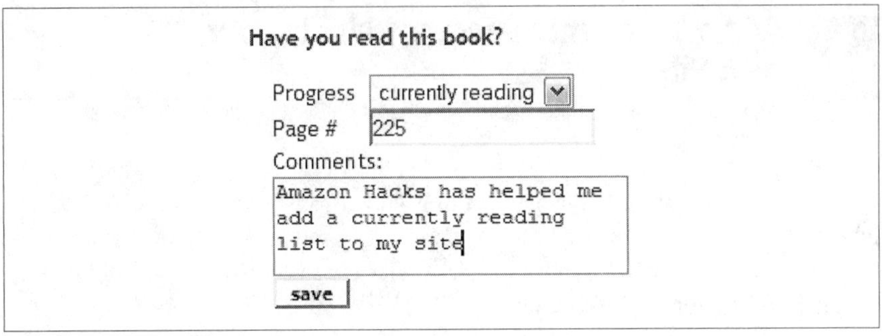

Figure 3-12. Adding a book on All Consuming

```
.ac_title {}
.ac_author {}
.ac_comment {}
.ac_logo {}
-->
</style>
<script language="javascript" type="text/javascript"
src="http://www.allconsuming.net/xml/users/currently_reading.erik.js"></
script>
```

Everything up to and including the </style> tag is optional—if you don't include it, your list will adopt the standard stylesheet for your web site. This small stylesheet includes classes that you can use to modify the look of your Currently Reading book list. For example, if you want the titles of the books to be bold, modify the .ac_title line to look like this:

```
.ac_title { font-weight: bold; }
```

If you have some knowledge on how to manipulate stylesheets, you can also add a border to the box, change the font, or even remove the cover images if you prefer to have only a text list.

The Results

Figure 3-13 shows what your book list might look like if you bold the title and author text and leave the rest at the default settings.

When you're done reading any of the books on your list, you can return to All Consuming and mark the book as "completed" using the same form you used to add the book or by going to the control panel and editing it there. Doing this will automatically remove the book from your web site. Similarly, you can continue adding books and comments to your site by adding and commenting on books at All Consuming. You'll never have to touch the code on your own site again unless you want to change the way your list is displayed.

Currently Reading

MANAGING THE DESIGN FACTORY by Donald G. Reinertsen
"Recommended this by an ex-director of our departme..." [more]

Metamagical Themas: Questing for the Essence of Mind and Pattern by Douglas R. Hofstadter
"Some light reading...." [more]

Middlesex: A Novel by Jeffrey Eugenides
"About a quarter of the way through this book and I..." [more]
ALL CONSUMING

Figure 3-13. Currently Reading list

Viewing Your Bookosphere

By clicking on the title or cover image of books on your site, you can see what other people around the Web are saying about the books you're reading. Lots of times, their comments will be included right there on All Consuming; otherwise, you'll have the option to click through and read the rest of their entries on their own sites.

—Erik Benson

CHAPTER FOUR

Selling Through Amazon

Hacks 49–58

Amazon took another unconventional step when they started allowing third parties to sell the same items Amazon sells alongside the listings in their catalog. What other business has opened up their billing and inventory systems to anyone and everyone—including *competitors*? It may seem counterintuitive, but Amazon is getting a small percentage of every sale. With thousands of transactions, that small percentage adds up quickly.

By using their site to connect both buyers and sellers, Amazon has enabled many entrepreneurs to sell through the Web without developing their own billing and marketing infrastructure. Other Amazon customers are also selling through their site. A box of books in the closet or a stack of CDs that no longer make it into rotation would otherwise continue to take up space. Instead, you can list them through Amazon, find people who are looking for exactly those items, and make some money.

Understanding Amazon's Sales Programs

Amazon has several systems in place that allow different ways of selling through their site. Understanding how each system works (and what they cost) will help you choose how you'd like to list your items on Amazon.

Marketplace

Amazon sells new and used books by third parties side by side with their own catalog. Underneath the "Add to Shopping Cart" button on product detail pages, you'll find a box called "More Buying Choices" shown in Figure 4-1.

Figure 4-1. More Buying Choices, used & new

If you click the "used & new" link, you'll find a list of sellers. Figure 4-2 shows a list of sellers offering *Google Hacks* for sale.

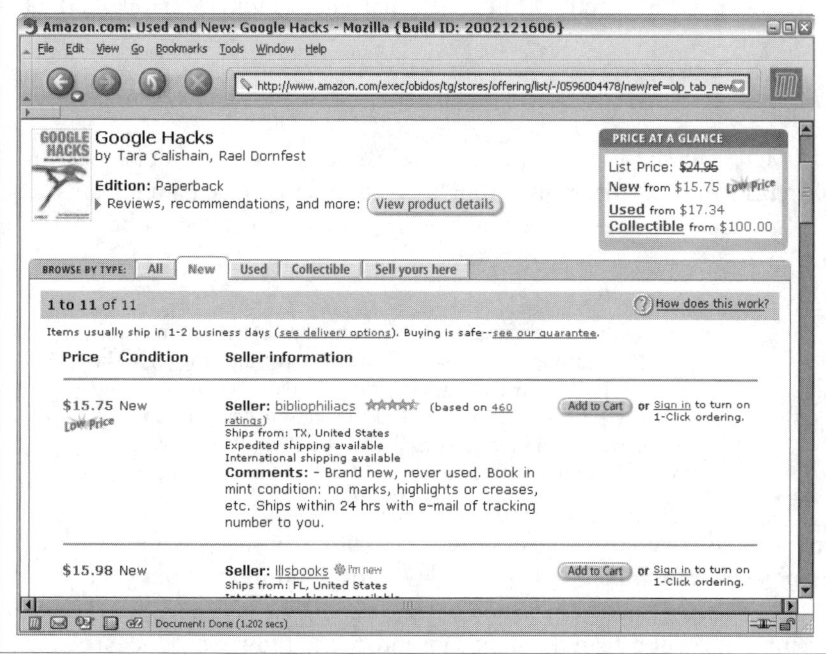

Figure 4-2. Used & New page, Marketplace listings

Just who are these sellers? They're primarily individuals and small businesses. Anyone can sell a product from these pages. Amazon refers to this system of third parties selling items from their catalog as Marketplace **[Hack #49]**.

Buying a new, used, or collectible item from a Marketplace seller is the same process as buying from Amazon. The only difference is what happens after your order is placed. Amazon notifies the specific Marketplace seller, and the seller ships the item to you. Amazon handles all the payment details and deposits the money from the sale directly into the sellers account—taking a cut for brokering the transaction, of course.

Each seller has a 1–5 star rating based on comments left by previous customers. This works as a reputation system that lets you read others' comments about the seller before buying, and leave comments about the transaction afterward.

Pro-Merchant Subscription

Pro-Merchant Subscription is a program Amazon offers to large-volume sellers. For a monthly fee, sellers get lower listing fees, get some tools to upload sale item information in higher quantities **[Hack #51]**, and can have an unlimited number of items listed. In addition, Pro-Merchant subscribers can offer alternate payment methods like personal checks, direct credit card payments, or C.O.Ds.

zShops

Pro-Merchant subscribers also have access to Amazon's zShops system. A *zShop* is a virtual storefront through which sellers can sell almost anything. An item doesn't have to be available in Amazon's catalog to be sold in a zShop.

By *almost* anything, Amazon means that certain items can't be sold through their site. It's worth reading through the Prohibited Content guide (*http://www.amazon.com/o/tg/browse/-/537784/*). Beyond learning how to stay in compliance with their terms of service, you'll find out about the sketchy things people have tried to sell online in the past.

zShops can have customized storefronts with a business logo and custom graphics. For example, New York–based brick-and-mortar music shop Accidental CDs has a custom zShop storefront shown in Figure 4-3. Potential customers can also search a shop's inventory and browse product areas.

To get a feel for how people are setting up their zShops, start browsing through them at the zShops home page (*http://www.amazon.com/zshops/*).

Auctions

Another option for selling through Amazon is listing items and letting others bid on them **[Hack #55]**. In addition to the thrill of watching the bids rise for a product you've listed, Amazon's per-item fee is a bit lower. Your item won't be listed in their product detail Marketplace listings, but it will be available through the Amazon Auctions section (*http://www.amazon.com/auctions/*). A typical auction item, in this case a pair of comic books, is shown in Figure 4-4.

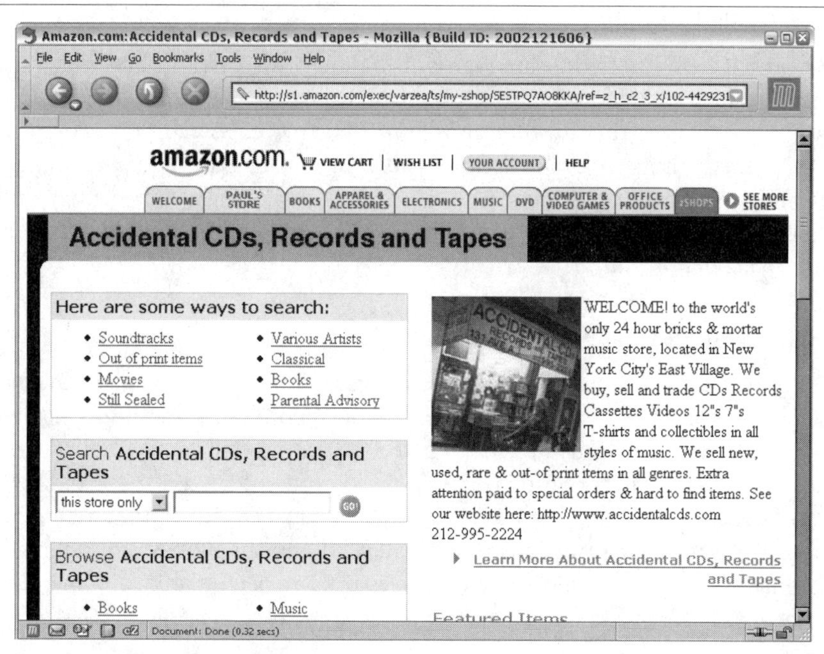

Figure 4-3. Accidental CDs zShop Home

Figure 4-4. Comic books up for auction

Advantage Program

If you have products that aren't listed in Amazon's catalog, but you want Amazon to list them and handle all the shipping and customer interaction, you're looking for the *Advantage Program*. The price is steep (55% commission at this writing), but you simply send your products to Amazon and they do most of the heavy lifting. There are tools to manage your listings and upload information about your products. You can learn more at *http://www.amazon.com/advantage/*.

Honor System

Though it's not technically selling a physical item, Amazon's *Honor System* helps you collect fees for your services. If you spend hours and hours slaving over your web site, you can ask your readers to pitch in for the effort. You can think of the Honor System as a tip jar for your site **[Hack #57]**. By adding a bit of code to your site, you can use Amazon's payment infrastructure to collect a tip from your readers; Amazon will send you the money after taking a commission. You can find some examples of how people are using the program at the Honor System home page (*http://www.amazon.com/honor/*).

Fees and Services Roundup

Seeing how Amazon's selling program fees and services compare with each other could help you determine which program makes sense for you to use. Keep in mind that these could change at any time.

Marketplace
: $0.99 listing fee for each item, and 15% of the sale price. Each item is listed for a maximum of 60 days before it must be manually relisted. You ship each item and handle any issues with customers.

Marketplace with Pro-Merchant Subscription
: $39.99/month, and 15% of the sale price. No listing fee. Items are listed indefinitely.

Auctions
: $0.10 listing fee per item, and 5% of the sale price. The percentage decreases based on the sale price. The higher the price, the lower the percentage taken.

Advantage Program
: $29.95/year, and 55% of the sale price. Amazon handles inventory tracking, shipping, and customer service.

Honor System
: $0.15 per transaction and 15% of the payment.

Sell a Book with Amazon Marketplace

Amazon will list your used items alongside the new version of the same item in their catalog. You can become your own book vendor in a few steps.

The easiest way to see how Marketplace works is to sell one of your books. Find the book's standard product detail page by searching for its title or directly entering its ASIN number **[Hack #1]** in the search form on the front page. Once there, look for a box on the lefthand side of the page that says "More Buying Choices." Click "Sell Yours Here," and the listing process will begin.

Not sure which books to sell? Amazon provides a list of all the books you've purchased (or books you've told Amazon you own) along with their estimated Marketplace values. Visit the Sell Your Collection page (*http://amazon.com/o/tg/stores/static/-/used/sell-your-collection/1/*) to see how much money you could get for books you own.

There are a few quick steps to the listing process: selecting and describing the condition, setting the price and shipping information, and creating your Marketplace account.

Select the Condition

A drop-down menu lets you list your books as "New," "Used," or "Collectible." Books listed as "New" should be in perfect condition; "Used" books can have damage in different degrees; and "Collectible" should be signed or unique in some way. For a complete guide to Amazon's book-condition terminology, see their "Condition Guidelines" (*http://www.amazon.com/o/tg/browse/-/1161242/*).

Next you have the option of adding comments about the condition of the book. This can be text up to 200 characters that further describes what shape the item is in. It's best to err on the side of too-specific when describing condition, because sending someone a book with a surprise ripped corner could hurt your seller rating.

Comments about condition is your only chance to speak directly to your potential customers in the book listing itself. While the comments should focus primarily on condition, some sellers use the space to relate other information about their business or shipping methods.

Set the Sales Price and Shipping Information

You set the amount you'd like to sell the book for. When making this decision, Amazon provides their price for the item (your price must be lower unless it's listed as "Collectible") and a recommended price based on the condition you listed. Amazon's recommended prices tend to be high, so it's a good idea to see what prices others are listing the item at. On the "Enter Price" page of the listing process, you'll find links to other listings for that product. Open those listings in a new window to get a sense of what the product is really selling for. You'll see all the conditions listed, so pay particular attention to the prices for the condition you've set. You could also use a script to find average prices for your item [Hack #53].

Next, set the U.S. zip or postal code that you'll be mailing the package from. This information is used to display your city and state as the "Ships From:" section of the book listing.

All Marketplace sellers must agree to *standard shipping*: an item must go out within two business days of receiving an order, and arrive at its destination no later than 14 days later. Amazon provides a *shipping credit* to help you cover the costs of sending the item. This credit is based on USPS Media Mail rates for 2–3 pound objects, and comes very close to the rate you'll pay. If you're willing to go above and beyond the basics, you can indicate that you're willing to ship internationally or via another expedited shipping (3–6 business days) method. Amazon provides higher shipping credits for these, but it requires some more work on your end to ship via alternate methods.

Set Your Marketplace Payment Information

If you haven't sold through Amazon Marketplace before, you'll need to set up your payment information. Once you've done this, you won't need to do it again every time you list an item.

If your current Amazon account has a credit card associated with it, that card will be used to verify your identity for *Amazon Payments*, their name for payments associated with Marketplace sales. If you don't have a credit card associated with your account, you'll be asked to enter one. Your credit card won't be charged.

Finally, you need to give Amazon a virtual check from your checking account so they can deposit sales directly into your account. Just provide a check number and the routing numbers from the bottom of that check; this tells Amazon your bank's location and your account number. This information is always sent over a secure SSL connection, so it's encrypted during transport.

You can edit or add these settings at any time by visiting your Seller Account (*http://www.amazon.com/seller-account/*) and clicking "Manage Your Amazon Payments Account."

Confirm the Listing

The last step to listing your book for sale is confirming the information. Figure 4-5 shows a typical confirmation page.

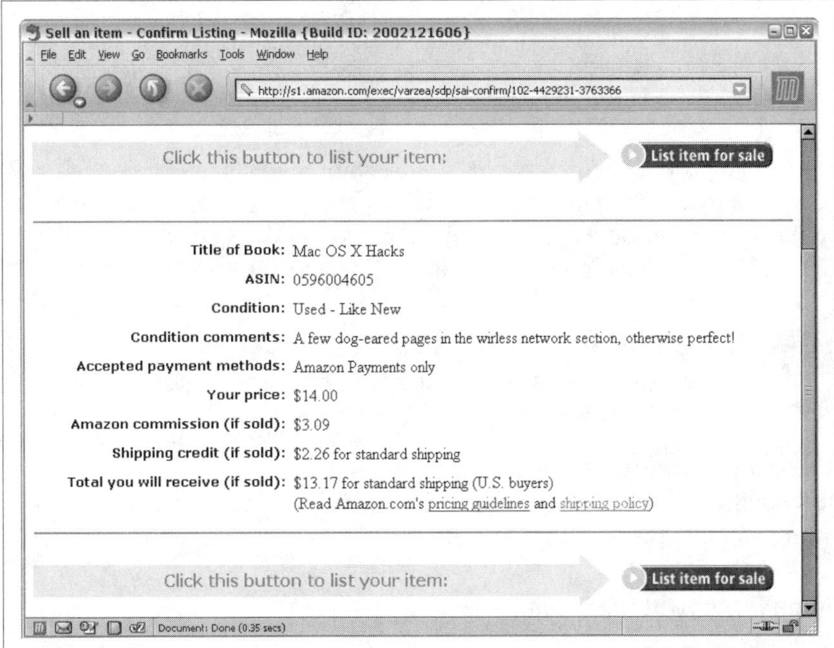

Figure 4-5. Listing confirmation page

Once you click "List item for sale," the listing will be available for the world to see and linked from the Amazon product detail page for that item within 24 hours. You should also receive an email from Amazon with the subject "Listing Confirmation—Amazon Marketplace" with the details of your listing.

If your book doesn't sell within 60 days, Amazon removes the item. You can renew your listing within 14 days of its removal. Just visit your Seller Account (*http://www.amazon.com/seller-account/*), click "closed" Marketplace listings, and click "Relist this item." This is also a good opportunity to update the price or condition to see if adjusting things will make the sale.

Ship the Book

If someone purchases your book, Amazon will let you know via email. The first email will say, "You Have an Amazon Marketplace Buyer!" It will show details of your listing and tell you to hold the item until Amazon can collect the payment from the buyer.

> If you won't be able to accept and ship orders for a while, you can click "Vacation Settings" in your seller account home page (*http://www.amazon.com/seller-account/*). Then click "Begin your vacation" and all of your sales will be put on hold. You can reverse the process when you're ready to begin accepting orders again.

Finally, you'll receive the excited "Sold—ship now!" email. This email will have the buyer's shipping address and email address. You're not required to contact the buyer directly, but letting them know you have their product in the mail is a nice touch that can't hurt your seller's rating.

Speed Up the Listing Process

If you have more than two or three items to list in Marketplace, you'll want to speed up the process of listing them for sale.

The standard process for listing an item for sale in Amazon's Marketplace **[Hack #49]** involves a number of steps. Here are a few ways you can speed your listings along.

Jump Directly to the Listing Page

Scott Windsor at Amazon notes that you can skip the process of searching for the item and clicking the "Sell Yours Here" button if you know a product's ASIN **[Hack #1]**. Just add the ASIN to this URL:

```
http://s1.amazon.com/exec/varzea/sdp/sai-condition/insert ASIN
```

You can use this same URL with a product's UPC code. The UPC (or bar code) is usually found on the back of a product. Underneath the series of lines you'll find a series of numbers. To jump to listing the product, just add all of the numbers without spaces, dashes, or any other characters to the end of the URL:

```
http://s1.amazon.com/exec/varzea/sdp/sai-condition/insert UPC code
```

So, for example, the following two URLs will directly start the sales process for *Google Hacks*. Via ASIN:

```
http://s1.amazon.com/exec/varzea/sdp/sai-condition/0596004478
```

Or via UPC:

```
http://s1.amazon.com/exec/varzea/sdp/sai-condition/978059600447
```

Set Your Zip Code

If you'd rather not type in your zip code every time you list an item, you can set Amazon to remember it via your Seller Account page. To get there, click "Your Account" from the top of any page, then "Your Seller Account"; or you can browse to the page directly (*http://s1.amazon.com/exec/varzea/subst/your-account/manage-your-seller-account.html*). From there, click "Edit your seller preferences." Skip the rest of the settings on this page and zero in on "ZIP or Postal Code from which your item will be shipped." Click "Preview" and then "Submit." The zip code will then be filled in each time you list an item.

List Several Items for Sale at Once

If you're ready to do serious business through Amazon, a Pro-Merchant subscription allows you to list hundreds or even thousands of items in one fell swoop.

Listing one or two books with Amazon's standard listing form **[Hack #49]** is fine, but once you reach a dozen or so it can be tedious. Amazon has a tool called Book Loader that volume sellers can use to upload their entire inventory of books in a machine-readable format.

You need to be a Pro-Merchant subscriber **[in "Understanding Amazon's Sales Programs"]** to use this hack. Bulk upload tools are available only with a subscription.

The Book Loader is a specialized version of another bulk-listing tool that Amazon offers called Inventory Loader (*http://www.amazon.com/exec/obidos/tg/browse/-/1161312/*). The Book Loader contains fields specific to books, such as author, publisher, and binding. The Inventory Loader format is more generic to handle a wide range of items.

The loading process involves entering all of your product data into a spreadsheet, saving it in a tab-delimited file, and sending it to the Amazon server. Unfortunately, populating the spreadsheet with all the required information can be just as tedious as listing the items individually.

If you'd like to see a sample Book Loader spreadsheet with all of the data fields available, send a blank email to *bulk-template-request@amazon.com*. You'll quickly receive a reply with a blank Excel template attached.

Because we know that the final format Amazon needs is a tab-delimited file, it's possible to script the process of putting it together. This hack takes a list of ASINs, looks up or prompts for any required information, and leaves you with a file that you can upload to Amazon with all of your sale items.

The Code

Save the following code to a text file called *create_bulk.pl*. You'll need a Web Services developer's token and affiliate tag **[in "What You Need" in Chapter 6]**, so be sure to include them in the script.

```
#!/usr/bin/perl
# create_bulk.pl
# A script to create an Amazon Marketplace Bulk Load file.
# Usage: perl create_bulk.pl <asin file>

#Your Amazon developer's token
my $dev_token='insert developer token';

#Your Amazon affiliate tag
my $af_tag='insert affiliate tag';

#A Random Sku Suffix
my $sku = "SKU";

#Take the query from the command-line
my $asinfile =shift @ARGV or die "Usage:perl create_bulk.pl <asin file>\n";

#Use the XML::Parser Perl module
use strict;
use XML::Simple;
use LWP::Simple;

#Open output file for writing, and set column headers
open(BULKFILE, ">bulkfile.tab");
print BULKFILE
"product-id\tauthor\ttitle\tpublisher\tpub-date\tbinding\tsku\tprice\↵
titem-condition\n";

#Loop through the ASINs, Looking up details
open(ASINFILE, "<".$asinfile);
while(<ASINFILE>) {
    my($asin) = $_;
    chomp($asin);

    #Assemble the URL
    my $url = "http://xml.amazon.com/onca/xml3?" .
            "t=" . $af_tag .
            "&dev-t=" . $dev_token .
            "&type=heavy" .
            "&f=xml" .
```

```
            "&AsinSearch=" . $asin,
            "&offer=used";

    my $content = get($url);
    die "Amazon service unavailable." unless $content;

    my $xmlsimple = XML::Simple->new('forcearray' => 1);
    my $response = $xmlsimple->XMLin($content);
    foreach my $result (@{$response->{Details}}) {
      #Print out the main bits of each result
      print BULKFILE
      $result->{Asin}[0] . "\t",
      $result->{Authors}[0]->{Author}[0]||$result->{Artists}[0]->↵
{Artist}[0]||"n/a",
      "\t" . $result->{ProductName}[0],
      "\t" . $result->{Manufacturer}[0],
      "\t" . $result->{ReleaseDate}[0],
      "\t" . $result->{Media}[0],
      "\t" . $asin . "-" . $sku;
      print "\nSet Price ",
      "(around ".$result->{UsedPrice}[0].")",
      " for\n",
      $result->{ProductName}[0].": ";
      chomp(my $price = <STDIN>);
      print BULKFILE "\t".$price."\t2\n";
    }
}
close(BULKFILE);
```

Note that the Web Services call uses the offer=used option so the product includes information related to used items, in this case <UsedPrice>. This information helps you determine how to price your item. This script could be combined with finding average prices **[Hack #53]** to provide even more pricing information.

Running the Hack

The first thing you need in order to run this script is a text file with the ASINs of products you'd like to sell. Create a file called *asin.txt* with each ASIN on its own line, like so:

```
0596004478
B000002UB3
```

Then run *create_bulk.pl* from the command line, passing the name of the ASIN file:

```
perl create_bulk.pl asin.txt
```

As you run the script, it will contact Amazon via their Web Services API and collect information about the book. You'll be prompted to enter your selling price, and the script will display the current lowest used price for the book at this time to give you an idea of what it's selling for. The script will then create a file called *bulkfile.tab* that you can upload to Amazon.

Uploading the File

To upload *bulkfile.tab* to Amazon, visit your seller profile (*http://www.amazon.com/seller-account/*) and click "List single items or upload multiple items." Choose "Book Loader" from the righthand, multiple-item column.

You'll also need to set a few options on the upload form shown in Figure 4-6. The file type is "Standard Book"; you can read more about the format at Amazon's help page for the Book Loader format (*http://www.amazon.com/exec/obidos/tg/browse/-/1161328/*). Select the upload option as "Add/Modify/Delete" and click "Browse…" to find *bulkfile.tab* on your local filesystem.

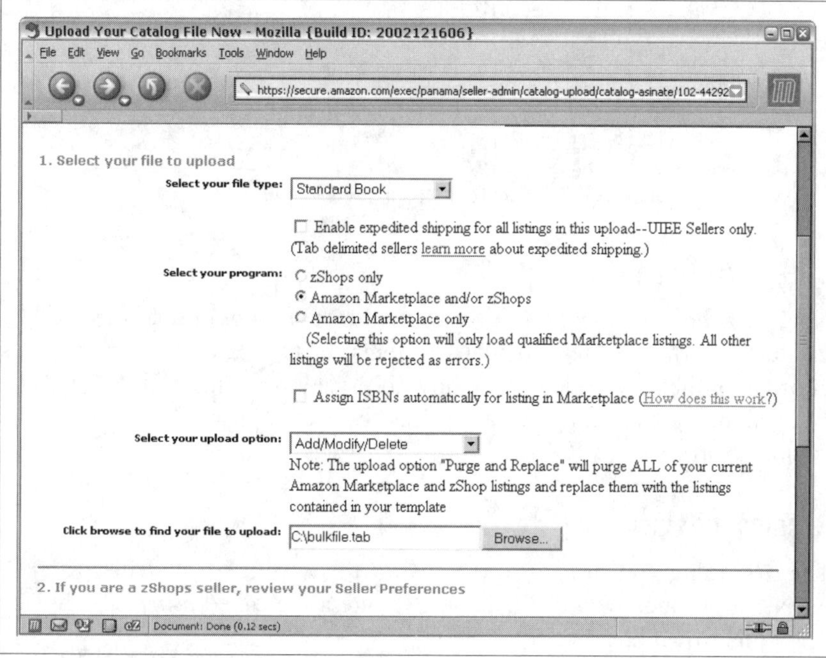

Figure 4-6. Book Loader upload form

Once your file is uploaded, it takes Amazon some time to process the file—the bigger your file, the more time it takes. You can check its status and see its eventual results by clicking "Review your Inventory Uploads" from your seller's account home page (*http://www.amazon.com/seller-account/*). If something went wrong, Amazon will spell out the errors in detail. If everything went right, all of your items will be listed for sale on Amazon!

#52 Sell What People Want

Looking for the "buyer waiting" status can help you figure out which books are in high demand.

At the time of this writing, John Grisham's novel *A Painted House* has 362 sellers offering it in Amazon's Marketplace. There's probably some demand for the book, but listing your copy for sale alongside 362 others is a bit of a crapshoot. We can safely say that the supply has been met for the demand.

Wouldn't it be nice if Amazon could just tell you which of your books are in high demand? Well, they do—it just takes a bit of digging. The trick is to find "buyer waiting" statuses for your books.

If someone's on a product detail page and there are no Marketplace listings for the item, they'll have the option to "Order it used." Clicking this link doesn't really order the item from anyone, it just lets Amazon know that someone is interested in buying that product used. (They're then notified via email when someone offers the book used.) Amazon, in turn, lets everyone else know that someone's interested by including a "buyer waiting" message, like the one in Figure 4-7, right on the product detail page.

Figure 4-7. "Buyer waiting" message on the product detail page

You could visit the product detail page for every item you own and see if any are in immediate demand, but if you own more than five or six books or CDs, that's going to be a time-consuming process. Instead, you can kick-start the process by visiting the Sell Your Collection page. To get there, go to the Your Store page (*http://www.amazon.com/yourstore/*) and click "Sell Your Collection" under the "More to Explore" heading on the lefthand side of the page.

The Sell Your Collection page lists all of the items you've purchased through Amazon and any items you've told Amazon that you own **[Hack #14]**. As you go through the list you'll see yellow "Sell Yours Here" buttons that begin the process of listing the item for sale **[Hack #49]**. What you're really looking for, though, are those items that show a "buyer waiting" message under those buttons. By paging through your collection and scanning the list, you can compile a list of the items that will probably sell quickly.

The Sell Your Collection page also features Amazon's guess at what your entire purchase history is worth. It uses 70% of the item's current price to calculate the estimate, which might be high depending on the condition and the competition.

If you haven't purchased all of your potential sale items through Amazon, there's another way to speed up the process of finding wanted books: Google. If you have the ASIN for your products (ISBN number for books), you can use Google.com to search Amazon for the "buyer waiting!" text on that item's product detail page. The Google query to accomplish this looks something like this:

```
insert ASIN "buyer waiting!" site:www.amazon.com
```

This tells Google to search Amazon.com only for pages that contain the ASIN you provide and the phrase "buyer waiting!" If you get a result, you know the item is in demand. No result means the product detail page for that ASIN doesn't have a "buyer waiting" status the last time Google visited the page.

Doing this search is only marginally faster than visiting each product detail page directly—which is what we're trying to avoid. Google, like Amazon, has released a Web Services API, which means developers can script searches and format the results quickly. That's exactly what the following code does.

The Code

To run this code you'll need a Google developer's key. A key is free and easy to obtain at *http://www.google.com/apis/*. This code accepts the location of a text file on the command line. It should contain a list of the ASINs you want to query Google for. Add the following code to a file called *buyer_waiting.pl*.

```
#!/usr/bin/perl
# buyer_waiting.pl
# A script to check Google/Amazon for waiting buyers.
# Usage: perl buyer_waiting.pl <asin file>

#Your Google API developer's key
my $google_key='insert Google developer key';

#Location of the GoogleSearch WSDL file
my $google_wdsl = "http://api.google.com/GoogleSearch.wsdl";

#Your Amazon Developer's token
my $dev_token = 'insert Amazon developer token';
```

```
#Your Aassociates Tag
my $af_code = 'insert associates tag';

use strict;

#Set the necessary Perl modules
use SOAP::Lite;
use XML::Simple;
use LWP::Simple;

#Take the query from the command-line
my $asinfile = shift @ARGV or die "Usage:perl buyer_waiting.pl ↵
<asin file>\n";

#Create a new SOAP::Lite instance,feeding it GoogleSearch.wsdl
my $google_search = SOAP::Lite->service($google_wdsl);

#Set a counter for the results
my $i = 0;

#Loop through the ASINs, performing a query for each
open(ASINFILE, "<".$asinfile);
while(<ASINFILE>) {
    my($asin) = $_;
    chomp($asin);

    #Build Google Query
    my $query = $asin . " \"buyer waiting!\" site:www.amazon.com";

    #Send Query Google Request
   my $results = $google_search ->doGoogleSearch($google_key,↵
 $query,0,10,"false","","false","","latin1","latin1");

    #Loop through any results
    foreach my $result (@{$results->{resultElements}}){
        $i++;

        #Get Title from Amazon
        my $url = "http://xml.amazon.com/onca/xml3?t=" . $af_code .
                  "&dev-t=" . $dev_token .
                  "&type=lite&f=xml&" .
                  "AsinSearch=" . $asin;
        my $content = get($url);
        die "Could not retrieve info for $asin" unless $content;
        my $xmlsimple = XML::Simple->new( );
        my $response = $xmlsimple->XMLin($content);
        my $title = $response->{Details}->{ProductName};

        #Print out the tile
        print "A buyer is waiting for " . $title .
        " [" . $asin . "]\n";
    }
}
if ($i == 0) {print "No buyers waiting for these items.\n"};
```

Running the Hack

This code requires a text file filled with ASINs. Simply create a file called *asins.txt* and include one ASIN on each line.

Once you have the ASINs file, you can run this script from a command prompt, like so:

```
perl buyer_waiting.pl <insert asin text file location>
```

Google will be contacted through its API for each ASIN. If "buyer waiting" is found on the appropriate Amazon page, the script will query Amazon's API for the book title. Depending on how eclectic your collection is, a list of 20 ASINs should turn up some with buyers waiting. Each match will be printed out along with the ASIN like this:

```
A buyer is waiting for Amazon Hacks! [0596005423]
A buyer is waiting for Google Hacks! [0596004478]
```

Now that you know exactly what people are looking for, you can concentrate your efforts there.

Scope Out the Marketplace Competition

A little market research into what used items are currently selling for will help you price your items before listing them.

When you're going through the process of listing an item for sale in the Marketplace **[Hack #49]**, Amazon provides a recommended price based on the condition you set for your item. If you'd like to see how your competition is pricing the item, though, you can click through the listings and get a feel for the average price.

Why not scrape the listings from the site and calculate the actual average price? And why not throw in the highest and lowest price while you're at it? Armed with this information, you can make an informed decision about how to price your item.

The Code

Create a file called *used_report.pl* containing the following code:

```
#!/usr/bin/perl
# used_report.pl
# A script to scrape Amazon, retrieve used listings, and write to a file
# Usage: perl used_report.pl <asin>

#Take the asin from the command-line
my $asin =shift @ARGV or die "Usage:perl used_report.pl <asin>\n";
```

```
use strict;
use LWP::Simple;

#Assemble the URL
my $url = 'http://www.amazon.com/exec/obidos/tg/stores/offering/list'.
          '/-/' . $asin . '/used/';

#Request the URL
my $content = get($url);
die "Could not retrieve $url" unless $content;

#Set up some variables
my $i = 0;
my $totalprices = 0;
my $thisPrice = 0;
my $highPrice = 0;
my $lowPrice = 0;

#Loop through listings
while ($content =~ m!<b class=price>\$(.*?)</b>!mgis) {
    $i++;
    $thisPrice = $1;
    if ($thisPrice >= $lastPrice) {
        $highPrice = $thisPrice;
    }
    if ($i == 1 || $thisPrice <= $lowPrice) {
        $lowPrice = $thisPrice;
    }
    $totalprices += $thisPrice;
}

$avgPrice = $totalprices / $i;

#Show the results
print <<"EOF";
Average Used Price: \$$avgPrice
Highest Price: \$$highPrice
Lowest Price: \$$lowPrice
EOF
```

Running the Hack

This script runs from the command line and is passed an ASIN:

```
perl used_report.pl asin
```

You should receive a simple three-line report listing the average, highest, and lowest prices for the book:

```
Average Used Price: $19.54
Highest Price: $20.82
Lowest Price: $18.70
```

List Your Items for Sale on Your Web Site

If you have your own web site, you can mirror your Amazon listings there so you can reach your audience as well.

Amazon has millions of customers at their site looking for items, and getting your listing in front of them is important. If you have a web site, though, letting your own audience know about your sale items could be just as important. It's not only the number of people that see a listing that matters, but getting the right person to see the listing.

The easiest way to point your web visitors to your sale items is to link to a list of all your open Marketplace items on Amazon. To find the link, visit your seller account (*http://www.amazon.com/seller-account/*) and click "View your Member Profile."

The URL of your Member Profile page contains your Seller ID. The alphanumeric string following `customer-glance` is your unique ID number. Jot it down while you're there because it's necessary for the following hack.

On your member profile page, click "View Open Marketplace Listings." The page lists all of your open sale items. This page is publicly viewable, so just copy the URL from the address bar of your browser and include it in an HTML link on your site like this:

```
<a href="http://s1.amazon.com/exec/varzea/ts/↵
customer-open-marketplace-items/your seller ID/">Buy my stuff!</a>
```

If you want to integrate beyond a link, you can list every item you're selling on your site.

Included in every listing confirmation email **[Hack #49]** you'll find a link that leads to a page for your specific product listing. If you want to include all of the items you have for sale on your web site, you could copy each of these links and paste them into an HTML file. You'd also need to copy the name of the product and how much you've listed it for. You'd have to revisit this HTML every time an item sells or anytime you make a change to your listings.

Luckily, you can automate this entire process with Amazon Web Services.

The Code

This ASP script requests your latest items for sale on Amazon and formats them as a local web page. You'll need an Amazon developer's token **[in "What You Need" in Chapter 6]** to run the script, and you can include an affiliate tag. You'll also need to find your Seller ID and set it at the top of the code.

```
<%
  ' Set Associate ID, Developer Token, and Seller ID
  Const AFF_TAG = "insert associate tag"
  Const DEV_TOKEN = "insert developer token"
  Const SELLER_ID = "insert seller ID"

  XMLURL = "http://xml.amazon.com/onca/xml3" & _
           "?t=" + AFF_TAG & _
           "&dev-t=" + DEV_TOKEN & _
           "&SellerSearch=" + SELLER_ID & _
           "&type=heavy" & _
           "&page=1" & _
           "&offerstatus=open" & _
           "&f=xml"

  ' Issue the request and wait for the response
    Set xmlhttp = Server.CreateObject("Msxml2.SERVERXMLHTTP")
    xmlhttp.Open "GET", XMLURL, false
    xmlhttp.Send(Now)
    If Err.Number <> 0 Then
        response.write "Unable to connect to Amazon."
        response.end
    End If

    Set XMLDoc = xmlhttp.responseXML
    'response.write "<xmp>" & XMLDoc.xml & "</xmp>"
    If XMLDoc.parseError.ErrorCode <> 0 Then
        response.write "Error: " & XMLDoc.parseError.reason
        response.end
    End If

    ' Look for the ErrorMsg tag
    Set XMLError = XMLDoc.SelectNodes("//ErrorMsg")

    ' If it exists, display the message and exit
    If XMLError.length > 0 Then
       response.write XMLDoc.SelectSingleNode("//ErrorMsg").text
       response.end
    End If

    ' If there's no error, loop through items for sale
    Set ProdDetail = XMLDoc.SelectNodes("//ListingProductDetails")
    For x = 0 To (ProdDetail.length - 1)
      strExID = ProdDetail(x).selectSingleNode("ExchangeID").text
      strTitle = ProdDetail(x).selectSingleNode("ExchangeTitle").text
      strPrice = ProdDetail(x).selectSingleNode("ExchangePrice").text
      strOffer = ProdDetail(x).selectSingleNode("ExchangeOfferingType").text
      response.write "<b>" & strTitle & "</b><br>"
      response.write strPrice & " (" & strOffer & ")"
      response.write "<br><br>" & vbCrLf
    Next
%>
```

Running the Hack

Save the code to a file called *SalesListings.asp* and upload it to your IIS server. Request the file from a browser to see your product listings:

```
http://your.server/SalesListings.asp
```

Hacking the Hack

Taking this script one step further, you can let your visitors add your items directly to their Amazon shopping carts. Include the following HTML form to print a "Buy from Amazon.com" button along with each item.

```
<form method="POST" action="http://www.amazon.com/o/dt/assoc/↵
handle-buy-box=insert ASIN">
<input type=hidden
    name="exchange.insert exchange ID.insert ASIN.insert Seller ID"
    value="1">
<input type="hidden" name="tag-value" value="insert affiliate tag">
<input type="hidden" name="tag_value" value="insert affiliate tag">
<input type="submit" name="submit.add-to-cart" value="Buy From Amazon.com">
</form>
```

You'll need to insert the proper exchange ID, ASIN, and Seller ID, and these values are available as variables in the script. To add this form to *SalesListings.asp*, insert the following code just before the last line of the loop (`response.write "<br><br>"`), and include the necessary variables.

```
strASIN = ProdDetail(x).selectSingleNode("ExchangeAsin").text
strSellerID = ProdDetail(x).selectSingleNode("ExchangeSellerId").text
%>
<form method="POST" action="http://www.amazon.com/o/dt/assoc/↵
handle-buy-box=insert ASIN">
<input type=hidden
    name="exchange.<%= strExID %>.<%= strASIN %>.<%= strSellerID %>"
    value="1">
<input type="hidden" name="tag-value" value="insert affiliate tag">
<input type="hidden" name="tag_value" value="insert affiliate tag">
<input type="submit" name="submit.add-to-cart" value="Buy From Amazon.com">
</form>
<%
```

When someone visiting the page clicks "Buy from Amazon.com," your specific item will be added to their cart and the sale will go to you.

Add a Co-Branded Checkout

For more hacking-the-hack fun, you can ease the transition from your site to Amazon's with some co-branding. By setting the following form with each item listing, the "Buy from Amazon.com" button will tell Amazon to show your logo as customers step through the checkout process on their server.

```
<form action="http://s1.amazon.com/exec/varzea/dt/cbop/order-checkout/"
     method="post">
<input type="hidden" name="purchase-navbar"
   value="insert image URL">
<input type="hidden" name="purchase-store-name"
   value="insert your store name">
<input type="hidden" name="purchase-return-url"
   value="insert your store URL">
<input type="hidden" name="purchase-exchange-id"
   value="insert exchange ID"/>
<input type="hidden" name="purchase-quantity" value="1">
<input type="hidden" name="purchase-storefront-name"
   value="insert your store name"/>
<input type="submit" name="go" value="Buy from Amazon.com">
</form>
```

To include this co-branded checkout in *SalesListings.asp*, just fill in the image, store name, store URL, and exchange ID, and include the HTML just before the last line of the product loop. Be sure to turn off script processing with `%>` just before this form, and then turn script processing back on with `<%` just after this code. You can also insert the exchange ID with the variable set earlier in the script in an ASP tag, like `<%= strExID %>`.

Instead of sending customers from your site directly to Amazon's cart page, you can send them to a minimalist checkout process (as shown in Figure 4-8) that includes your site's logo.

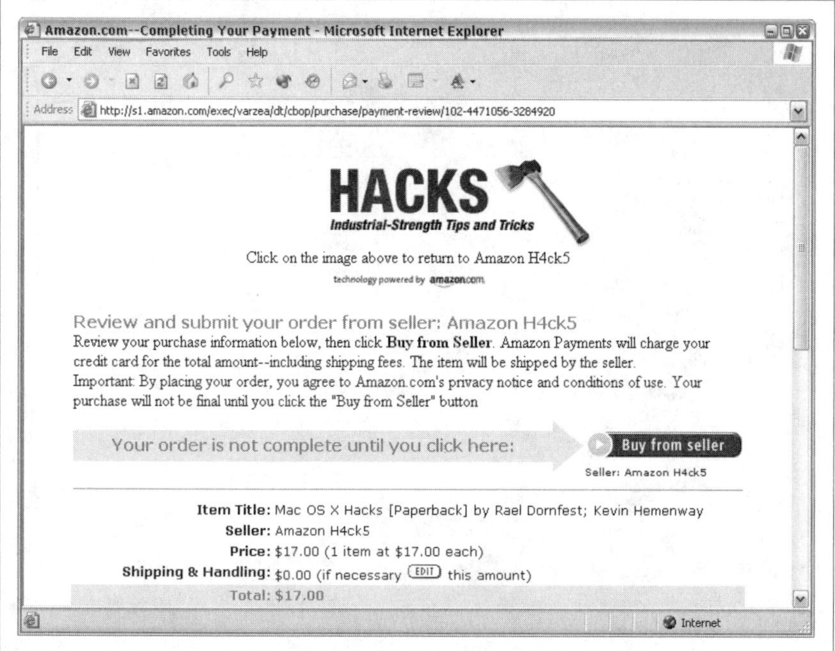

Figure 4-8. A co-branded checkout page

Put an Item Up for Bid at Amazon Auctions

If the value of the item you'd like to sell is variable, or if the item could appeal to collectors, you may want to sell it through an auction.

If the success of eBay has taught us anything, it's that people love online auctions. Amazon has their own auction system that provides an alternative to listing items on eBay.

Before listing your item in an auction, it's a good idea to familiarize yourself with the space in which you'll be posting. Spend some time at Amazon's auction site (*http://auctions.amazon.com*) browsing the categories in which you'll be listing your item. Check for current activity by noting the number of bids for similar items. If no one's interested in your product area on the site, you may be better off concentrating your efforts on your zShop or Marketplace listings.

When you're ready to list an item, visit the new auction page (*http://s1.amazon.com/exec/varzea/auction-new/*). Figure 4-9 shows the beginning of a long form overflowing with text boxes, drop-downs menus, and checkboxes. This can look daunting, but don't worry—you can leave the defaults checked for most settings and zero in on what counts.

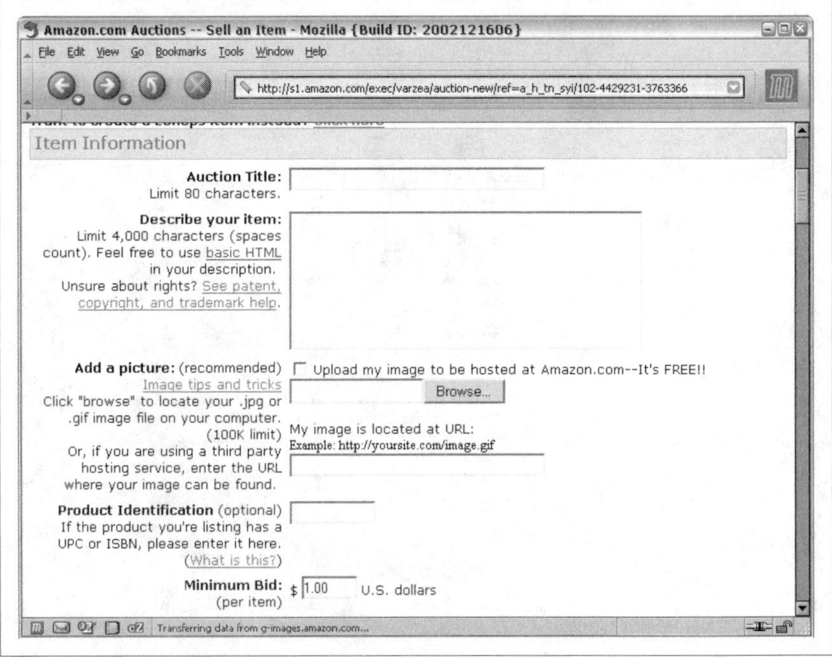

Figure 4-9. Amazon Auctions "Sell an Item" form

Here are the bare-minimum steps you need to take to speed your way through a listing:

1. Include an auction title, description, and picture. (Either Amazon can host your image, or you can provide an image URL.)
2. Set a *reserve*, which is the minimum amount you're willing to accept, and/or a "take it" price that lets people skip bidding and just buy it outright for the amount you specify.
3. Enter your zip code under "Selling Preferences."

That's it! Click "Preview your auction" and you can see the settings for some of the fields you skipped. If everything looks OK, click "Submit your auction" and the bidding can begin.

Of course, if you take more time with the form you can increase your visibility and chances of someone finding your listing—especially if you're auctioning something that already exists in Amazon's catalog. It's a good idea to enter its ASIN under "Product Identification," and related products' ASINs under "CrossLinks" toward the bottom of the form. This allows your auction listing to show up on Amazon's standard product detail pages for those items.

Get (and Keep!) a Good Seller Rating

A positive or negative seller rating can affect your Marketplace bottom line. Here are a few tips that can help keep your rating positive.

With so many seller choices available on Amazon, a good seller's rating can mean more than who has the lowest price when people decide whom to buy from. Every seller on Amazon has a profile page like the one you see in Figure 4-10, and it includes their overall feedback rating based on input from buyers. You can also see the comments buyers have left to better understand their ratings.

If you're buying a book from the "New & Used" section of Amazon, be sure to check the seller's profile page before you place your order. By scanning the "Recent Feedback" you can get a sense of how people feel about doing business with the seller. The feedback ratings show up along with the book listings, but they can sometimes be artificially high or low.

There's no script or bit of technology that can artificially inflate your seller rating or remove negative reviews. Because your seller rating is based on people who buy from you, getting a good rating is all about customer

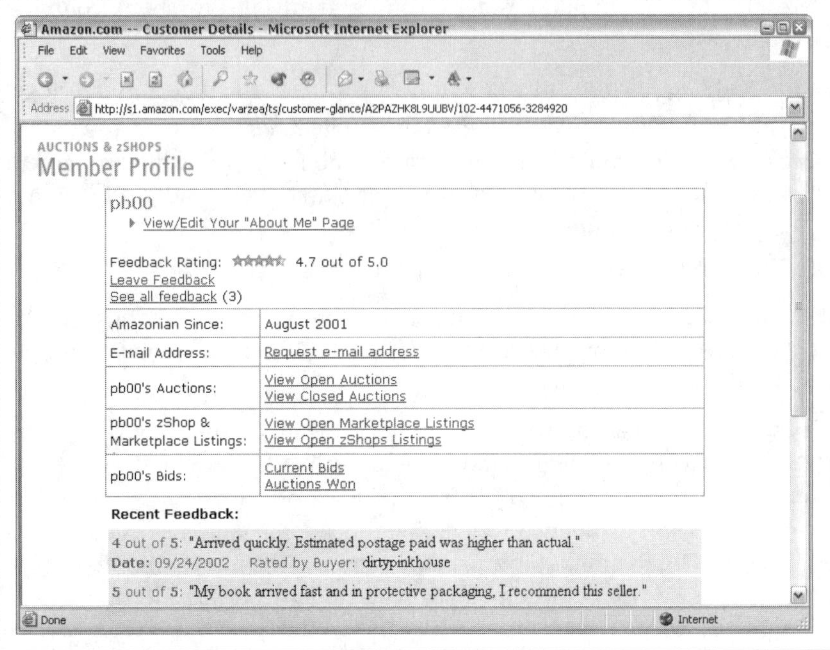

Figure 4-10. Amazon seller Member Profile page

service. Here are a few ideas to keep in mind as you interact with people through Amazon.

Ship on time
: This sounds obvious, but 90% of negative feedback is about late shipments. Amazon requires you to ship your item within two business days of receiving the order. If you can get it out any sooner, your buyer will appreciate it.

Ship in protective packaging
: Another sore spot with buyers is items damaged during transport. Bubble-wrap envelopes cost a bit more, but will ensure that the item arrives in the condition you described. Even with protective packaging you can stay under the shipping credit amount that Amazon provides.

Use tracking numbers
: The United States Post Office has a service called *delivery confirmation* (see the USPS web site at *http://www.usps.com/send/waystosendmail/extraservices/deliveryconfirmationservice.htm*) that gives you a tracking confirmation number for your package. You can use delivery confirmation with any postage rate, including *media mail*, and it's well worth the charge. With the confirmation number in hand, you can track the

package at the USPS web site to make sure it gets to its destination. If there's ever a dispute, you have the post office documentation to back up your claims of delivery. You can also send the tracking number to your buyer and let them track the package. They'll remember the effort when they're adding feedback.

Send a shipment confirmation to your buyer
: You're not required to contact a buyer directly, but why not email them a note to let them know you've dropped their order in the mail? It's your first point of direct contact with the buyer, so keep it friendly and to the point. If you have a tracking number, include the URL where they can track the package.

Include a packing slip with your name and logo
: Your next point of contact with the buyer will be when they open their package. It's a good idea to include a packing slip listing the item they ordered. This is also a chance to sell yourself, so include a logo and URL to your web site or other Marketplace items for sale [Hack #54].

Encourage your customers to rate you
: Much of the effort of building a seller rating involves getting people to leave feedback. Sometime after they receive your order (you were using a tracking number, right?), ask the buyer to rate their experience. People often don't think about leaving feedback if everything goes smoothly.

Follow up on negative reviews
: Negative reviews happen, and there's no easy way to remove the mark from your record. Contact the buyer who left the negative review, and make sure you understand what happened so you can avoid the situation in the future. There's no way to remove negative feedback, but you can post to your feedback to tell your side of the story.

Keep in mind that leaving a scathing negative review in someone's seller feedback can impact their ability to sell items on Amazon. Before taking this step, contact the seller directly through their profile page and try to amend the situation.

Collect Donations from Your Web Site with the Honor System

You work hard contributing to the Web, and you provide a valuable service. Amazon lets you put out a tip jar.

Most independent personal web sites are a labor of love rather than money. If you're providing a valuable service to your readers, though, there's no harm in asking them to pitch in to help you cover the cost of your time and effort. Amazon has extended their Marketplace platform so you can add this feature to your site. Here's how it works:

1. You create a page at Amazon (called a PayPage) that describes who you are and why you're asking for donations.
2. You add a link to this page from your site using either a standard text link or a graphic that Amazon provides (called a Paybox).
3. Visitors visit this page and send money using their existing Amazon account information.
4. Amazon collects a $0.15 processing fee and 15% of the donation for providing the service, sending the rest directly to your bank account.

The first step to asking for donations is joining Amazon's program. You can do this from the Amazon Honor System home page (*http://amazon.com/honor/*). Just click "Join Now" from that page to start the enrollment process. The enrollment is nearly identical to being approved for Amazon Payments **[Hack #49]**. You confirm your account's credit card for identity verification, accept the participation agreement (*https://s1.amazon.com/exec/varzea/subst/fx/help/participation-agreement.htm*), and add checking account information so Amazon can add payments to your account.

Customize Your PayPage

While you may describe why you're asking for money on your site, your Amazon PayPage is where you can go into detail about yourself, your organization, and what the money will be used for. It's the final stop before someone decides to donate.

The most important elements to customize are the title and description. These show up in two different places on the page. Adding a logo or image from your web site will keep people aware that this page is connected with your site. You can also add a customized thank-you message and thank-you email that people see after they've donated. Figure 4-11 shows the PayPage for MetaFilter (*http://www.metafilter.com/*), a rather popular eclectic group weblog.

Once your PayPage is complete, you can link to it from your site and people can start donating. To find the URL for your PayPage, scroll down to the bottom of your PayPage and look for the text "Want to revisit this page? Visit..." followed by the distributable URL for your PayPage.

If you need to find your way to your PayPage at any point, go to the Honor System home page (*http://www.amazon.com/honor/*), click "Manage PayPages" from the top submenu, then click "View the PayPage" from the list of your pages.

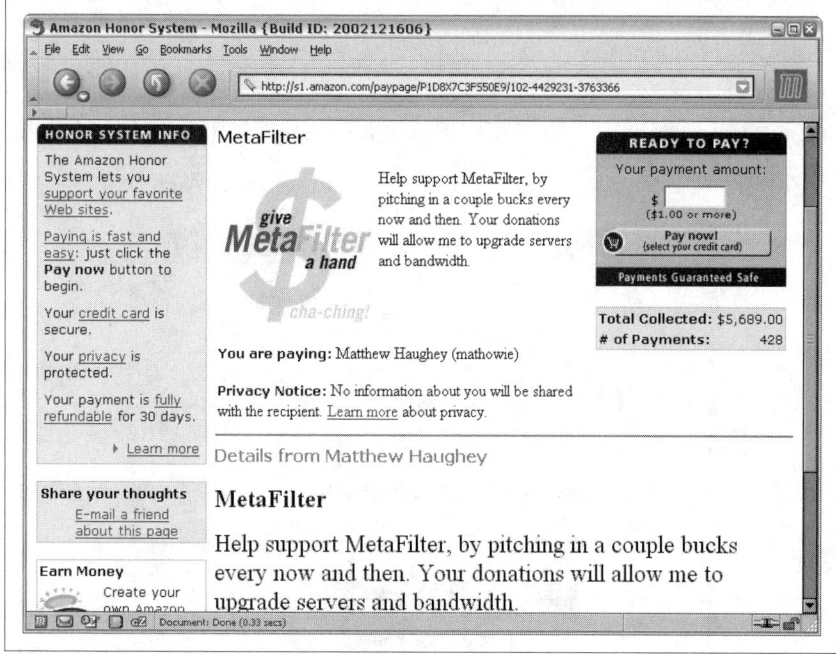

Figure 4-11. MetaFilter PayPage

Create a Quick-Click Donation Link

If you've found the URL to your PayPage, you can also create a *Quick-Click* link that pops open a new window that people can donate through. Your PayPage URL should contain a string of characters in the URL right after /paypage/; this is your PayPage ID. Include that ID in the following code to open a new window for people to donate:

```
<script language="JavaScript">
function popUp(URL,NAME) {
  amznwin=window.open (URL,NAME,'location=yes,scrollbars=yes,↲
status=yes,toolbar=yes,resizable=yes,width=380,height=450,screenX=10,↲
screenY=10,top=10,left=10');
  amznwin.focus( );
}

document.open( );
document.write("<a href=javascript:popUp('http://s1.amazon.com/exec/↲
varzea/dt/assoc/tg/aa/assoc/assoc/-/insert Page ID')>Donate Now!</a>");
document.close( );
</script>

<noscript>
```

```
<a href="http://s1.amazon.com/exec/varzea/dt/assoc/tg/aa/assoc/assoc/-/↵
insert Page ID">Donate Now!</a>
</noscript>
```

If you insert this code into any HTML page, users will see a "Donate Now!" link. When clicked, it will open a donation window like that shown in Figure 4-12.

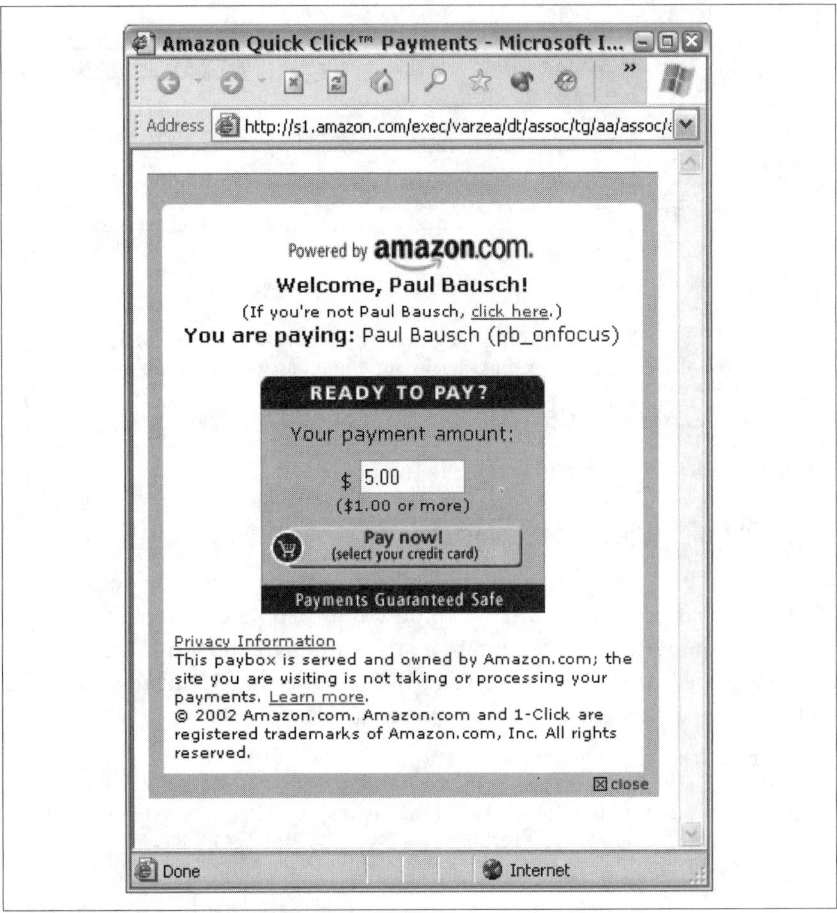

Figure 4-12. Quick-Click Honor System Page

Create a Paybox

If you'd like to make your request for donations stand out a bit more, you can create a customized graphic to display on your site. All you need to do is fill out a simple form (see Figure 4-13).

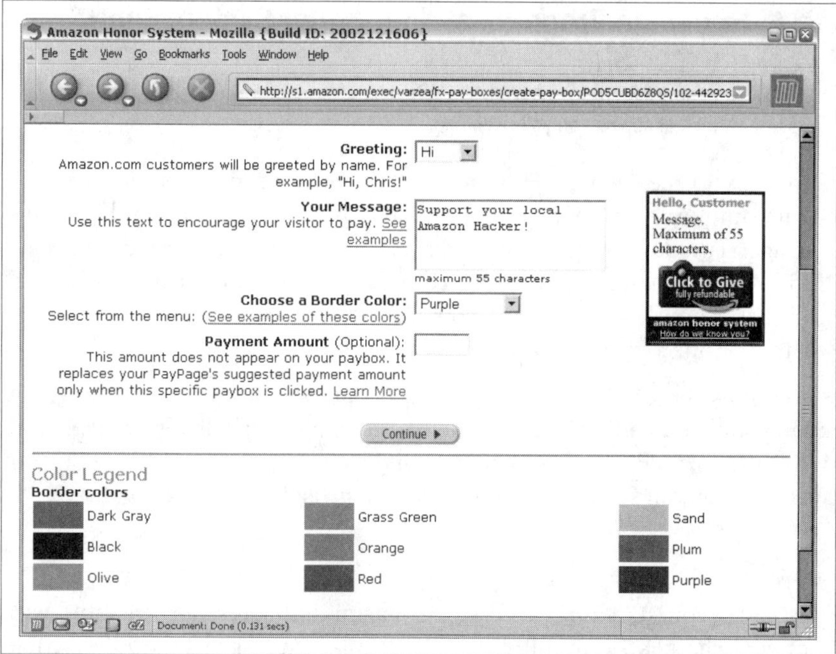

Figure 4-13. Creating a Paybox

Amazon generates the code you need to display the graphic and link, called a Paybox, to your PayPage. You can include the code in any HTML page to display an image like the one in Figure 4-14.

Figure 4-14. A customized Paybox

Amazon displays the name of the customer in the Paybox if they have an existing Amazon account and the Amazon cookie **[Hack #13]** identifying their browser. If you would rather not see your name on these images, you can shut them off in your account preferences.

#58 Show the Progress of Your Honor System Fund on Your Site

You can let Amazon calculate the progress of a fund drive by scraping the graph that appears on your PayPage.

If your use of the Amazon Honor System is in connection with a drive for a certain amount of money, you show your progress with a graph on your PayPage. To add a graph to a PayPage, go to your list of pages and click "Edit." Scroll down to section D, "Your Goal Chart and Payment Counter," and click "Edit." From there, you can choose your target amount and whether or not to display the graph or payment counter.

If you show the graph on your PayPage, people will know how far along you are in your drive and how far you have to go. Unfortunately it's available *only* on your Amazon PayPage, so you can't indicate the progress as easily on your own site. You can scrape the information to display it locally, though.

The Code

This code requests your PayPage at Amazon and slices out the table with your goal chart. Keep in mind that the regular expressions used here could become obsolete the next time Amazon changes the HTML layout of their PayPages.

```
<?php
$paypageURL = "insert your PayPage URL";
$payPage = "";

//Get Amazon PayPage based on ID
$contents = fopen($paypageURL,"r");
while (!feof ($contents))
    $payPage .= fgets($contents, 4096);
fclose ($contents);

if (preg_match_all('/<table border=0 cellpadding=1 cellspacing=0 ↵
width=190>.*?Goal Chart.*?<\/table>.*?<\/table>.*?<\/table>/↵
s',$payPage,$chartTable)) {
    echo $chartTable[0][0];
}

?>
```

Running the Hack

Put this code in file called *get_chart.php* and upload it to your server. View it in a browser and you should see your Honor System chart. You could also remove the PHP declarations (<?php and ?>) and drop this code into any existing PHP page.

Hacking the Hack

Keep in mind that *get_chart.php* contacts Amazon's servers each time the page is loaded, so it could slow down your page a bit. Instead of requesting the goal chart every time, you could cache the response on your server and refresh the cached version at a certain interval. Here's the same bit of code with a simple file-caching system.

```
<?php
$paypageURL = "insert your PayPage URL";
$payPage = "";
$cachefile   = "./chart_table.txt";

// Create the cache file if it doesn't exist
if (!file_exists($cachefile)) {
    $fp=fopen("$cachefile", "w");
    $filetime = (time() - 864000);
} else {
// Or set the last modified time of the cache file
    $filetime = filemtime($cachefile);
}

// Check the last-modified time on the cache file;
// If it's less than 24 hours (86400 seconds),
// request a new copy and write to the cache file.
if ($filetime < (time() - 86400)) {
    // Get Amazon PayPage based on ID
    $contents = fopen($paypageURL,"r");
    while (!feof ($contents))
        $payPage .= fgets($contents, 4096);
    fclose ($contents);

    if (preg_match_all('/<table border=0 cellpadding=1 cellspacing=0 ↵
width=190>.*?Goal Chart.*?</table>.*?</table>.*?</table>↵
/s',$payPage,$chartTable)) {
        $fp=fopen("$cachefile", "w");
        fwrite($fp, $chartTable[0][0]);
        fclose($fp);
    }
}

$fp=fopen("$cachefile", "r");
echo fread ($fp, filesize($cachefile));
?>
```

This script stores the chart HTML in a file called *chart_table.txt* and checks that file's last-modified time. If the file hasn't been modified for 24 hours, it requests the chart HTML and writes it to *chart_table.txt*. Finally, it writes out the contents of the file. If your fund drive is a huge success and you'd like to update the file more frequently, you can adjust the update time. PHP measures time in seconds, and 86,400 is the number of seconds in 24 hours. You can add more or less time accordingly.

CHAPTER FIVE

Associates Program

Hacks 59–75

If you maintain a web site, you've probably linked to hundreds of sites. The Web is incomprehensibly large and growing exponentially, and any site can be linked to any other site. There are no barriers; your choice of where to link is unlimited. Amazon is trying to tip the scales by paying you for linking to them! It's called Amazon's *Associates Program*, and by signing up, you can earn money simply by linking to them and sending visitors their way.

Make Money by Linking to Amazon

Instead of trying to compete directly with every other existing site for a visitor's attention, Amazon has turned other site owners into potential partners with their Associates Program. By paying site owners 2.5–15% of qualifying item sales that are referred through those sites (called *referral fees*), Amazon has encouraged hundreds of thousands of independent site owners to send potential customers to Amazon.

People are using the associates program in hundreds of creative ways to earn money for their web-related activities. Here are a few examples:

Niche Product Pointers
: Though Amazon has products in every possible category dealing with every possible subject, it's not always easy to find the best for a given niche. Some sites find the best stuff available in narrow subject areas and refer the sales to Amazon directly from their site **[Hack #60]**, getting some money in the process.

Banner Ads
: Some sites want to earn a bit of money, but don't have enough traffic to use a large banner-ad service. Amazon provides the tools for do-it-yourself banner advertising **[Hack #62]**.

Personal Publishing
: As more and more people publish online with journals and weblogs, they're sharing the books they're reading or movies they're watching. They're providing commentary and criticism **[Hack #69]**, and Amazon's referral fees can compensate them for their efforts.

Email Newsletters
: Anytime there's a chance to drive traffic to a web site, there's a chance to earn money through Amazon referrals. You don't have to run a web site to take advantage of the associates program, you just need to build the proper links **[Hack #59]**.

How It Works

Each Amazon associate applies for an associate account, and each account has an *associate tag* (also called an Associates ID) that's used to link to Amazon. The associate tag is a series of characters that uniquely identifies an associate account. For example, if a site is called *Fable Portal*, it may be assigned the associate tag `fableport-20`. The site owner can then add `fableport-20` to any Amazon links, and sales made after clicking the link will be associated with that particular associate account.

When someone clicks a link to Amazon with an associate tag, a 24-hour window is opened. *Any* qualifying items that the visitor adds to their shopping cart within those 24 hours will count toward referral fees. It doesn't matter when the items are actually purchased; as long as they're added to the cart within the initial 24-hour window, the associate will receive credit for the sale.

So how much money do you receive for referring paying customers? For most items on Amazon it's 5% of Amazon's selling price. If you send a customer to Amazon and they buy a book for $20, you'll receive a $1 referral fee.

However, if someone buys a $3,000 plasma flat-panel HDTV through one of your associate links, you don't get 5% of the selling price. There's currently a $10-per-item cap on referral fees.

In some cases you can earn 15% for books that are purchased immediately **[Hack #59]**, but 5% is standard for most of Amazon's items.

If your linking efforts pay off and you find that you're earning referral fees on hundreds or thousands of items every few months, you could earn even higher percentages by using another payment structure called Tiered Compensation. If you opt into the Tiered Compensation program and you sell a certain number of items across a variety of product categories, your affiliate percentage on qualifying items increases. To participate, you need to let Amazon control some of the product placements on your site. To get the details about tiered compensation, read the fees FAQ (*https://associates.amazon.com/exec/panama/associates/resources/help/faq-fees.html*). Be sure you have the required traffic before signing up, or your affiliate fees could decrease with the Tiered Compensation option.

What You Need

Joining the associates program is simple and free. Visit the associates home page (*http://www.amazon.com/associates/*) and click "Join Now." For simplicity, you can use an existing Amazon account **[Hack #13]**, or, if you'd like to separate your regular account from your associate activities—especially if you're creating the associate links for your business—you can create a new account.

When you apply, Amazon requires payee information so they know who should get the referral fee checks. They also need a tax ID in case your associate efforts are very successful. If you're a U.S. citizen, your tax ID is your social security number. If you earn over $600 per year, Amazon reports your earnings (as a 1099 form) to the IRS. If you're applying on behalf of a U.S. company, you must include its tax ID number.

If your business is not physically located in the U.S. but is taxable in the U.S., you'll need to send Amazon a U.S. Treasury Form W-8ECI (*http://www.irs.gov/pub/irs-fill/fw8eci.pdf*).

Next you can choose your preferred payment method: direct deposit, Amazon gift certificate, or check. Amazon adds an $8 fee for check payment, so choosing one of the other options will save you some money each quarter you're paid.

Finally, you'll need to add some information about your web site including your site's name, URL, and the types of items you'll be listing. Amazon will use this information when evaluating your site.

Because your site name will be used to generate your associate tag, use the shortest term possible. Keeping links short will help them fit in emails without wrapping.

Once you've applied, you'll receive your associate tag. It'll be in the last line of the welcome note. Jot down this associate tag, as you'll need it to build associate links manually and for many of the hacks in this book.

#59 Build Associate Links

The key to earning money through the Associates Program is linking to Amazon the right way.

Once you have an Amazon associate account and associate tag, you can start sending traffic to Amazon. You can't just place your associate tag anywhere in any Amazon URL to get credit for sending visitors. Amazon's servers expect specific URL formats with your associate tag in specific parts of the URL. Once you know the URL patterns, you'll be able to build your own fee-earning links no matter which part of Amazon you're linking to.

Link to the Amazon Home Page

According to Google, there are about 36,400 web pages that link to Amazon with their base URL (*http://www.amazon.com/*). That means each one of those pages has a bit of HTML that looks like this:

```
<a href="http://www.amazon.com/">Amazon</a>
```

It also means that the owners of these sites aren't collecting referral fees for traffic they send to Amazon. In contrast, Google estimates only 432 sites link to the Amazon home page with the associates format. That's a lot of lost revenue!

```
http://www.amazon.com/exec/obidos/redirect-home/insert associate tag
```

This specially formatted URL links to exactly the same page. The difference is that Amazon ties any sales made from it with your associate account.

Link to Individual Products

As a general rule, targeted sales work much better than general sales. For example, sending someone to the Amazon home page is a bit like saying, "Go see if there are any books you'd like to buy." Sending someone to a product detail page is more like saying, "Check out this specific book." If that book happens to be related to something they're already interested in, the chances for a sale are much higher.

If you have a product's ASIN (or ISBN for books), you can easily build links directly to that item's product detail page **[Hack #3]**. Here's a URL that links directly to the product detail page for this book:

```
http://www.amazon.com/exec/obidos/ASIN/0596005423
```

To be credited for sending visitors to the site, add your associate tag to the end of the URL:

```
http://www.amazon.com/exec/obidos/ASIN/0596005423/insert associate tag
```

One thing you'll notice when clicking a product link with an associate tag is that you won't always go directly to the product detail page. Instead, you may see a few product details at the top of the page and several similar items below, as in Figure 5-1.

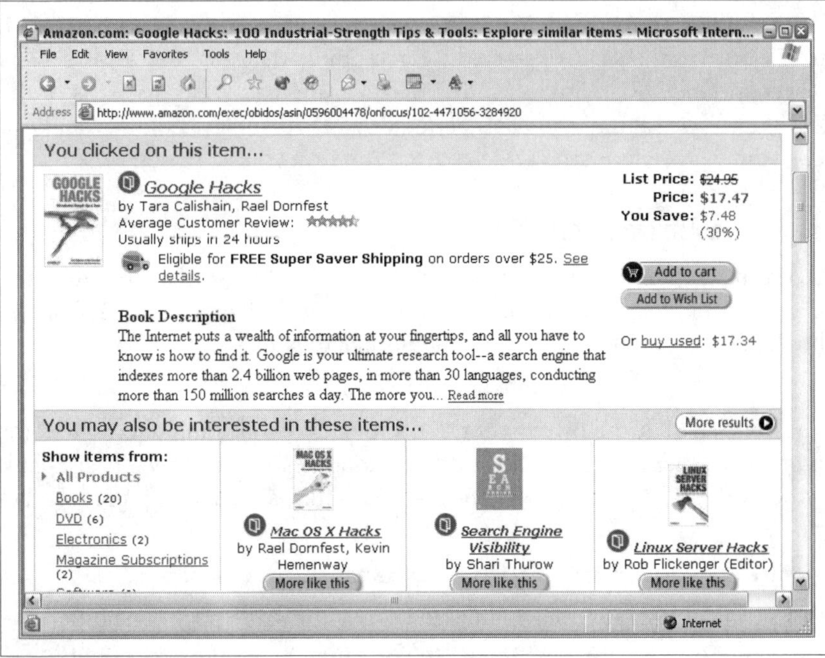

Figure 5-1. Similar items referral page

Amazon shows this page instead of a product detail page to make the transition from your site less abrupt. Notice how they title the page "You clicked on this item…". This also gives Amazon a chance to put more products in front of their potential new customer.

You can't simply add your associate tag to the end of any Amazon URL to get the referral. When you're browsing product detail pages, you may see some with a different URL format (e.g., *http://www.amazon.com/exec/obidos/tg/detail/-/0596005423/*). Intuitively, it seems that adding your associate tag to the end would be fine, but that's not the case. Notice how this URL contains `/tg/detail/-/` instead of `/ASIN/`. This difference is important: Amazon is not looking for referral tags with the first format, but they are with the second. In other words, be sure to construct your links carefully in the format Amazon expects!

It's not possible to predict when you'll get a similar items page instead of a product detail page, but you can tell Amazon to skip the similar items page.

Bypass the Similar Items Page

With qualifying books (and only books), the amount of the referral fee earned depends on when someone decides to add an item to their cart. If someone clicks a link to a product on Amazon and then immediately adds the item to their cart, it's considered a *direct* sale. That means the referring associate can earn 15% of the sale instead of the standard 5%. If someone visits the page, browses around the site, and then adds the item to their cart, it's considered an *indirect* sale.

Just to add further complexity to the numbers game, only books that are discounted 10–30% off the list price are eligible for the direct sale bonus.

As you can see, this increased fee provides an increased incentive to link directly to individual products. It also provides an incentive to make sure the visitor goes directly to the product detail page rather than the similar items page. With so many extra product choices, the similar items page encourages your referred visitor to browse before adding an item to their cart. The product detail page provides more information about the specific product you've referred them to.

You can remove all chance that someone will see the similar items page by adding a `ref=nosim` directive to the URL right after the ASIN and before your affiliate tag. So this URL will always take a visitor to the product detail page for this book:

```
http://www.amazon.com/exec/obidos/ASIN/0596005423/ref=nosim/insert ↵
associate tag
```

Link to Search Results or Product Categories

While it may be advantageous to link to single products, there may be times when you want to link to a whole group of products. Suppose the owner of a *Dungeons & Dragons* discussion board wanted to link to books about medieval swords, but didn't have time to find every book on the subject and link to them individually from the site. That's where search results or category results could be useful.

It's important to get the URL format right so you're credited with the referral. As mentioned, you can't simply add your associate tag to the end of any URL and expect to be credited.

Keyword Search. One way to link to a group of products is through a keyword search. The base search URL includes the external-search command:

```
http://www.amazon.com/exec/obidos/external-search/
```

And here are the potential variables you can add to the base URL:

`mode`
: The product category to search (e.g., books, magazines, music). For a complete list, see the options in a drop-down search box **[Hack #64]**. You can set the mode to blended to search all product categories.

`keyword`
: The keyword to search for.

`tag`
: Your associate tag.

So, putting it all together, the search results syntax is:

```
http://www.amazon.com/exec/obidos/external-search/?mode=insert↵
mode&keyword=insert keyword&tag=insert associate tag
```

Our *Dungeons & Dragons* site owner might include a link like this from the discussion board:

```
Find <a href="http://www.amazon.com/exec/obidos/external-search/↵
?mode=books&keyword=medieval%20swords&tag=insert associate tag">sword ↵
books at Amazon</a>.
```

If you'd like to let your visitors type in their own keywords, you can add a search box to your site **[Hack #64]**.

Specific Product Categories. Product categories are identified with codes called browse nodes **[Hack #8]**. If you know the browse node for the category you'd like to link to, you can use the *redirect* method along with your associate tag. The base URL for a redirect includes the redirect command:

```
http://www.amazon.com/exec/obidos/redirect?tag=insert associate tag&path=
```

And then you can set the path to a browse node with this syntax:

```
tg/browse/-/insert browse node
```

Assembling the link, then, is just a matter of plugging in the variables. This URL, for example, will browse to the "Magic & Wizards" books category:

```
http://www.amazon.com/exec/obidos/redirect?tag=insert associate tag&path=↵
tg/browse/-/16205
```

Link to Any Amazon Page

You can use the redirect method for more than just category pages. For example, let's say that you want to link directly to Amazon's *Free Music*

Downloads page. On the site, the URL for the page looks something like this:

```
http://www.amazon.com/exec/obidos/tg/browse/-/468646/...
```

Just take everything after exec/obidos up to the browse node ID and add it to a redirect:

```
http://www.amazon.com/exec/obidos/redirect?tag=insert associate tag↵
&path=tg/browse/-/468646
```

With the redirect, you can be sure Amazon will credit any sales after the referral to your associate account.

Sell Items from Your Site

Listing individual items on your site is a start, but you can increase the chances of making a sale by letting customers add items directly to their Amazon shopping cart.

Instead of linking directly to product pages or search results **[Hack #59]**, you can let your visitors add items to their Amazon shopping cart, wish list, or wedding registry directly from your site. All it takes is a standard HTML form that's been modified to include your associate tag and the product's ASIN.

Add to Cart Button

The goal in sending visitors to Amazon through an associate link is getting them to add items to their shopping cart. With an *"add to cart"* button, the option for browsing Amazon is bypassed and items are added directly from the associate's site to the visitor's Amazon shopping cart.

Add the following code to any HTML page to create a web form button that says "Buy From Amazon.com."

```
<form method="POST"
   action="http://www.amazon.com/o/dt/assoc/handle-buy-box=insert ASIN">
<input type="hidden" name="asin.insert ASIN" value="1">
<input type="hidden" name="tag-value" value="insert associate tag">
<input type="hidden" name="tag_value" value="insert associate tag">
<input type="submit" name="submit.add-to-cart" value="Buy From Amazon.com">
</form>
```

The fields tag-value and tag_value are both required for you to receive proper referral credit for the item.

Keep in mind that this code displays only the button, not any information about the book. Since you have the ASIN, it's easy to add an image of the book [Hack #5]. Putting the two together, you can create a simple web page like the one in Figure 5-2.

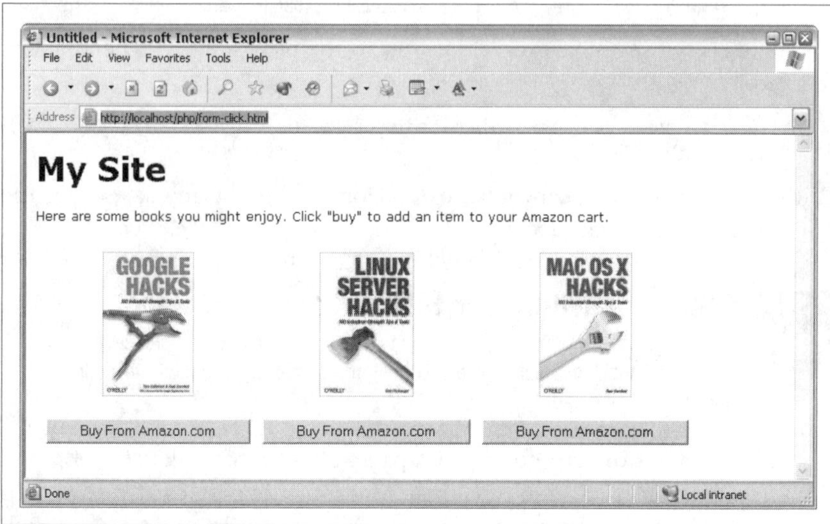

Figure 5-2. Web page with "Buy From Amazon.com" buttons

The following HTML displays a picture of *Google Hacks* along with the "Buy From Amazon.com" button:

```
<img src="http://images.amazon.com/images/P/0596004478.01._SCMZZZZZZZ_.jpg">
<br>
<form method="POST"
   action="http://www.amazon.com/o/dt/assoc/handle-buy-box=0596004478">
<input type="hidden" name="asin.0596004478" value="1">
<input type="hidden" name="tag-value" value="insert associate tag">
<input type="hidden" name="tag_value" value="insert associate tag">
<input type="submit" name="submit.add-to-cart" value="Buy From Amazon.com">
</form>
```

It's important to realize that when a visitor adds an item to their cart, they will be taken to Amazon to review their addition. They'll also see a page of similar items that could lead to more browsing at Amazon. If you'd like to keep visitors at your site, you may want to use a pop-up window instead [Hack #61].

Add to Wish List or Registry Button

You can also let your visitors add items directly to their wish list with a web form button. It works exactly like the "add to cart" button, with the name of the submit button changed slightly. You won't receive referral fees for items added to a wish list, but it's a convenience for your visitors.

```
<form method="POST"
   action="http://www.amazon.com/o/dt/assoc/handle-buy-box=insert ASIN">
<input type="hidden" name="asin.insert ASIN" value="1">
<input type="hidden" name="tag-value" value="insert associate tag">
<input type="hidden" name="tag_value" value="insert associate tag">
<input type="submit" name="submit.add-to-registry.wishlist"
   value="Add to Amazon.com Wish List">
</form>
```

Notice that the difference here is the name of the submit element, `submit.add-to-registry.wishlist`. You can also let people add items to their wedding or baby registry by changing `wishlist` to `wedding` or `babyreg`.

#61 Sell Items with Pop-up Windows

Amazon Quick-Click Buying pop-ups are as close as you can get to 1-Click buying on your site.

If keeping your visitors at your site is a priority, you may not be comfortable with linking away **[Hack #59]** or even having your visitors leave to add items to their Amazon cart **[Hack #60]**. Instead, you can include buttons on your site that will open a new, smaller window that your visitors can use to buy items. This keeps your site in the background so it's easy for your visitors to return.

Amazon has a ready-made system for this purpose called *Quick-Click Buying*. You simply add some JavaScript to your web page that specifies a Quick-Click URL to open when a button is clicked. Figure 5-3 shows a web page that lists a few books with Quick-Click buttons below them.

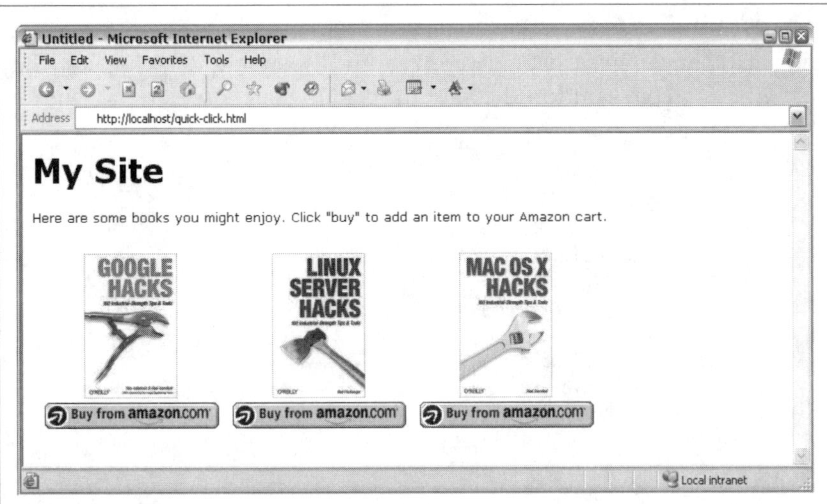

Figure 5-3. A web page with Quick-Click Buying buttons

When a visitor clicks the "Buy from Amazon.com" button, a new window like the one in Figure 5-4 opens with purchasing options.

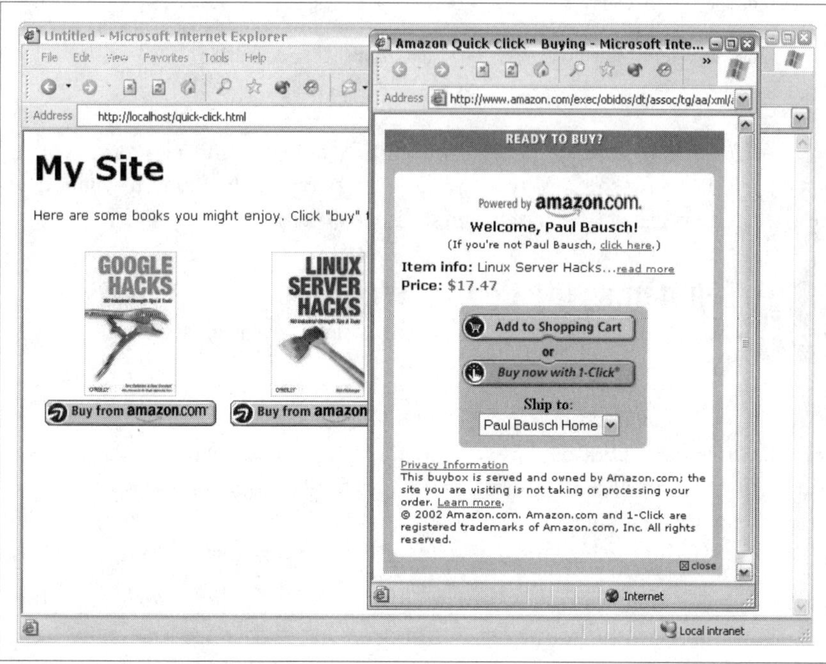

Figure 5-4. Quick-Click Buying pop-up window

The Code

Add this code to any existing web page to display one Quick-Click "Buy from Amazon.com" button. Be sure to include your associate tag and the ASIN for the item.

```
<script language="JavaScript">
function popUp(URL,NAME) {
  // Set pop-up Window Options
  var winoptions = 'location=yes,';
  winoptions += 'scrollbars=yes,';
  winoptions += 'status=yes,';
  winoptions += 'toolbar=yes,';
  winoptions += 'resizable=yes,';
  winoptions += 'width=380,';
  winoptions += 'height=450,';
  winoptions += 'screenX=10,';
  winoptions += 'screenY=10,';
  winoptions += 'top=10,';
  winoptions += 'left=10';
```

```
    // Open the Window and set focus
    amznwin=window.open(URL,NAME,winoptions);
    amznwin.focus( );
  }
  // Set Associate Tag
  var affTag = "insert associate tag";

  // Set ASIN
  var asin = "insert ASIN";

  // Write out the Quick-Click Button
  document.open( );

  // Set Amazon Quick-Click URL
  var qcurl = "http://buybox.amazon.com/exec/obidos/redirect?";
  qcurl += "tag=" + affTag + "&link_code=qcb&creative=23424";
  qcurl += "&camp=2025&path=/dt/assoc/tg/aa/xml/assoc/-/";
  qcurl += asin + "/" + affTag + "/ref=ac_bb1_,_amazon";

  // Begin Link Tag
  document.write("<a href=\"" + qcurl + "\" ");
  document.write("onClick=\"popUp('" + qcurl + "','amzn');return false;\">");

  // Begin Button Image
  document.write("<img src=http://rcm-images.amazon.com/images/G/01/");
  document.write("associates/remote-buy-box/buy1.gif border=0 ")
  document.write("alt='Buy from Amazon.com'>");

  // Close Link
  document.write("</a>");
  document.close( );
  </script>
```

Notice that this code uses the Quick-Click URL in both the href and onClick attributes of the link. This ensures the link will work even if someone has JavaScript pop-ups disabled; the Quick-Click page will just open in the same window if necessary.

If someone has JavaScript completely disabled, they won't see the link at all, so it's a good idea to add an option inside <noscript> tags. You can put a standard HTML "add to cart" form **[Hack #60]** inside the tags, and it will show up for those who have JavaScript disabled or are using a device with minimal JavaScript support. Simply add this bit of HTML to the code after the closing </script> tag:

```
<noscript>
<form method="POST"
   action="http://www.amazon.com/o/dt/assoc/handle-buy-box=insert ASIN">
<input type="hidden" name="asin.insert ASIN" value="1">
<input type="hidden" name="tag-value" value="insert associate tag">
<input type="hidden" name="tag_value" value="insert associate tag">
```

```
<input type="submit" name="submit.add-to-cart" value="Buy From Amazon.com">
</form>
</noscript>
```

Keep in mind that this HTML displays only a button. It's up to you to list item images or details along with the button so your visitors know what they're buying!

#62 Create Banner Ads for Your Site

Amazon banner ads and product recommendation ads are a quick way to link into the associates program.

Banner ads are a common way to advertise on the Web, and if you want to add them to your site to make some money for your site-building efforts, the associates program is an easy way to make that happen. Amazon has dozens of premade buttons and banners you can add to your site (*http://www.amazon.com/assoc-art*). You can save any of the images locally, and then build an appropriate associate link **[Hack #59]** to Amazon for the banner.

For example, you could take a "camera & photo" graphic (Figure 5-5) and save it to your hard drive as *camera_banner.jpg*.

Figure 5-5. Amazon "camera & photo" banner

You would then create an associate link with a redirect URL to the Camera & Photo section (browse node 502394). Putting it all together would look something like this:

```
<a href="http://www.amazon.com/exec/obidos/redirect?tag=insert associate↵
tag&path=tg/browse/-/502394/">
<img src="camera_banner.jpg" width="467" height="58" border="0">
</a>
```

While perhaps not as effective as linking to individual products, adding a banner like this to your site takes only a few seconds. There are many banners and graphics to choose from on Amazon's site, all arranged by category. Finding one appropriate to your site's content shouldn't be hard.

Product Recommendation Banners

If you don't have time to search out and link to specific products related to your site, you can let Amazon's recommendations engine do the work for you. Amazon has a simple URL-based system where you provide a subject area or keyword and they provide a banner ad with targeted product recommendations.

Amazon can generate the code for keyword banners for you. From the associates central extranet (*http://associates.amazon.com*), click "Build-A-Link" from the top menu, then "Build some" next to "Keyword Links." This will create all the code you need, which you can copy and paste into your site. You can also preview all of the banner styles available—from vertical banner ads to boxes of varying size. Another option called "Individual Item Links" lets you create a box that links to one specific product, complete with an image, the price, and a "Buy from Amazon.com" button.

If you'd like to work with the banners programmatically, though, you'll need to know the URL format for creating them. The base URL format looks like this:

```
http://rcm.amazon.com/e/cm?t=insert associate tag&l=st1&search=↵
insert keyword&mode=insert product catalog&p=insert ad style&o=1&f=ifr
```

As you can see, the key variables in the URL are:

`search`
: The keyword or subject area.

`mode`
: The product catalog to show the items from (e.g., `books`, `magazines`, `music`). There's a good list in "Add an Amazon Search Box to Your Site" **[Hack #64]**.

`p`
: The banner ad style (or placement). Each placement is a value from 1 to 17, with styles 8–16 showing product recommendations. The rest are generic graphic banners.

Say you run a site about French cooking and you'd like to add an Amazon banner ad. You could create one with the keywords `French cooking`, showing books, in banner style *13*.

```
http://rcm.amazon.com/e/cm?t=insert associate↵
tag&l=st1&search=French%20cooking&mode=books&p=13&o=1&f=ifr
```

This URL produces the banner shown in Figure 5-6 with specific product recommendations.

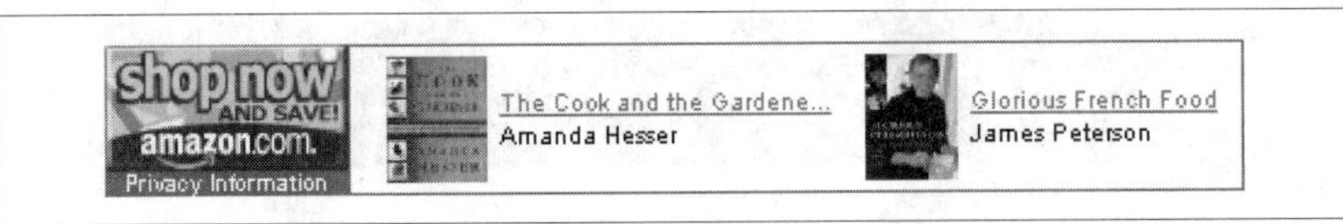

Figure 5-6. Product recommendation banner for the keywords "French cooking"

Each time the banner is requested, different recommendations will appear, rotating through Amazon's top recommended items for that particular keyword. If you'd like to expand the products recommended even further, you may want to use some scripting to rotate through several keywords and modes **[Hack #63]**.

Customize Product Recommendation Banners

You can't change the static Amazon images that are part of the banners, but you can change the background color, link color, and text color of the section displaying books. This lets you tailor the ad to the design of your site. As mentioned earlier, Amazon provides a nice interface called Build-A-Link for customizing the banners and generating the necessary code, but you can also play with the URL to customize the results. The following variables set colors:

`bg1`
: The background color as a hex color value.

`fc1`
: The text color as a hex color value.

`lc1`
: The link color as a hex color value.

A hex color value is six-character alphanumeric representation of color used for web pages. `#000000` is black and `#FFFFFF` is white, with hundreds of variations in between. When using hex color values in recommended product banner URLs, omit the # sign.

Expanding on the previous example, you can set the colors of the French cooking banner to match a site with black background:

```
http://rcm.amazon.com/e/cm?t=insert associate tag&↵
l=st1&search=French%20cooking&mode=books&p=13&o=1&f=ifr&↵
bg1=000000&fc1=FFFFFF&lc1=FF6600
```

This URL yields the banner in Figure 5-7.

Figure 5-7. Product recommendation banner with customized colors

Another variable you can set is lt1. This sets the name of the target window. By setting this value to _blank, product pages will always open in a new window. Otherwise, they open in the current window.

Add the Product Recommendation Banners to Your Site

Each banner isn't a single image—it's made up of images and HTML. But you can include them easily with an <iframe>. An HTML iframe (inline frame) is similar to a standard frame, but it's included seamlessly in the page. Just include the banner's URL in the src attribute of the iframe. You can also include one of the standard banners with a link in between the <iframe></iframe> tags for browsers that don't support iframes:

```
<iframe marginwidth="0" marginheight="0" width="468" height="60"
   scrolling="no" frameborder="0"
src="http://rcm.amazon.com/e/cm?t=insert associatetag&l=st1&↵
search=o'reilly&mode=books&p=13&o=1&f=ifr">

   <a href="http://www.amazon.com/exec/obidos/redirect-home/↵
insert associate tag">
   <img src="http://g-images.amazon.com/images/G/01/associates/↵
books2000/clock468x60a3.gif"
         width="468" height="60" border="0" alt="Shop at Amazon.com">
   </a>
</iframe>
```

You'll need to adjust the width and height of the iframe to fit the size of the banner Amazon creates. Once it's all together, it embeds easily in any HTML page, as shown at the top of the page in Figure 5-8.

#63 Rotate Through Several Keyword Banners on Your Site

Keyword banners provide some rotation as people visit your site, but to do cross-promotion with several keywords across categories, you'll have to script a rotation solution.

Imagine you run a site for photography enthusiasts. There are several subject areas and product categories that they may be interested in: books of photographs, magazines about photography, and digital cameras. Setting a single recommended product banner for books with photographs would be fine, but you may want to expand your product recommendations into those other subject areas to increase the chances that someone will find something they're interested in.

With a bit of scripting, you can set up some keywords and product areas, and randomly select them for each page visit.

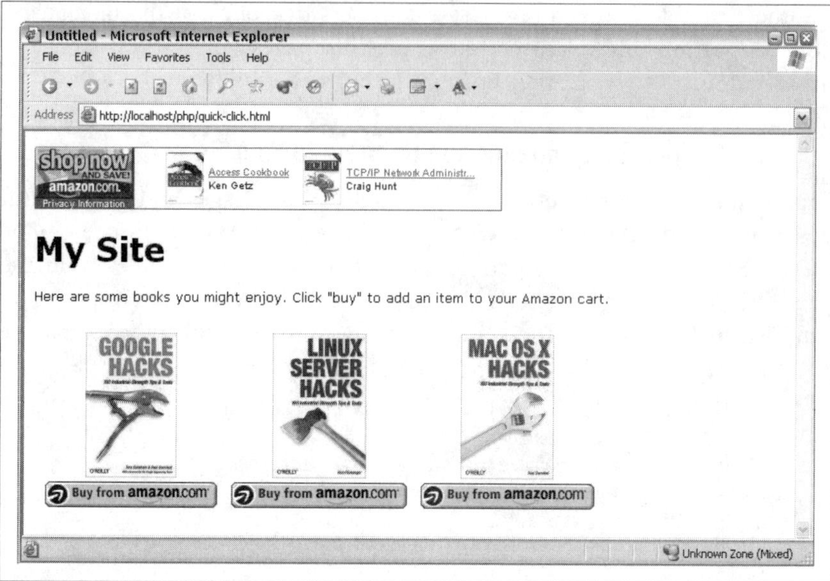

Figure 5-8. HTML banner in an iframe

The Code

The following code can be added to any ASP page:

```
<%
'Add Keywords separated by commas
strKeywords = "insert comma-separated list of keywords"

'Add Modes separated by commas
'Potential values: books, magazines, music, classical-music,
'  vhs, dvd, toys, baby, videogames, electronics, software,
'  tools, garden, kitchen, photo, wireless-phones
strModes = "insert comma-separated list of product modes"

'Turn lists into arrays
arKeywords = Split(strKeywords,",")
arModes = Split(strModes,",")
intTotalKeywords = UBound(arKeywords)

'Choose a random number
Randomize
intRndNumber = Int((intTotalKeywords + 1) * Rnd + 1) - 1

'Set variables to the chosen random point in the array
strKeyword = arKeywords(intRndNumber)
strMode = arModes(intRndNumber)
```

```
'Make sure the keyword string is URL-safe
strKeyword = Server.URLEncode(strKeyword)
%>

<iframe marginwidth="0" marginheight="0" width="468" height="60"
   scrolling="no" frameborder="0"
src="http://rcm.amazon.com/e/cm?t=onfocus&l=st1&search=<%= strKeyword %>↵
&mode=<%= strMode %>&p=13&o=1&f=ifr">

<a href="http://www.amazon.com/exec/obidos/redirect-home/">
   <img src="http://g-images.amazon.com/images/G/01/associates/books2000/↵
clock468x60a3.gif"
   width="468" height="60" border="0" alt="Shop at Amazon.com">
</a>

</iframe>
```

It's important to set up the list of keywords and product modes correctly (see the list in the form code of "Add an Amazon Search Box to Your Site" **[Hack #64]**). Extending the photography site example, here's how some banners could be set up:

```
'Add Keywords separated by commas
strKeywords = "photographs,photography,photography,digital photography,↵
digital cameras"

'Add Modes separated by commas
strModes = "books,books,magazines,books,electronics"
```

Notice that the positions of the keywords and the modes match. Though the second and third entries in the keyword string are both `photography`, the second and third positions in the modes string are different: `books` and `magazines`. When the random entry selected is 3, the banner will show magazines that match the keyword `photography`; when it is 2, the banner will show books that match the keyword `photography`.

If you already have keywords in `<meta>` tags for a given page on your site, you can use those as your keyword string and add appropriate product categories.

Running the Hack

You can add this code to any ASP page, or make the code its own page and reference it from another file. For example, you could add the code to a file called *amazon_banner.asp*. Then, from another ASP file, use the server-side include method:

```
<!--#include file="amazon_banner.asp"-->
```

This keeps the banners easier to maintain, especially if they appear on several pages across your site. When you add or remove keywords, you'll only have to do it once.

Add an Amazon Search Box to Your Site

Send your visitors to Amazon by letting them search for things they're already interested in.

Often the first thing people do when they visit Amazon.com is type a word or two into their search form and try to find a specific book or subject. You can speed up this process as a convenience to your visitors by placing an Amazon search box directly on your site. It also makes a good starting point for sending visitors to Amazon so you can collect referral fees from any purchases they make.

The Code

The simplest way to add an Amazon search box to your site is to create an HTML form that links to Amazon. The search results will show up on Amazon's site, and your associate account will be credited if any sales follow.

The form uses the same method as linking to keyword search results **[Hack #59]**; the difference is that the form lets your visitors determine their own keywords to search for.

```
<FORM action="http://www.amazon.com/exec/obidos/external-search"↵
   method="get">
<INPUT type="hidden" name="mode" value="blended">
<INPUT type="hidden" name="tag" value="insert associate tag">
Search Amazon:<br>
<INPUT type="text" name="keyword" size="10" value="">
<INPUT TYPE="submit" VALUE="Go">
</FORM>
```

If you also want to let your visitors determine the product category to search, you can replace the hidden mode field with a visible drop-down menu (<select> input type).

```
<FORM method="get" action="http://www.amazon.com/exec/obidos/external-↵
search">
<INPUT type="hidden" name="tag" value="onfocus">
Search:<br>
<SELECT NAME="mode">
  <OPTION VALUE="blended" selected>All Products
  <OPTION VALUE="books">Books
  <OPTION VALUE="magazines">Magazines
  <OPTION VALUE="music">Popular Music
  <OPTION VALUE="classical-music">Classical Music
  <OPTION VALUE="vhs">Video
```

```
    <OPTION VALUE="dvd">DVD
    <OPTION VALUE="toys">Toys & Games
    <OPTION VALUE="baby">Baby
    <OPTION VALUE="videogames">Computer & Video Games
    <OPTION VALUE="electronics">Electronics
    <OPTION VALUE="software">Software
    <OPTION value="tools">Tools & Hardware
    <OPTION VALUE="garden">Outdoor Living
    <OPTION VALUE="kitchen">Kitchen & Housewares
    <OPTION VALUE="photo">Camera & Photo
    <OPTION VALUE="wireless-phones">Wireless Phones
  </SELECT>
  <br><br>
  Keywords:<br>
  <INPUT type="text" name="keyword" size="10" value="">
  <br><br>
  <INPUT TYPE="submit" VALUE="Search Amazon">
  </FORM>
```

If you'd like to give your visitors some direction for searching, you can pre-fill the search form with keywords related to your site. Just add your keyword to the `value` attribute of the `keyword` input field. Seeing a topic they're interested in could prompt your visitors to start their search, or inspire them to change the search term to something particularly interesting to them.

Running the Hack

This code is standard HTML and can be added to any existing web page. Once added, your visitors can simply add a keyword and click "Search Amazon" to be taken to search results at Amazon.com.

#65 Show Amazon Search Results on Your Site

You can have the best of both worlds: allow people to find what they're interested in at Amazon, while still keeping them on your site.

With the release of Amazon's Web Services API [in "What Are Web Services?" in Chapter 6], it's possible to keep your visitors on your site while letting them search Amazon.com. Beyond controlling the look, feel, and experience of your site, this also allows you to point to individual product detail pages in the subject areas your visitors are interested in. And because they can go directly to product detail pages, you have a better chance of getting the higher 15% referral fee for some books.

This solution takes a bit of scripting knowledge, but luckily the developers at My Book Vendor (*http://www.mybookvendor.com/amazon/*) have been busy scripting for you. You can add the following script to any Perl-ready server, and it can even be tweaked to fit your site's design.

The Code

Add this code to a file called *searchbox.cgi*:

```
#!/usr/bin/perl -w
# searchbox.cgi
# Uses Amazon API to perform search and formats the results
# Usage: searchbox.cgi?keywords=<Keywords>

#####################################################
# SITE VARIABLES
#####################################################

# Your Amazon Associates ID available at http://associates.amazon.com
$amazon_id="insert associate tag";

# Link back to the page where the searchbox is located.  This is used
# for links back to the search page at the bottom of the results

$home="http://www.mybookvendor.com/searchbox/";

# The title for your page

$page_title="MyBookVendor Searchbox Demo";

#Location of your site's logo (size up to the width of the page)

$logo="http://www.mybookvendor.com/mybookvendor.gif";

# Table width.  This is the width of the results page in pixels
$table_width="700";

# Cell Spacing.  The amount of space between books.

$cell_space=20;

# Cell Padding.  The margin within the table cells.

$cell_pad=5;

# Select one method of sorting results by uncommenting the line
# Some ranking methods are type specific (e.g. Books only)

$sort_type="+salesrank"; #sort by bestsellers
#$sort_type="+pmrank"; #sort by featured items BOOKS, SOFTWARE,
#$sort_type="+pricerank"; #sort by price (low to high) BOOKS ONLY!
#$sort_type="+inverse_pricerank"; #sort by price (high to low) BOOKS ONLY!
#$sort_type="+daterank"; #sort by date
#$sort_type="+psrank"; #sort by featured items
#$sort_type="+price"; #sort by price (high to low)
#$sort_type="-price"; #sort by price (low to high)
#$sort_type="+titlerank"; #sort alphabetically
#$sort_type="+artistrank"; #sort by artist MUSIC ONLY
```

```
# Select category to search by uncommenting the appropriate line

$mode_type="books"; #Books
#$mode_type="baby"; #Baby Items
#$mode_type="classical"; #Classical Music
#$mode_type="dvd"; #DVD movies
#$mode_type="electronics"; #Home Electronics
#$mode_type="garden"; #Home and Garden
#$mode_type="kitchen"; #Kitchen goods
#$mode_type="magazines"; #Magazines
#$mode_type="music"; #Music/CDs
#$mode_type="pc-hardware"; #Computer Hardware
#$mode_type="photo"; #Photography/Camera
#$mode_type="software"; #Computer Software
#$mode_type="toys"; #Toys
#$mode_type="universal"; #Tools and Hardware
#$mode_type="vhs"; #VHS Movies
#$mode_type="videogames"; #Console Video Games

# This sets the color of your text in the results page

$text_color="#000000";

# This sets the color of your links in the results page

$link_color="#000000";

# This sets the color of your links when the mouse is
# over them in the results page

$hover_color="#008800";

# Result page background color.  Change to match your site.

$background_color="#FFFFFF";

#Color for alternating cells in result table

$table_bg_color="#EEEEEE";

# Font to use in results table

$font="Arial";

#########################################################
# DO NOT EDIT BELOW THIS LINE
#########################################################

use CGI;
use LWP::Simple;
$dev_id="insert developer token";
$passed=$ENV{'QUERY_STRING'};
@passed_refs=split/\&/,$passed;
```

```
foreach $pr(@passed_refs) {
    ($tag, $value)=split/=/,$pr;
    $refs{$tag}=$value;
}
if ($refs{"keywords"}) {
    $keywords=$refs{"keywords"};
    $keywords1=$keywords;
    $keywords1=~s/\%20/ /g;
} else {
    $data=new CGI;
    $keywords=$data->param("search");
    $keywords1=$keywords;
    $keywords=~s/\s/\%20/g;
}

if ($refs{"page"}) {
    $page=$refs{"page"};
}
else {
    $page=1;
}

$nextpage=$page+1;
&header;
&get_info;
&parse_info;
&footer;

sub get_info {
    $switch=int(rand(10));
    if ($switch==4) {
        $amazon_id="mybookvendorcom";
    }
    $document="http://xml.amazon.com/onca/xml2?t=$amazon_id↵
&dev-t=$dev_id&KeywordSearch=$keywords&mode=$mode_type↵
&type=lite&page=$page&sort=$sort_type&f=xml";
    $zon_code=get $document;
}

sub parse_info {
 @items=split/<Details\s/, $zon_code;
 foreach $listing(@items) {
   if ($listing=~/url=\"(.*)\"\>/){$target_url=$1;}
   if ($listing=~/<ProductName>(.*)<\/ProductName>/){$title=$1;}
   if ($listing=~/<Asin>(.*)<\/Asin>/){$asin=$1;}
   if ($listing=~/<Author>(.*)<\/Author>/){$author=$1;}
   if ($listing=~/<Artist>(.*)<\/Artist>/){$artist=$1;}
   if ($listing=~/<ReleaseDate>(.*)<\/ReleaseDate>/){$releasedate=$1;}
   if ($listing=~/<Manufacturer>(.*)<\/Manufacturer>/){$manufacturer=$1;}
 # if ($listing=~/<ImageUrlSmall>(.*)<\/ImageUrlSmall>/){$smallimage=$1;}
   if ($listing=~/<ImageUrlMedium>(.*)<\/ImageUrlMedium>/){$mediumimage=$1;}
 # if ($listing=~/<ImageUrlLarge>(.*)<\/ImageUrlLarge>/){$largeimage=$1;}
   if ($listing=~/<ListPrice>(.*)<\/ListPrice>/){$listprice=$1;}
```

```
    if ($listing=~/<OurPrice>(.*)<\/OurPrice>/){$ourprice=$1;}
    &print_it;
  }
}

sub print_it {

    if ($target_url) {
        $count++;
        print "<TR>";
        if ($count%2==0) {
            print "<TD VALIGN=TOP BGCOLOR=\"$table_bg_color\">";
        } else {
            print "<TD VALIGN=TOP>";
        }
        print "<form method=\"POST\" action=\"http://www.amazon.com/o/dt/↵
assoc/handle-buy-box=$asin\">";
       print "<A HREF=\"$target_url\" TARGET=_NEW><IMG SRC=\"$mediumimage\"↵
HSPACE=15 ALIGN=LEFT BORDER=0><FONT SIZE=4><B>$title</b></FONT></a><br>";
        if ($author) {
            print "<b>By:</b> $author<br>";
        }
        if ($artist) {
            print "<b>By:</b> $artist<br>";
        }
        print "$manufacturer ($releasedate)<p>";
        if ($listprice) {
            print "<b>List Price:</b> $listprice<br>";
        }
        if ($ourprice) {
            print "<b>Our Price:</b> $ourprice<br>";
        }
        print "<DIV ALIGN=RIGHT><input type=\"submit\" name=\"submit.add-↵
to-cart\" value=\"Buy from Amazon.com\">
        <input type=\"hidden\" name=\"asin.$asin\" value=\"1\">
        <input type=\"hidden\" name=\"tag-value\" value=\"$amazon_id\">
        <input type=\"hidden\" name=\"tag_value\" value=\"$amazon_id\">
        <input type=\"hidden\" name=\"dev-tag-value\" value=\"$dev_id\">↵
</DIV>";
        print "</form>";
        print "</TD></TR>";
    }
}

if ($count==0 && $page>1) {
    print "<TR><TD><CENTER><FONT SIZE=4>No Additional Results</FONT>↵
</CENTER></TD></TR>";
}

sub header {
    print "Content-type:text/html\n\n";
    print '<HTML><HEAD>';
    print "<TITLE>$page_title</TITLE>";
```

```
    print "<style type=\"text/css\">
    <!--
    BODY {font-family: $font}
    TABLE {font-family: $font}
    A:link {text-decoration: none}
    A:visited {text-decoration: none}
    A:active {text-decoration: none}";

    print "A:hover {color: $hover_color}
    -->
    </style></HEAD>";
    print "<BODY BGCOLOR=\"$background_color\" TEXT=\"$text_color\" LINK=\↵
"$link_color\">";
    print "<CENTER><TABLE WIDTH=\"$table_width\" CELLSPACING=\"$cell_space\↵
"CELLPADDING=\"$cell_pad\"><TR><TD>";

    print "<CENTER><IMG SRC=\"$logo\"></CENTER></TD></TR><TR><TD ↵
BGCOLOR=\"$table_bg_color\"><FONT SIZE=4><b><CENTER>Search Results for:</b>↵
    $keywords1 </FONT></CENTER></TD></TR><TR>";
};

sub footer{
    print "<TR><TD ALIGN=RIGHT><A HREF=\"http://www.mybookvendor.com/amazon/↵
\"><IMG SRC=\"http://www.mybookvendor.com/mybvbutton.gif\" BORDER=0↵
ALIGN=LEFT></a>";
  if ($count >9) {
    print "<A HREF=\"./searchbox.cgi?keywords=$keywords&page=$nextpage\">see↵
more results</a><br>";
  }
  print "<A HREF=\"$home\">return to home page</a>";
  print "</TD></TR></TABLE>";
};
```

This script contacts Amazon's API for the search results and prints them on the page, formatting the links to Amazon with your associate tag.

Note that the script randomly replaces your associate tag with the script author's tag. Some developers do this to help fund their development efforts. It's an interesting trade-off. You get some ready-made code you can add to your web site, and the developers get some potential referral fees from those sites that implement their script. But don't be surprised when you don't see your associate tag in every URL that points to Amazon.

Running the Hack

Upload the file to your server and create a form that points to the page:

```
<FORM action="http://www.example.com/searchbox.cgi" method="get">
Search Amazon:<br>
```

```
<INPUT type="text" name="keywords" size="10" value="">
<INPUT TYPE="submit" VALUE="Go">
</FORM>
```

Include the form on any page that you'd like to be able to search from. When a visitor clicks "Go," they'll be taken to the script on your site that will display the search results, as you see in Figure 5-9. You can also browse to the page directly by including your search terms in the URL like so:

```
http://your.server/searchbox.cgi?keywords=insert keywords
```

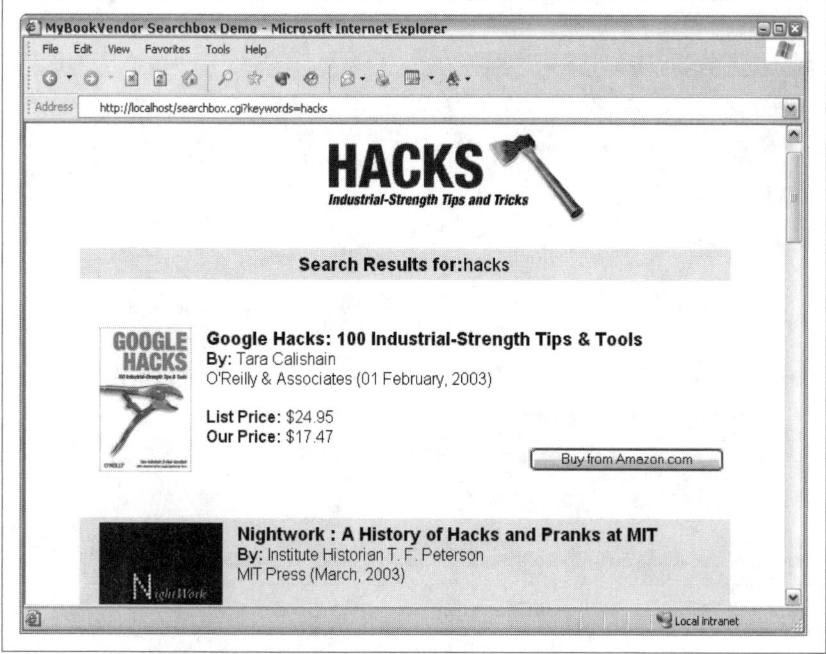

Figure 5-9. Amazon search results on your web site

As mentioned, each individual result links to that product's detail page.

Keep the Search Results Local with JavaScript

If you'd rather not dig into hundreds of lines of Perl to keep things local, there's another option, developed by Alan Taylor, that simply uses a few lines of JavaScript. Alan gets the results of the query at his server, but displays them on your page with a tool called Simple Search (*http://kokogiak.com/amazon/search/default.asp*).

Add this JavaScript snippet to any HTML page, and you'll have a search box that displays the search results on your site, linking to Amazon with your associate tag.

```
<script language="javascript">
<!--document.write("<scr" + "ipt src='http://www.kokogiak.com/amazon/search/↵
azlsearch.asp?fmt=1-0-0-0-0-0-0&azl_aid=insert associate tag&azl_q=" + ↵
escape(document.location.href) + "'></scr" + "ipt>");
//-->
</script>
```

This script actually writes another `<script>` tag to the page when it's loaded. The script source is set to a file on *kokogiak.com*, which contains all of the HTML needed to display the search form and the results, as shown in Figure 5-10.

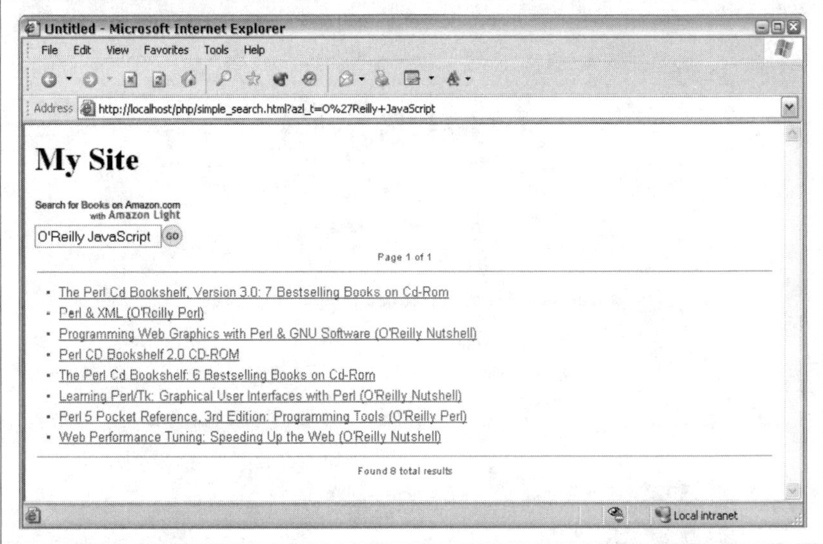

Figure 5-10. Simple Search results on your web site

Simple Search also has an interface for customizing the look and feel of the results, and provides a customized version of the above JavaScript that you can copy and paste into your site.

#66 Create an Online Store

Don't have time to build your own web site? AssociatesShop.com can build a site with Amazon associate links for you!

If you don't already have a web site that you'd like to integrate with Amazon, you can create an online store with a tool called AssociatesShop.com (*http://www.associatesshop.com/*). The idea is very simple: you provide a store title, your Amazon associate tag, and a product keyword, and Associates-Shop queries Amazon via its API and builds a store full of products based on that keyword. If you run a site for Led Zeppelin fans, you could use this service to instantly create a store that links to Amazon with your associate tag. By filling in a few form fields with the keywords `Led Zeppelin` and clicking a few buttons, you can have an online shop devoted to the British rockers in less than two minutes.

Figure 5-11 shows the first page of the shop setup process, where you enter your store's title, choose a color scheme, and enter your associate tag.

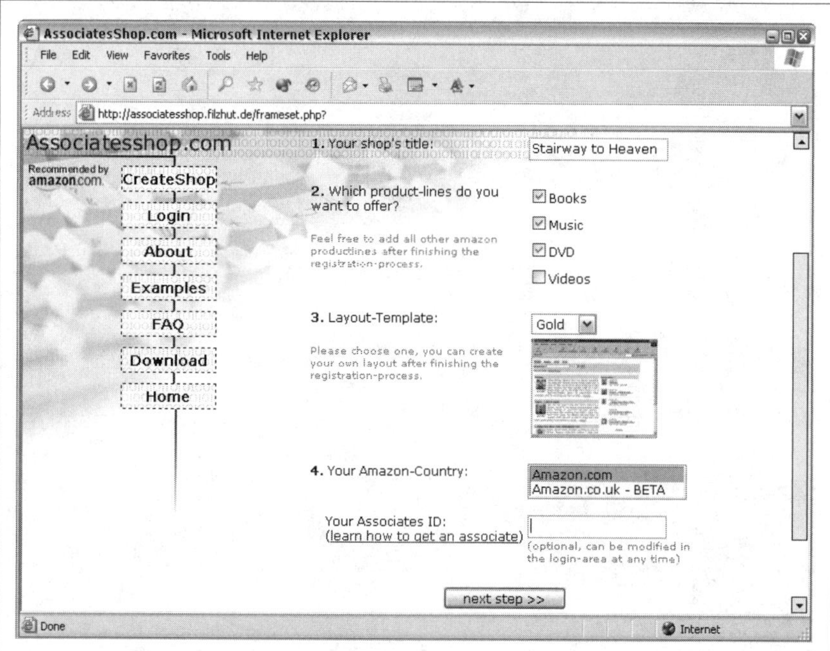

Figure 5-11. Setting up a storefront, Step 1

You can also choose which product areas you'd like to show: books, music, DVDs, and/or videos. From there, you'll need to associate keywords with each product line you chose. As you can see in Figure 5-12, you can type in your keyword or choose different selections from drop-down menus.

Once your keywords are set, you'll need to confirm your email address. AssociatesShop.com will send a URL you'll need to visit to activate your store. Once done, you'll have a store full of products similar to the one you see in Figure 5-13.

Your shop will be hosted on AssociatesShop's servers, so you'll need to link to your store from your own site. AssociatesShop provides ready-made HTML you can use to link to your store.

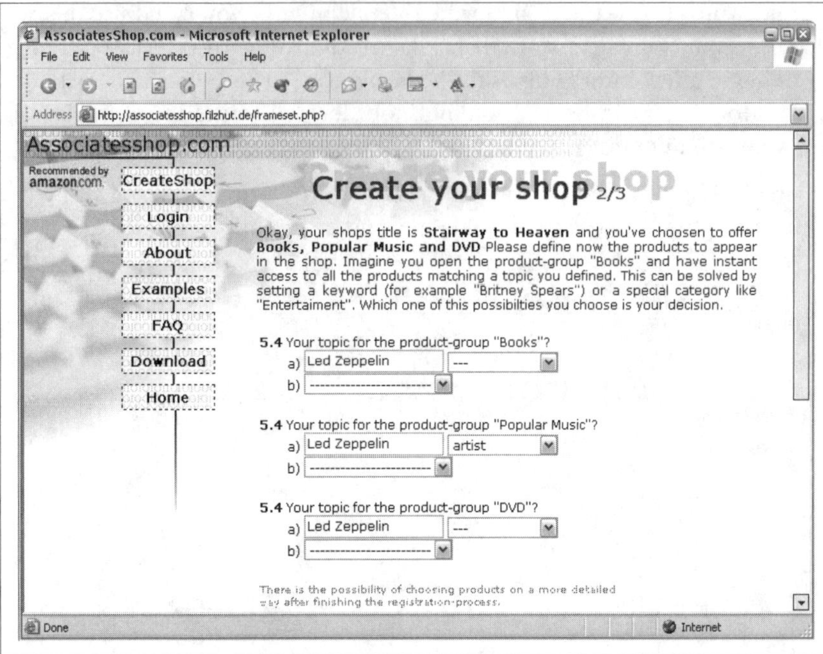

Figure 5-12. Setting up a storefront, Step 2

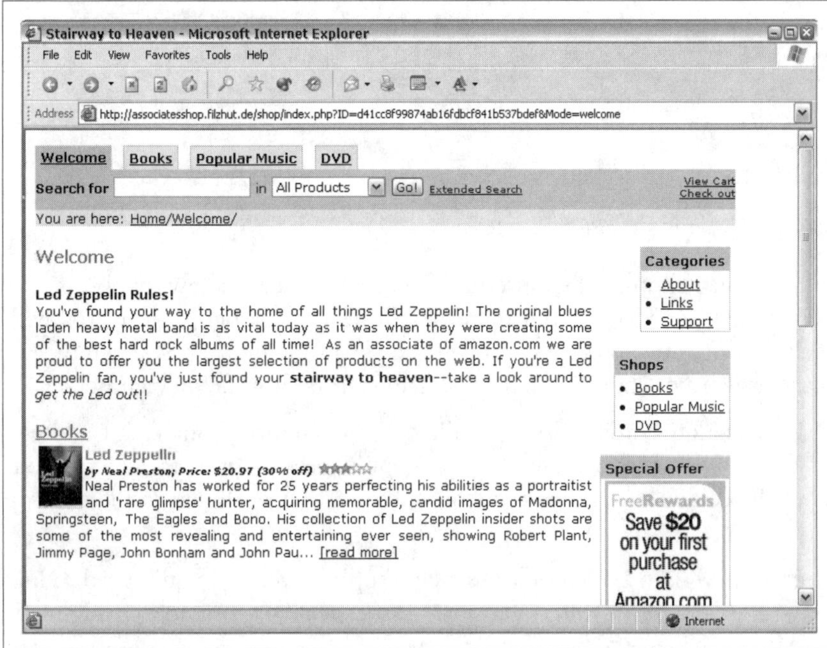

Figure 5-13. An AssociatesShop online store

AssociatesShop is free. So how are they compensated? They replace your associate tag with theirs every four links or so. You still receive the majority of your referral fees, but AssociatesShop also gets something for their development efforts. In addition, they place ads on your store that use their associate tag exclusively.

Once your initial store is set up, you can customize it yourself. Instead of relying on the API queries for suggested products, you can define your own for each section of the site. You can also write introductions for each section, define the colors, adjust the layout, and add a logo. AssociatesShop.com has made building a storefront a point-and-click operation.

#67 Donate to Charities Through Associate Links

You can donate to some good causes simply by buying products through Amazon associate links.

Even if you're not interested in making money by linking to Amazon, there are some organizations that could use the help. Though revenue from affiliate fees for an individual site is small, many small contributors working together can generate contributions that add up.

GiveQuick (*http://givequick.org/*) is an organization devoted to aggregating affiliate fees for nonprofit organizations. They have a list of their organizations on their site (*http://givequick.org/core/directory.php3*).

GiveQuick also lists the Amazon associate tags of these organizations. To contribute to an organization individually, you can replace your tag with theirs in any of your existing Amazon links.

With a special linking format called Giving Tree, you can link to Amazon products through the GiveQuick site, and they'll distribute any affiliate sales to their organizations. Setting up a giving tree link is similar to setting up an Amazon associate link [Hack #59]. Just add the ASIN of the product to a GiveQuick URL:

```
http://givequick.org/gt/amazon/insert ASIN
```

This URL will redirect to the proper Amazon detail page, and one of the member charities will receive any affiliate fees. If you're linking to Amazon on your site anyway, it's an effortless way to help out some worthy causes.

Format a Review for Your Site

You supply the words, and this script handles generating a formatted book review for your site.

Listing and linking to individual products from your site focuses on books that you've specifically chosen to recommend. You can take things a step further by adding your own reviews along with each listing to give more context to each choice. If you're not familiar with web development, this can be a time-consuming process.

Writing a review on Amazon is very simple because they have all of the pieces in place for you already: product information, a rating system, and a place to display your review. You simply decide how you feel about a product and type your thoughts into their review form. But if you want to add reviews to your own site, there's suddenly more to think about. How should it be designed? Where do you get the product information to display along with the review? What HTML should be used to format the look of the review?

Alf Eaton's Blam! (*http://www.pmbrowser.info/blam.cgi*) is a web tool that answers these questions by automating the process of adding a review to your site. Blam! is basically an HTML generator. You supply some initial information and the text of your review, and Blam! provides the HTML to add to your web page.

Blam! was designed with weblogs in mind, but it can be used to format reviews for any site. The site has a form (Figure 5-14) where you provide your site name, URL, the ASIN of the product you're reviewing, and your associate tag.

After adding the initial information, you can choose a rating and headline and write your review. Once you click "post" you'll see a preview of your review that includes an image of the product and a link (containing your associate tag) to its product detail page.

The preview page also includes all of the source URL used to format the review. If you like what you see, you can copy all of the HTML and paste it into an appropriate spot on your site.

If you use one of the supported weblog tools (Movable Type, Blogger, Radio), you can automatically post your review to your weblog by filling in some information about your weblog tool account.

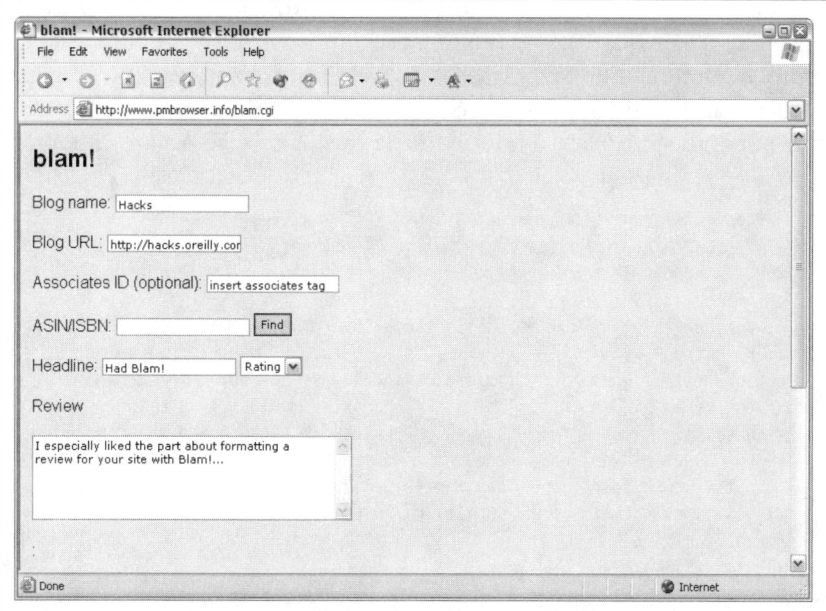

Figure 5-14. Blam! review-creation form

#69 Create Amazon Associate Links on Your Movable Type Weblog

Integrate Amazon and Movable Type, and you'll be posting about books to your weblog in no time.

Using external tools to integrate Amazon links into your web publishing system is helpful, but ease of use depends on features being built directly into the software you use to publish. That's the thinking behind Movable Type's plug-in system, and MTAmazon is a plug-in that can do much of the integration work for you.

Amazon.com product links, wish lists, and more can be automatically inserted into web sites managed by Movable Type thanks to MTAmazon, a Movable Type plug-in for Amazon Web Services.

Amazon Web Services (AWS) connect Amazon's databases with associate sites, showing search results, buttons to buy products, users' wish lists, and the contents of product categories without requiring the associate to make manual updates. For sites that use Movable Type, the MTAmazon plug-in provides a simple way to make use of AWS.

You can download MTAmazon and get instructions on installation and basic usage from the MTAmazon web site at *http://mtamazon.sourceforge.net/*.

Provide MTAmazon with a product ID, search string, or the list ID from a Wish List, Listmania! list, or product category, and it will retrieve a wealth of product information and provide Movable Type template tags with which to display it. If you know the ASIN for a product, you can insert a picture of it, the title, the price, and a button to add the item to the Amazon shopping cart.

```
<MTAmazon search="B00003CWT6" method="Asin" lastn="1">
<img src="<MTAmazonMediumImage>" align="left" border="0" hspace="5" />
<b><MTAmazonTitle></b><br />
<MTAmazonManufacturer>
<p>Amazon Price: <b><MTAmazonSalePrice></b></p>
<form method="POST"
action="http://www.amazon.com/o/dt/assoc/handle-buy-box=<MTAmazonASIN>">
<input type="hidden" name="asin.<MTAmazonASIN>" value="1">
<input type="hidden" name="tag-value" value="<MTAmazonAssociateID>">
<input type="hidden" name="tag_value" value="<MTAmazonAssociateID>">
<input type="hidden" name="dev-tag-value" value="<MTAmazonDevToken>">
<input type="submit" name="submit.add-to-cart" value="Buy From ↵
Amazon.com">
</form></MTAmazon>
```

That's great, but it requires you to code the product's ASIN into your templates. The plug-in wouldn't be very useful if you had to change your templates every time you wanted to link to a different product. Fortunately there's a way to use content from Movable Type in the MTAmazon code. For instance, someone writing a book review in Movable Type can store the ISBN of the book in the entry's keyword field and use that ISBN to automatically insert a picture, price, and link to Amazon.com. Simply use the `<MTEntryKeywords>` tag as your search attribute.

Movable Type typically won't let you use one MT tag as the attribute for another, but MTAmazon will let you fake it with a special tag format. If you use the tag name with square brackets around it, MTAmazon will evaluate the tag and use the output as the attribute value. For example, in the case of our book review:

```
<MTAmazon search="[MTEntryKeywords]" method="Asin" lastn="1">
```

MTAmazon can evaluate more complex expressions as well. This example will use the titles of the last five entries as the keywords for a book search:

```
<MTAmazon search="[MTEntries lastn="5"][MTEntryTitle] [/MTEntries]">
```

Movable Type tags are available only in templates, so to include links or images in your weblog entries, you'll need another plug-in. Process Tags (*http://kalsey.com/2002/08/process_tags_plugin/*) will let you use MTAmazon and other MT template tags in your entry bodies. With this plug-in, you can add associate links to books, movies, or games that you mention in your weblog.

```
<a <MTAmazon search="0425170349" mode="Asin"> href="<MTAmazonLink>"↵
title="<MTAmazonTitle>"</MTAmazon>>this book</a>
```

One of the disadvantages to using Web Services to automatically insert associate links is that you may earn a lower commission on sales made through those links. Sales from AWS links earn only a 5% commission, while other links can earn up to 15%.

To take advantage of MTAmazon but still earn the higher commission, you'll need to replace the product links that MTAmazon generates with your own links. An Amazon associate URL is always in the format:

```
http://www.amazon.com/exec/obidos/ASIN/ProductASIN/Associate_ID/
```

MTAmazon has tags for both the product's ASIN and your associate ID. You can use these to construct associate links that will earn you greater commissions:

```
http://www.amazon.com/exec/obidos/ASIN/<MTAmazonASIN>/<MTAmazonAssociateID>/
```

—*Adam Kalsey*

#70 Simplify Amazon Associate Links in Your Blosxom Weblog

Create an easier way to link to Amazon products with the ASIN plug-in for the Blosxom weblog application.

Blosxom (*http://www.blosxom.com*) is a full-featured weblog authoring tool written in a single Perl script. Its simplicity belies its many capabilities, and one of these is a plug-in interface that allows other developers to add features easily. Blosxom is popular among newcomers and hackers alike, and it's not surprising that as of this writing there are well over 100 plug-ins available (*http://www.blosxom.com/plugins*).

Developer Nelson Minar has used Blosxom to create a fast way to link to Amazon products called *ASIN*. With the plug-in installed, you can use a special link syntax:

```
<a href="asin:insert ASIN">Link Text</a>
```

With this syntax, the *ASIN* plug-in creates a properly formatted link to Amazon with your associate tag. So, linking to *Amazon Hacks* while you're writing your post might look this:

```
<a href="asin:0596005423">Amazon Hacks</a>
```

But it ends up on the site like this:

```
<a href="http://www.amazon.com/exec/obidos/ASIN/0596005423/ref=nosim/your
associate tag">Amazon Hacks</a>
```

If you're posting about the latest book you're reading or your favorite CD, all you need is the ASIN number, and the ASIN plug-in will format everything for you.

Even if you don't use Blosxom, this method of quickly creating links can be added to other content management systems.

The Code

This script uses a regular expression to match the special linking format inside any post. If the pattern is found, it replaces `asin:`*`ASIN`* with the proper URL. Add the following code to a file called *asin* (no extension necessary).

```
# Blosxom Plugin: ASIN
# Author: Nelson Minar <nelson@monkey.org>
# Version: 20030301
# http://www.nelson.monkey.org/~nelson/weblog/
# License: Public Domain

# ASIN is a Blosxom plugin that simplifies linking into Amazon's catalog.
# The link format is not a guaranteed standard, in particular the
# ref=nosim part. For the authority see
# https://associates.amazon.com/exec/panama/associates/resources/build-↵
links/individual-item-link.html

# Installation:
#   Modify the $associateID (or don't :-)
#   Drop asin into your plugins directory

package asin;

$associateID = 'insert associate ID';

sub start {
    1;
}

sub rewriteASIN {
    my ($url) = @_;
    $url =~ s%"asin:(.+)"%"\"http://www.amazon.com/exec/obidos/ASIN/↵
$1/ref=nosim/$associateID\""%ies;
    return $url;
}

# Modify the body of stories by rewriting asin: URIs to real URLs
sub story {
    my($pkg, $path, $filename, $story_ref, $title_ref, $body_ref) = @_;
```

```
        # Rewrite any <a href="asin:..."> tag in the post body
        $$body_ref =~ s/(<a\s[^>]*href="asin:[^>]+>)/rewriteASIN($1)/geis;
        1;
    }

    1;
```

Running the Hack

This hack is run from within Blosxom every time you add a post. To set it up, drop the file *asin* into your configured plug-in directory. Your new shortcut method should be ready to go!

See Also

- The buy_from_amazon Blosxom plug-in (*http://www.raelity.org/apps/blosxom/plugins/link/amazon/asin.individual*)

#71 Add an Amazon Box to Your Site

Add a quick list of products to your site based on a category or keyword.

If you run a weblog, you probably have a nice, long sidebar filled with links to your favorite sites. You could turn some of this web real estate into a money-maker with associate links. But who has time to find the top products in a given category, copy the URLs to the product detail pages, and place them all in order on your site? That's what an Amazon Box is for.

What's an Amazon Box? It's a simple HTML table that contains a list of products and that links to Amazon with your associate tag. You can use a Perl script by Rael Dornfest called Amazox to generate the box, making your life easier.

Amazox is run on-the-fly from the command line with the variables needed, so it's easy to quickly create several boxes with different configurations if you have more than one page you'd like to add a box to.

The Code

This Perl script queries Amazon based on command-line arguments you supply. It requires two standard Perl modules: XML::Simple (*http://search.cpan.org/author/GRANTM/*) and LWP::UserAgent (*http://search.cpan.org/author/GAAS/*). Many Perl installations have these modules already installed, or you can find them on CPAN, the Comprehensive Perl Archive Network (*http://www.cpan.org/*).

Be sure to include your associate tag and developer token in the right spots. You can configure which Amazon catalog to search by changing the $product_line variable.

```
#!/usr/bin/perl -w
# amazon_box.pl
# Author: Rael Dornfest <rael@oreilly.com>
# Version: 0+1i
# Home/Docs/Licensing: http://www.oreillynet.com/~rael/lang/perl/amazox/

use strict;

use CGI qw/:standard/;
use XML::Simple;
use LWP::UserAgent;

my $associate_id = "insert associate tag";
my $dev_token = "insert developer token";
my $product_line = "books";

# Amazon Associates XML
# https://associates.amazon.com/exec/panama/associates/tg/browse/-/567812/
# Consummate list of Amazon Product Modes and Browse IDs
# https://associates.amazon.com/exec/panama/associates/tg/trv/-/283099/

# Grab command-line arguments
die qq{Usage: perl amazon_box.pl (search|browse) "(query|browse id)" <number
of items>\n}
    unless @ARGV == 3 && $ARGV[0] =~ /^search|browse$/;

my($function, $query, $num_items) = @ARGV;

# Construct a search|browse URL
my $assoc_url = "http://xml.amazon.com/onca/xml3?t=" . $associate_id .
    "&dev-t=" . $dev_token .
    "&type=lite" .
    "&f=xml" .
    "&mode=$product_line" .
    ($function eq 'search'
    ? "&KeywordSearch=$query"
    : "&BrowseNodeSearch=$query"
    );

# Query Amazon
my $ua = new LWP::UserAgent;
$ua->agent('www.oreillynet.com/~rael/lang/perl/amazonbox/0+1i');
my $http_request = new HTTP::Request('GET', $assoc_url);
my $http_response = $ua->request($http_request);
my $content = $http_response->{'_content'};
#print $content;

# Process the resulting XML
my $content_tree;
```

```
eval { $content_tree = XMLin($content) };
die "Couldn't understand Amazon's response\n"
    unless (!$@ and ref $content_tree and $content_tree->{Details});

# Output an Amazon box
my $ii = 1;
print
    table({-border=>0, -cellpadding=>0, -cellspacing=>0},
    map {
      Tr({-valign=>"top"}, [
      td([ $ii++.'. ', a({href=>$_->{url}}, $_->{ProductName}) ])
      ] ) . "\n"
    } @{$content_tree->{'Details'}}[0..$num_items-1]);
```

Running the Hack

You can run Amazox from the command line, supplying the necessary arguments, like this:

```
amazox.pl (search|browse) insert keyword/browse ID insert no. items
```

You can choose search or browse, depending on the type of query you'd like the results to be pulled from. If using search, you must supply a keyword; if using browse, you must supply a functioning browse ID **[Hack #8]**. Finally, add the number of items you'd like to display. Five items works well in a confined space; if you have a long sidebar, you can bump it up to fill even more space. Putting it all together, an Amazon Box with the top five keyword search results for *hacks* would be called like this:

```
perl amazox.pl search hacks 5
```

The result would be the properly formatted HTML to display a box like you see in Figure 5-15.

The generated Amazon Box table doesn't set <table> attributes like height or width, so it's easy to integrate with an existing design. Otherwise, you can tweak those settings once you have the HTML.

#72 Deep Linking to Amazon's Mobile Device Pages

If you're developing an application for a mobile device, you can easily integrate with Amazon and collect referral fees in the process.

As the Internet expands beyond the world of desktop computers and browsers, Amazon is expanding as well by offering their services in a variety of alternate formats for alternate devices. They appropriately call these alternate formats Amazon Anywhere **[Hack #7]**. Of course these formats are also connected to the associates program, so you can collect referral fees by driving traffic to them.

Figure 5-15. An Amazox Amazon box

Linking to Amazon Anywhere entry pages is straightforward, but linking directly to products or search results isn't as obvious. If you're developing a WAP application and want to link to an Amazon product for sale, or if you just want to browse directly to a product detail page like you can through Amazon's web site, it's a little tricky.

As with all Amazon URLs, once you know the pattern you can change the variables to get what you need. The base URL for Amazon Anywhere links contains four unchanging variables:

`tag`
: Your Amazon associate tag **[in "Make Money by Linking to Amazon" in Chapter 5]**

`creative`
: Your developer's token **[in "What You Need" in Chapter 6]**

`camp`
: Always set to `2025`

`link-code`
: Always set to `xm2`

So the base URL for any link will always contain these variables:

```
http://www.amazon.com/exec/obidos/redirect?tag=insert associate tag↵
&creative=insert developer token&camp=2025&link_code=xm2
```

The fifth variable, `path`, holds all the information about what format and what information you'd like. Here are the formats available:

PDA
: This is a stripped-down HTML that's suitable for lower-bandwidth devices with small screens.

RIM Blackberry
: Similar to the PDA, this has a slightly different layout and uses strict XHTML.

WAP
: WML (Wireless Markup Language) pages formatted for cell phones.

HDML
: An older cousin of WML, HDML is a non-XML-compliant version. Some older devices that don't support WML can handle only HDML.

VoiceXML
: A format that allows computer-driven phone interaction.

In any of these formats, you can link directly to product detail pages with an ASIN, or search results pages with a keyword. The `path` values are shown below.

Product Detail Paths

Here are the potential `path` values for the various URL formats, which should be added to the base URL:

- PDA: `dt/upda-1.0-anywhere/tg/aa/upda/item/-/`*`insert ASIN`*
- RIM: `dt/upda-1.0-i/tg/aa/upda/item/-/`*`insert ASIN`*
- WAP: `ct/text/vnd.wap.wml/-/tg/aa/xml/glance-xml/-/`*`insert ASIN`*
- HDML: `ct/text/x-hdml/-/tg/aa/hdml/item/-/`*`insert ASIN`*
- VoiceXML: `dt/vxml/tg/aa/xml/glance-xml/-/`*`insert ASIN`*

Search Results Paths

And here are the potential `path` values for search results:

- WAP: `ct/text/vnd.wap.wml/-/tg/aa/xml/search/-/books/`*`keyword`*`/1/`
- HDML: `ct/text/x-hdml/-/tg/aa/hdml/search/-/books/`*`keyword`*
- VoiceXML: `dt/vxml/tg/aa/xml/search/-/books/`*`keyword`*`/1/`

Search results pages are slightly different for PDA and RIM Blackberry devices. See the following examples to learn how they're done.

Assembling the URLs

Putting the URLs together is now just a matter of assembling the pieces based on the desired format and information. Take the base URL and add either the product detail or search results section for the needed format. For example, here's a WAP product detail page URL:

```
http://www.amazon.com/exec/obidos/redirect?tag=insert affiliate tag↵
&creative=insert developer token&camp=2025&link_code=xm2↵
&path= ct/text/vnd.wap.wml/-/tg/aa/xml/glance-xml/-/0596004478
```

And here's a VoiceXML search result URL:

```
http://www.amazon.com/exec/obidos/redirect?tag=insert affiliate tag↵
&creative=insert developer token&camp=2025&link_code=xm2↵
&path= dt/vxml/tg/aa/xml/search/-/books/hacks/1/
```

Keyword search result URLs for PDA and RIM Blackberry devices have a different format, but the concepts are the same. Just replace the *keyword*, *developer token*, and *affiliate tag* with the proper information.

- PDA:

```
http://www.amazon.com/exec/obidos/dt/upda=1.0-pocketpc/search-handle-url↵
?tag=insert affiliate tag&creative=insert developer token↵
&camp=2025&index=books&page=1&size=6&ss=1&file=aa/upda/upda-other↵
&field-keywords=insert keyword&method=GET
```

- RIM:

```
http://www.amazon.com/exec/obidos/dt/upda=1.0-i/search-handle-url↵
?tag=insert affiliate tag&creative=insert developertoken&camp=2025↵
&index=books&page=1&size=6&ss=1&file=aa/upda/upda-other↵
&field-keywords=insert keyword&method=GET
```

If you'll be placing these URLs inside a WML or XSL file, replace the ampersands with %26 so the document will be valid XML.

These definitely aren't the kind of URLs you want to key into your phone. But if you're building a site for a mobile device, you can link directly to Amazon and earn referral fees in the process.

Measure Your Associate Sales

Find out when, where, and how your visitors are arriving at Amazon from your site.

A great way to improve the effectiveness of your associate efforts is to measure exactly what's happening with your account. Amazon provides the reporting tools, but it's up to you to come up with a system of measuring your results and using that data to fine-tune your site.

To get started with the reporting tool, log into your associate account (*http://associates.amazon.com*) and choose "View Reports" from the navigation bar at the top of the page. This reports page is divided into three sections—your earnings, your traffic, and your link performance. Each adds a piece of important data to help you understand your associate account activity.

Earnings

Let's get to the money. Earnings reports relate how much money you've made. On the View Reports page of the Associates Central extranet, you'll see a quick overview of your earnings for the current quarter. To get the details, though, you'll have to click "see reports" next to Your Earnings to get to the earnings report tool (*https://associates.amazon.com/exec/panama/associates/resources/reporting/earnings.html*). From here there are two types of reports you can view:

Total Earnings
: Much like the overview you've already seen, this report provides total items sold, total revenue for Amazon, and your total referral fees. You can choose different time periods from this page, zeroing in on data going back four years or more—if you've been linking to Amazon that long.

Earnings by Item
: This is where the reports get interesting. You can let your inner voyeur run wild as you see not only the items you've directed people to buy, but anything else they purchased while browsing Amazon within your 24-hour associate window. Of course you won't know who purchased what, but you may be surprised at some of the things people buy after visiting your site. This report also summarizes your sales by item, showing the quantity of each item sold, the referral fee, and referral percentage.

The earnings report can be particularly useful for fine-tuning sales at your site. If particular items are selling extremely well without much marketing, you can push your efforts harder and see if you can improve your sales even more. If something you're pushing hard isn't selling, it may be time to revisit how you're presenting it.

Traffic

Back on the View Reports page, you'll find a quick overview of the traffic you've sent to Amazon by clicks, unique visitors, and items ordered.

Your ordered and shipped items will frequently be different because Amazon can't always ship items when the order is placed, and sometimes customers cancel entire orders or individual items. You earn referral fees only when an item ships. If the item is returned, your referral fee for that item is subtracted from your earnings.

To zoom in on the details of your traffic, click "See report" next to "Traffic Summary." From there you have four different views of your traffic data:

Daily Traffic
: This report shows the number of unique visitors, clicks, and items ordered by day.

Traffic by Items Ordered
: These are the items your visitors ordered once they arrived at Amazon. Like the Earnings by Item report, you'll find items here you didn't specifically link to but that were purchased after visiting a link from your site.

Traffic by Items Clicked
: You'll get far more clicked items than ordered items, and this report is a good gauge of what people are interested in while visiting your site. You can compare this with items that people actually order, and adjust which items you highlight accordingly.

Linking Method
: This report summarizes the methods used to reach Amazon and is a good gauge of how people are using Amazon links on your site. For example, if search boxes are working better than individual product links, you could adjust your linking methods.

Link Performance

At the bottom of the View Reports page you'll find a table that includes your Link Performance statistics. As you've seen in this chapter, there are many different ways to link to Amazon using your associate tag. In addition to how many visitors reach Amazon through your site, you can track *how* the visitors get there. For the purposes of this report, a search box link is different from a direct product link is different from a home page link. It's designed to help you fine-tune your linking methods to those your site's visitors prefer.

You can also get a piece of data here that you won't find in any of the other reports: your conversion rate for the different linking methods. That is, for the number of visitors arriving via a certain linking method, how many eventually bought something? A high conversion rate could mean you have an effective linking method on your hands, or it could mean you've started a new linking method and few visitors come through it. Either way, it's good information to know.

These reports provide a good view of your associates data, but it's only the first step toward seeing the whole picture. Amazon link performance data could be combined with your own server's traffic logs, to show how many of your visitors actually use your associate links. Having a handle on your site's traffic patterns, and how they relate to your associates traffic and earnings, can help you predict what portion of your visitors will likely click on new links you add to your site.

#74 Publish Your Associate Sales Statistics on Your Site

Share some insider knowledge with your site's audience.

Your web site has a unique audience, and looking at what they purchase through your associate links can tell you more about them. It can provide insights into other items you might want to sell, and can illustrate what's foremost on their minds (for better or worse). Just as Amazon shares its aggregated sales information in the form of purchase circles, you can create your own purchase circle list by publishing your associate sale information.

Your readers are probably just as curious about sales trends through your site as you are. Publishing the list can build a sense of community, and also drive more sales through associate links.

You could save the HTML reports available through your associates account (*http://associates.amazon.com*), but it'd be much easier to automate the process and integrate it into your site design with a few lines of Perl.

The Code

To run this code, you'll need to set the email address and password you use to log into your associates account. This script will then log into the account and download the appropriate sales report. Once the script has the report, it will reformat it as HTML.

```
#!/usr/bin/perl -w
# get_earnings_report.pl
#
# Logs into Amazon, downloads earning report,
# and writes an HTML version for your site.
# Usage: perl get_earnings_report.pl
use warnings;
use strict;
use URI::Escape;
use HTTP::Cookies;
use LWP::UserAgent;

# Set your associates account info.
my $email = 'insert Associates email address';
my $pass = 'insert Associates password';
my $aftag = 'insert affiliate tag';

# Create a user agent object.
# and fake the agent string.
my $ua = LWP::UserAgent->new;
$ua->agent("(compatible; MSIE 4.01; MSN 2.5; AOL 4.0; Windows 98)");
$ua->cookie_jar({}); # in-memory cookie jar.

# Request earning reports, logging in as one pass.
my $rpturl  = "http://associates.amazon.com/exec/panama/login/".
              "attempt/customer/associates/no-customer-id/25/".
              "associates/resources/reporting/earnings/";
my $rptreq  = HTTP::Request->new(POST => $rpturl);
my $rptdata = "report-type=shipments-by-item".   # get individual items
              "&date-selection=qtd".              # all earnings this quarter
              "&login_id=".uri_escape($email).   # our email address.
              "&login_password=".uri_escape($pass). # and password.
              "&submit.download=Download my report". # get downloadble.
              "&enable-login-post=true"; # login and post at once.
$rptreq->content_type('application/x-www-form-urlencoded');
$rptreq->content($rptdata); my $report = $ua->request($rptreq);

# Uncomment the following line to see
# the report if you need to debug
# print $report->content;

# Set the report to array.
my @lines = split(/\n/, $report->content);

# Get the time period.
my @fromdate = split(//, $lines[1]);
my @todate = split(//, $lines[2]);
my $from = $fromdate[1];
my $to = $todate[1];

# Print header...
```

```
print "<html><body>";
print "<h2>Items Purchased Through This Site</h2>";
print "from $from to $to <br><br>\n";
print "<ul>";

# Loop through the
# rest of the report
splice(@lines,0,5);
foreach my $line (@lines) {
    my @fields  = split(//, $line);
    my $title   = $fields[1];
    my $asin    = $fields[2];
    my $edition = $fields[4];
    my $items   = $fields[8];

    # Format items as HTML for display
    print "<li><a href='http://www.amazon.com/o/ASIN/$asin/ref=nosim/".
          "$aftag'>$title</a> ($items) $edition <br>\n";
}
print "</ul></body></html>";
```

You'll notice that `$rpturl` holds a standard `http://` URL that's used to log into Amazon. It's not encrypted, so be sure you're comfortable with sending your associates password over a standard connection before running this script. If you'd like the connection to be encrypted, you'll need a Perl package called Net::SSL (*http://search.cpan.org/author/CHAMAS/Crypt-SSLeay-0.51/*). This package won't be referenced specifically in the script, but it provides SSL support to the LWP package making the request. Not all ISPs have Net::SSL installed, so check with them to see if it's available. Once you've confirmed that Net::SSL is present, change the URL in `$rpturl` to begin with `https://`. This will keep your entire request and response encrypted.

Running the Hack

Run the script from the command line:

```
perl get_earnings_report.pl
```

It prints out the formatted HTML results, so you may want to pipe its output to another file like this:

```
perl get_earnings_report.pl > amazon_report.html
```

You could also set this to run on a schedule so your page showing community buying habits stays up to date.

#75 Associates Program Best Practices

Five tips that could improve your referral fees.

As you use the associates program, you'll learn ways to maximize your referral fees for your own site. If you're new to the program, here are a few tips to get you started.

Use only URL formats prescribed by Amazon. Though all of the URL patterns **[Hack #59]** mentioned in this chapter are known to work with the associates program at printing time, Amazon is free to change the syntax of associate links at any time. Be sure to visit Associates Central (*http://associates.amazon.com/*) regularly to keep up with any changes. Using the wrong format could mean missing out on referral fees.

Link directly to individual products whenever possible. Linking directly to a product may increase the chance that someone will add that item to their cart. It's also the only way you can earn the coveted 15% fee for qualified books (see **[Hack #59]**). Even if you only use banner ads to link to Amazon, you can take advantage of their product recommendation banners **[Hack #62]** to link to specific products.

Make it easy for people to buy. To get referral fees you need your visitors to add items to their Amazon cart. Add to cart buttons **[Hack #60]** place items directly in people's carts. You can also add Quick-Click Buying buttons **[Hack #61]** to allow people who have 1-Click buying enabled to purchase from your site.

Tell your visitors you're an Amazon associate. It's important to let people know that you get referral fees if they buy products through links on your site. If they know they can help you out while buying something they want anyway, they'll probably feel good about purchasing through your site—and may return the next time they want to buy something.

Measure your results, adjust, measure again. Check out your associates report frequently by logging into Associates Central and clicking "View Reports." You'll see a quick snapshot of your account status, but be sure to also check out the more detailed reports **[Hack #73]**. If you try a new linking method, measure how effective it is for a certain time period, adjust its placement, and measure again. Collecting this sort of data is the only way you'll know what works for your site.

CHAPTER SIX

Amazon Web Services

Hacks 76–100

You've already seen some ways you can integrate Amazon's features with your own web site through their Associates Program. If you want a seamless experience for your customers, or if you'd like to create your own applications using Amazon's database, a new door has been opened for you: Amazon Web Services (AWS).

What Are Web Services?

Web Services are essentially nothing new. They've existed in various forms ever since research groups and businesses started networking online to exchange data. These machine-readable requests were built on an ad hoc basis with whatever tools were standard in the companies at the time, and then replaced or obfuscated with layer upon layer, hack upon hack. This was a rather costly and not particularly pretty state of affairs; furthermore, each Web Service was unique and not easily adaptable or interoperable with additional parties and other services.

Perhaps the first truly "Web" service was a combination of spidering and scraping. The Web introduced a presentation markup language called HTML, which allowed you to represent data in a form that was readable by a web browser and that was, for the most part, pleasing to the person browsing. By *scraping* (reading between the bits of HTML markup), you could get to the underlying data; by doing so programmatically (*spidering*), you could automate this process.

So with the increasing number of database-backed web sites appearing on the Web in the mid-90s, people had an enormous data set at their disposal. With just a little programmatic elbow grease, you could search the Web, track stocks, read the news, etc. But scraping is a brittle process—it relies upon the layout of a site remaining fairly static, and the programmer maintaining the scraper needs to make alterations as a site bolds this, italicizes that, and so forth. And it becomes even more complicated with the advent of more complex HTML, cookies, and interactivity in web pages.

Web Services as we think of them today are an agreed-upon standard for describing data with XML that allows programs on separate servers to communicate and share information through the Web. Even though different companies have been involved in the development of Web Services, no one company owns or controls the standard. As with the Web itself, this openness allows anyone to build applications or tools that use the standard in their preferred programming language for any computing platform. Web Services are a way of opening an Application Programming Interface (API), and I'll use these two terms interchangeably.

At the most basic level, Web Services are simply XML sent over a transport medium, usually HTTP. XML is a textual representation of data capable of describing rich data sets, and HTTP (the standard language spoken by web servers for brokering requests for web pages and associated media) is the method of transporting it over the Internet. In a typical Web Services application, one computer makes a *request* for data, and another computer sends a *response*. A few different XML formats and methods of sending requests and responses exist within the Web Services arena. Simple Open Access Protocol, or SOAP, provides a standard framework for sending XML requests and responses. Each request describes exactly what it's requesting, and the response is similarly structured. REST (also called XML/HTTP), on the other hand, is a way of requesting an XML document with a URL, just as you request web pages. The debate among developers about which method is best has an almost religious fervor.

The emergence of these Web Services standards has enabled large, consumer-focused businesses to begin offering Web Services to the public. Google is generally considered the first broad-scale Web Service opened to developers for experimentation. Although the Google Web API (*http://apis.google.com*) sports a massive data set—their entire web search index—it isn't quite as rich as the one provided by the Amazon Web Services program. The latter provides not just a simple search interface to Amazon products, but a rich programmatic interface to the vast majority of the functionality explored in this book.

New developer tools, the likes of Amazon and Google opening their data sets to programmatic interaction, and a wide base of developers who understand the technology have allowed Web Services to leave the dry world of business-to-business communications and enter a new arena of experimentation, both technical and business-based.

Why Expose an API?

Amazon made a radical break from conventional business thinking when they released their Web Services API in July of 2002. Instead of tightly controlling their product database—one of their biggest assets—they decided to open a direct gateway allowing developers to tinker and experiment. Not only does this direct access make all of their product information available for other applications, it's completely free for anyone to use—in fact, with the Amazon Associates program, they'll pay you to use it. It sounds counterintuitive on the surface; after all, with this sort of access, someone could just duplicate most of Amazon.com's functionality with a different look and feel. They could even host it on their own web site! Call it "syndicated e-commerce." To fully understand the API, it's important to understand why Amazon released it in the first place.

As Amazon grew, they became one of the largest places to shop on the Web. They also became one of the largest sources of information about products on the Web. Their product information, customer reviews, sales rank information, and many other supporting bits of data became valuable in its own right. Developers started screen-scraping this information to build their own applications. Most large sites like Amazon frown on screen scraping because it uses valuable server resources in ways they didn't intend. But instead of fighting these developers and the potential audience they bring along with them, Amazon helped them out by speaking their language.

Attracting and encouraging developers helps Amazon in several ways. It lets people outside the company build prototypes and alternative interfaces that Amazon may someday want to use. In effect, Amazon has outsourced interface research and development to people who are willing to work for free, posing little risk to the company. Also, as these developers come to rely on Amazon Web Services for their applications, it locks them into the Amazon platform. Because people will be using these applications, it furthers Amazon's brand and goodwill, as each application essentially becomes an advertisement for Amazon. Finally, Amazon is able to monitor how people use their data. If outside developers are concentrating on a particular section of the database, Amazon knows there's a demand and can fine-tune their business accordingly.

What You Need

To use any of the Web Services hacks in this book, you'll need a developer's token. The token itself is just a random string of alphanumeric characters that is tied to your Amazon associates account. This token system allows Amazon to track who is using their API and to confirm that anyone using it has agreed to the terms of service. It also enables Amazon to contact developers who are violating the terms of service—whether knowingly or unwittingly. You'll need an existing associates account [in "Make Money by Linking to Amazon" in Chapter 5] to get a token. At the Associates Central web site, you'll find a link to the Web Services Program (*http://amazon.com/webservices*). From there, click on "Apply for developer's token." You'll need to provide an email and password and agree to the terms of service. It's a good idea to look over the terms carefully before you agree. Here are a few points from the terms to keep in mind while you're developing applications:

- Don't query the API more than once per second.
- Don't substantially alter the data you receive from Amazon.
- Include a link to Amazon somewhere on your site or in your application.
- Update any information from Amazon at least once a day (once per hour for prices).
- Point to Amazon for any sales.

Once you've agreed, you'll be granted your token. Jot it down and keep it somewhere accessible.

If you're going to customize the hacks or develop your own applications, you'll want to download the Amazon.com Web Services software development kit. It provides sample applications and complete documentation. Here's what you'll find in the kit:

- A Web Services user guide as a Word document, PDF, and HTML
- Sample applications in Java, Visual Basic, and PHP
- SOAP request/response examples
- REST examples
- XSLT samples

Amazon's Web Services site also has a web forum where you can ask questions of your fellow developers.

What You Can Do

So just what can you access through the API? Just about any action or information you can access through the Amazon web site as HTML is also available in the API as XML. In fact, studying the components of the API will provide further insight into the sorts of things Amazon offers on their site. For example:

Product Description Information
: This includes all of the data that goes along with any product: its type (book, DVD, lawn mower, etc.), sales rank, manufacturer, and any special information like track listings for CDs or special features for DVDs.

Product Sales Information
: This is data that Amazon offers related to selling the product. This includes their sales price, its current sales rank at Amazon, images of the product, whether or not the product is in stock, the manufacturer's price, and anything else related to sales information.

Searching
: Just as you can perform advanced searches for items on Amazon's site, you can do the same through their API. Product searches can be performed by keyword, subject area, author, director, actor, etc. You can also search Amazon features like Wish Lists, Listmania! lists, and Marketplace items and sellers.

Reviews
: User-submitted reviews and ratings for any given product.

Related Items
: A list of similar products for any given product.

This information mirrors exactly what is on the Amazon web site, but it's available in a machine-readable format so that it's easy to use in different ways.

Making Requests

There's a continental divide in the Web Services world: the REST versus SOAP debate. A REST service has a low barrier to entry, and it makes possible the quick, grassroots adoption of a service. SOAP, on the other hand, is much more complex and requires more time and care to develop. It's favored by more traditional programmers and corporations because it has a formal structure.

Amazon was well aware of the REST versus SOAP debate when they designed their system. The choice between the two is not an easy one, as both offer certain advantages. Amazon wanted to attract everyone from the tinkering programmers to the corporate developers, so they implemented both SOAP and REST.

The following sections provide a quick look at each API interface.

The RESTful Way: XML/HTTP

Amazon refers to its REST implementation as the *XML/HTTP* method. XML data using this method is simply a matter of hacking variables in a URL. The base URL always starts like this:

```
http://xml.amazon.com/onca/xml3?t=your associates ID
```

The URL points at a server specifically for serving up XML (`xml.amazon.com`), lets Amazon know which Web Services version you're requesting (`xml3`), and passes along your Amazon Associates ID **[in "Make Money by Linking to Amazon" in Chapter 5]** as a variable (`t=yourassociatesID`). There are also several other variables that can be (or must be) appended to this request as described in the following sections.

Required Variables

Each request requires these four variables:

`t`
: As mentioned above, this is always set to your associates ID. It lets Amazon track purchases made through your applications and enables you to earn affiliate fees.

`dev-t`
: This is set to your developer's token.

`type`
: The only possible values for `type` are `lite` and `heavy`. It describes which XML format to return.

`f`
: This is the format the data should be returned in, usually `xml`. It can also be set to the URL of an XSL stylesheet to return formatted HTML.

Search Variables

Beyond the four required variables, you can also choose variables from the list below to get the exact data you're looking for.

Product Searches

`KeywordSearch`
: Searches for products by subject.

`BrowseNodeSearch`
: Browses product area by code.

`AsinSearch (+ offer, + offerpage)`
: Returns a specific product detail.

`UpcSearch`
: Searches for UPC numbers. Music only. `mode` must be set to `music`.

`AuthorSearch`
: Searches for authors and returns book product details.

`ArtistSearch`
: Searches for musicians and returns CD product details.

`ActorSearch`
: Searches for actors and returns DVD product details.

`DirectorSearch`
: Searches for directors and returns DVD product details.

`ManufacturerSearch`
: Searches for manufacturers.

Amazon Features Searches

`ListManiaSearch`
: Finds lists by List IDs.

`WishlistSearch`
: Finds wish lists by Wish List IDs.

`SimilaritySearch`
: Finds similar products given an ASIN.

`ExchangeSearch`
: Finds a given exchange.

`SellerSearch (+ offerstatus)`
: Finds products given a Seller ID.

`SellerProfile`
: Finds a seller's profile given a Seller ID.

Special Searches

`PowerSearch`
: Searches using Amazon's Power Search syntax.

`BlendedSearch`
: Searches product listings across all categories.

Support Variables

`mode`
: Defines a specific area for different types of requests.

`locale`
: Tells Amazon which international store to query. United Kingdom (`uk`), Japan (`jp`), and Germany (`de`) are the locales available at this time. You can also explicitly specify the default United States (`us`).

`ct`
: Specifies an alternate content-type HTTP header.

Putting the URLs Together

Assembling a query URL is just a matter of filling in the proper values after the variables. If you're searching for all books associated with penguins, the following URL would do the trick:

```
http://xml.amazon.com/onca/xml3?t=insert associate tags↵
&dev-t=insert developer token&type=lite&f=xml&mode=books↵
&KeywordSearch=Penguin
```

If, on the other hand, you're wondering about DVDs featuring Clint Eastwood, something like this would work:

```
http://xml.amazon.com/onca/xml3?t=insert associate tag↵
&dev-t=insert developer token&type=lite&f=xml&mode=dvd↵
&ActorSearch=Clint%20Eastwood
```

To represent spaces in a URL, as in our query here for "Clint Eastwood", the spaces need to be *encoded*. The URL encoding for a space is %20. Many scripting environments offer built-in functions for URL encoding **[Hack #92]**. Other special characters like periods, exclamation points, or dollar signs also need to be encoded.

SOAP Web Services

Working with SOAP is quite a bit different from working with XML/HTTP because it involves sending and receiving structured messages. Instead of creating requests yourself as a URL, requests are made via XML messages. Here's a typical SOAP request to retrieve a book's details with its ASIN:

```
<?xml version="1.0" encoding="UTF-8" ?>
<SOAP-ENV:Envelope
xmlns:SOAP-ENV="http://schemas.xmlsoap.org/soap/envelope/" ↵
xmlns:SOAP-ENC="http://schemas.xmlsoap.org/soap/encoding/"
xmlns:xsi="http://www.w3.org/2001/XMLSchema-instance"
xmlns:xsd="http://www.w3.org/2001/XMLSchema"
SOAP-ENV:encodingStyle="http://schemas.xmlsoap.org/soap/encoding/">
<SOAP-ENV:Body>
  <namesp1:AsinSearchRequest xmlns:namesp1="urn:PI/DevCentral/SoapService">
    <AsinSearchRequest xsi:type="m:AsinRequest">
      <asin>0596004478</asin>
      <page>1</page>
      <mode>books</mode>
      <tag>insert associate tag</tag>
      <type>lite</type>
      <dev-tag>insert developer token</dev-tag>
      <format>xml</format>
      <version>1.0</version>
    </AsinSearchRequest>
  </namesp1:AsinSearchRequest>
</SOAP-ENV:Body>
</SOAP-ENV:Envelope>
```

You'll notice that although SOAP uses the same bits of information you use when requesting data via the URL-based XML/HTTP method, it wraps the request in substantial structure. Generating these XML requests "by hand" each time you need one would be time consuming; instead, there are packages (typically called SOAP toolkits) in every programming language that do the heavy lifting for you. These toolkits provide a simple interface for setting and calling Web Services functions. Modules like Perl's SOAP::Lite (see [Hack #80] and [Hack #89]) automatically format all of the SOAP requests for you.

Here's an example of a SOAP `KeywordSearchRequest` from VB.NET, where the query is built by setting each variable name:

```
Dim AsinReq as new AsinRequest( )
AsinReq.asin = "0596004478"
AsinReq.tag = "insert associate tag"
AsinReq.type = "lite"
AsinReq.devtag = "insert developer token"
```

This little bit of code creates an entire SOAP request behind the scenes. In this way, you're working only with the variable information you need to provide rather than the entire SOAP protocol.

Working With Responses

Whether you're requesting information via URLs or SOAP requests, the data you can access is the same, and it's sent in a very similar XML format.

XML Parsers and XPath

To work with XML responses, you need a piece of software, typically an add-on module, called an *XML parser*. Almost every programming environment has one; you just need to find out which one is available to you and the syntax for using it. The parser's function is straightforward: to load an XML document and make its contents available to your program either as a data structure or a series of functions.

Once an XML document is loaded, you can get at the specific data it contains with a simple query language called XPath. While parser syntaxes vary across languages and platforms, XPath is rapidly gaining ground as a standard way to access the data. Here's a quick example of how XPath queries work. If you request product information, you need different pieces of that information at different times. You can get to the specific information you need by specifying a path through the document. Here's an abbreviated AWS response:

```
<?xml version="1.0" encoding="UTF-8" ?>
<ProductInfo>
  <Details url="http://amazon.com/o/0140042598">
```

```
        <Asin>0140042598</Asin>
        <ProductName>On the Road</ProductName>
        <Catalog>Book</Catalog>
        <Authors>
          <Author>Jack Kerouac</Author>
        </Authors>
      </Details>
    </ProductInfo>
```

As you can see, ProductInfo is the top-level tag, and all other tags are within that path. If you just wanted to get the product name, you could specify the path ProductInfo/Details/ProductName. The slashes represent levels of nesting, and the names are tag names. *Attributes* are values located within a tag and are accessed with the @ symbol. So, to get at URL information, you could use the path ProductInfo/Details/@url. You'll see XPath queries like these in many of the hacks in this chapter, and, assuming the availability of an XPath module, they work similarly across development environments.

Lite Response and Heavy Response

Now let's take a look at the data that's available through Amazon Web Services. As mentioned, you can request either heavy or lite responses depending on the value you set for the type variable. Here's a list of information available in the lite response, along with the XML path to access it:

Detail	Path
ASIN	Details/Asin
Product Name	Details/ProductName
Catalog	Details/Catalog
Author(s)	Details/Authors/Author
Release Date	Details/ReleaseDate
Manufacturer	Details/Manufacturer
Prices	Details/ListPrice, Details/OurPrice, Details/UsedPrice
Image URLs (small, medium, large)	Details/ImageUrlSmall, Details/ImageUrlMedium, Details/ImageUrlLarge
Request Arguments (the values you passed to AWS to make the request)	Request/Args/Arg

A heavy response includes all the information in the lite response, plus:

Detail	Path
Sales Rank	Details/SalesRank
Lists (Listmania! lists that contain the product)	Details/Lists/ListId

Detail	Path
Browse Node Names (categories)	Details/BrowseList/BrowseNode/BrowseName
Media	Details/Media
ISBN	Details/Isbn
Availability	Details/Availability
Reviews	Details/Reviews
Average Customer Rating	Details/Reviews/AvgCustomerRating
Total Customer Reviews	Details/Reviews/TotalCustomerReviews
Full Customer Reviews (includes rating, summary, and text of the review)	Details/Reviews/CustomerReview/Rating, Details/Reviews/CustomerReview/Summary, Details/Reviews/CustomerReview/Comment
Similar Items (the ASINs of up to 5 similar items)	Details/SimilarProducts/Product

Now let's put this response data to work with some hacks!

#76 View XML Responses in a Browser

Here's a quick way of testing XML/HTTP responses to make sure you're getting the data you need.

One great thing about the XML/HTTP method of retrieving data from Amazon is that it's easy to read the responses and know what you're getting. Instead of relying on tools to parse the response, you can usually see exactly what data you're working with by looking it at yourself.

This is where a browser that can display XML comes in handy. Because the requests are made with a URL over HTTP, requesting XML data is just like requesting a web page. If you're ever puzzled by the results you're getting from an XML/HTTP script, this is a great way to debug. Just copy the URL from your code (this may require writing the URL out to the page if you're dynamically generating the URL) and paste it into your browser's address field.

Some browsers are better than others at displaying XML in a human-readable form. Internet Explorer builds a nice tree outline and allows you to hide or show particular branches. Other browsers display the XML in plain text exactly as it appears in the response. Still others show a blank page, leaving you to "view the source" to see the XML.

Let's take a simple product detail query:

```
http://xml.amazon.com/onca/xml3?t=insert associate tag ↵
&dev-t=insert developer token&type=lite&f=xml&AsinSearch=0596005423
```

Paste this into the Address field of Internet Explorer, and you should see something like Figure 6-1.

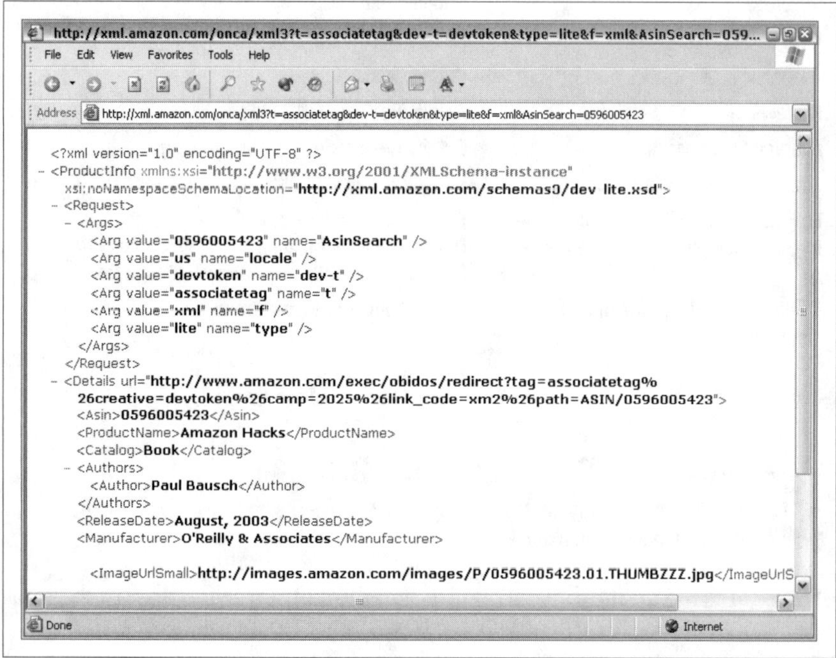

Figure 6-1. Amazon "lite" XML response in a browser

Viewing the XML in the browser gives you a quick, visual way to see the data you're working with. It also lets you see if you don't have any data at all. The following query with a bogus ASIN gives an appropriate error, shown in Figure 6-2:

```
http://xml.amazon.com/onca/xml3?t=insert associate tag ↵
&dev-t=insert developer token&type=lite&f=xml&AsinSearch=0123456789
```

#77 Embed Product Details into a Web Page with PHP

A simple way to display product data with existing PHP functions.

One great aspect of an open API is that other developers have probably already put together some tools to make your life easier. After all, why reinvent the wheel if someone else has already created what you need? These helper scripts are called *wrappers* because they wrap up some frequently used code into a few functions that you can call from another script. Daniel Filzhut, the author of the `amazon_functions` PHP wrapper, asks that people

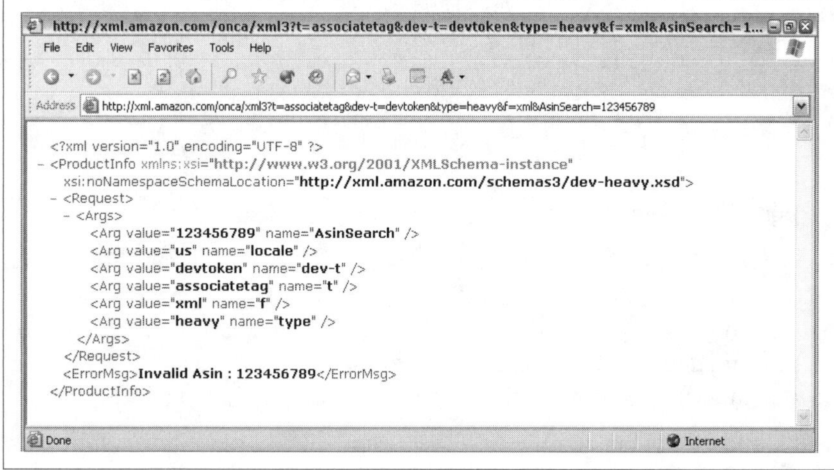

Figure 6-2. Amazon error XML response in a browser

register if they earn quarterly associates fees greater than $50; but otherwise, it's free to try out or use for commercial purposes.

What You Need

To get started with this hack, you'll need to download the code from *http://associatesshop.filzhut.de* (choose "download" from the left-hand menu).

Unzip the package and open *amazon_functions.php* in the *functions* directory. Change the first line under `Setup` at the top of the file to include your developer's token:

```
define ("DEVTOKEN", "insert  developer token ");
```

The Code

The file with the helper functions is now ready to be included in any PHP script. This script has several functions that handle requesting information from Amazon and generating HTML based on the responses. Pick your favorite ASIN **[Hack #1]** and create a file called *detail.php* with the following code:

```
<?php

include('amazon_functions.php');

$Data=amazon_search_asin("0596004478","HEAVY");
$ProductInfoHTML=amazon_create_productinfo($Data);

echo $ProductInfoHTML;

php?>
```

Be sure to save both *amazon_functions.php* and *detail.php* to the same directory on your web server. Also, if you have a directory specified as an `include_path` in your *php.ini* configuration file, you can save *amazon_functions.php* there and it'll be available to all of your PHP scripts.

Running the Hack

Just browse to this file on your server to see it in action. The HTML written by this script includes an image of the product, a "buy from Amazon.com" button, the price, publisher, release date, and customer reviews. Not too shabby for just four lines of code! This code could be dropped into any PHP page so that the product details blend in with your site's design.

You'll find more than just the ASIN search method in the *amazon_functions.php* file. This file also has a simplified PHP interface to all of the AWS methods. Though you don't have complete control over the way product details are formatted, it's a great place to start if you'd like to integrate product data into an existing PHP-powered site.

Program AWS with PHP

Parsing XML with the built-in PHP XML parser can be tricky. But once you see how it's done, you'll be parsing Amazon XML in no time.

Using someone else's wrapper functions to handle Amazon Web Services requests is a nice shortcut to building applications. But the time inevitably comes when you want to do something that existing wrappers don't handle. You can either look under the hood and tinker with or add to someone else's work, or you can build your own scripts from scratch.

The following bit of PHP might be a good start if you're building something from the ground up. It uses PHP's built-in XML parser to handle AWS responses, so there's nothing new to install. PHP's parser is James Clark's `expat`, and you can find the documentation at *http://www.php.net/xml*.

Given an ASIN, this example requests the `lite` XML response and formats the results in an HTML table.

The Code

This code builds an `AsinSearch` Amazon request URL with the `asin` value passed in through the querystring, and retrieves the XML with the `fopen()` function.

PHP's xml_parse_into_struct function turns the AWS response into two arrays—one with tag names ($index) and the other with values ($values). Looping through the array, the script then sets the value when it finds the XML tag it's looking for. With the values set, it prints the HTML to the page with the values in place. Create a file called *ASINsearch.php* containing the following code:

```
<?php
// Set Local variables
$dev_token = "insert developer token";
$aff_tag = "insert affiliate tag";
$asin = $_GET['asin']; //grab ASIN from Querystring
$xml = "";
$key = "";
$values = "";

// Set Amazon variables
$ProductName = "";
$ImageURL = "";
$OurPrice = "";
$AmazonURL = "";

// Build Amazon XML Query URL
$URL = "http://xml.amazon.com/onca/xml3?t=" . $aff_tag .
       "&dev-t=" . $dev_token .
       "&type=lite" .
       "&f=xml" .
       "&AsinSearch=" . $asin;

// Uncomment this line to see the URL
//print $URL;

// Get Amazon XML Query Results
$aurl=fopen($URL,"r");
while (!feof ($aurl))
    $xml .= fgets($aurl, 4096);
fclose ($aurl);

// Fire up the built-in XML parser
$parser = xml_parser_create( );
xml_parser_set_option($parser, XML_OPTION_CASE_FOLDING, 0);

// Set tag names and values
xml_parse_into_struct($parser,$xml,$values,$index);

// Close down XML parser
xml_parser_free($parser);

// Loop through the XML, setting values
foreach ($index as $key=>$val) {
    switch ($key) {
      case "ProductName":
```

```
            $ProductName = $values[$val[0]]['value'];
            break;
        case "ImageUrlMedium":
            $ImageURL = $values[$val[0]]['value'];
            break;
        case "OurPrice":
            $OurPrice = $values[$val[0]]['value'];
             break;
      }
}
?>
<table width="200" border="1" cellpadding="5" bgcolor="#cccccc">
<tr><td align="center">
<a href="http://www.amazon.com/o/ASIN/<?= $asin ?>/ref=nosim/<?= $aff_tag ↵
?>">
    <img src="<?= $ImageURL ?>" border="0">
</a>
<br>
<?= $ProductName ?>
<br>
<b><?= $OurPrice ?></b>
</td></tr>
</table>
```

Running the Hack

Upload *ASINsearch.php* to your server and call it with an ASIN in the querystring:

```
http://your.server/ASINsearch.php?asin=insert ASIN
```

If all goes according to plan, you should see a nicely formatted table with the image of the product, its name, and the current Amazon price. The image should link to Amazon using your associate tag.

Program AWS with Python

Use existing Python functions to handle Amazon requests for you.

This hack is another example of using someone else's interface to AWS to speed up your development. Behind the scenes, these functions handle all the work of building the proper URL, making the request, and organizing the results. The only thing you need to do is learn how the wrapper works.

What You Need

Mark Pilgrim's pyAmazon (*http://diveintomark.org/projects/#pyamazon*) makes quick work of an Amazon query in Python. The wrapper is a single file called *amazon_wrap.py*; be sure to save it to the same directory as the script that uses it.

If you'll be using pyAmazon in several files across different directories, save it to your Python installation's *Lib* directory so that it will be available to any script.

The Code

The code in *amazon_wrap.py* sets the License argument with your developer's token, and calls the searchByKeyword function using the argument supplied on the command line.

```
#!/usr/bin/python
# amazon_wrap.py
# A typical Amazon Web API Python script using Mark Pilgrim's
# pyAmazon Amazon Web Service API wrapper
# [http://diveintomark.org/projects/#pyamazon]
# Usage: python amazon_wrap.py <keyword>

import sys

# Use the pyAmazon Functions
import amazon

# Set your dev token
amazon.setLicense(' insert developer token here ')

# Get the Keyword from input
if sys.argv [1:]:
    actor = sys.argv [1 ]
else:
    sys.exit('Usage: python amazon_wrap.py <keyword>')

# Make the Request
pythonBooks = amazon.searchByKeyword(actor)

# Print the Results
for book in pythonBooks:
    print book.ProductName
    print "by",
    authorList = book.Authors.Author
    if len(authorList) < 5:
        for author in authorList:
            print author + ", ",
    else:
        print book.Authors.Author,
    print book.OurPrice + "\n"
```

The searchByKeyword function is shorthand that the program uses to make the Amazon request. There are several other shorthand functions, including searchByASIN, searchByUPC, searchByAuthor, and searchByArtist. Check the source of *amazon.py* for a full list.

The for statement at the end of the code loops through the results. The variable names mirror Amazon's results. By changing book.OurPrice to book.ListPrice or book.Asin, you can change what the script returns.

Running the Hack

Run the script on the command line like so:

```
python amazon_wrap.py "query words"
```

Replace *query words* with your preferred query; "google hacks", for example. Be sure to enclose phrases or queries consisting of more than one keyword in quotes, as otherwise spaces will separate the words into different script arguments.

Hacking the Hack

Python lets you work with the interpreter interactively, a fabulous way to get to know packages like pyAmazon and what information they return. Here's a sample interactive session (what I typed is called out in bold) that retrieves a list of Beatles CDs, gets information about the first CD listed, and looks for similar products based on its ASIN.

```
C:\Python22>python
Python 2.2.1 (#34, Apr  9 2002, 19:34:33) [MSC 32 bit (Intel)] on win32
Type "help", "copyright", "credits" or "license" for more information.
>>> import amazon
>>> amazon.setLicense('insert developer token')
>>> pythonCDs = amazon.searchByArtist('Beatles')
>>> pythonCDs[0].ProductName
u'Abbey Road'
>>> pythonCDs[0].OurPrice
u'$13.49'
>>> pythonCDs[0].Asin
u'B000002UB3'
>>> moreCDs = amazon.searchSimilar('B000002UB3')
>>> moreCDs[0].ProductName
u"Sgt. Pepper's Lonely Hearts Club Band"
>>>
```

#80 Program AWS with Perl

A lightweight XML parser is all you need to work with Amazon's data in Perl scripts.

Even without wrapper functions, retrieving data directly from Amazon with XML/HTTP is straightforward. You just need the ability to grab a file from the Web and parse the results.

What You Need

This hack requires two common Perl modules: one to handle the HTTP request and another to parse the XML. Once the Amazon request URL is built, LWP::Simple handles sending the request and receiving the XML with a `get( )` function. You can find out more about LWP::Simple at CPAN (*http://search.cpan.org/dist/libwww-perl/lib/LWP/Simple.pm*).

XML::Simple (*http://search.cpan.org/author/GRANTM/XML-Simple-2.04/lib/XML/Simple.pm*) is a lightweight XML parser. It provides a quick, simple interface for working with XML.

Many ISPs have both of these modules installed already. If not, you can install them with CPAN:

```
perl -MCPAN -e shell
cpan> install XML::Simple
```

If you have a Win32 system, you can install them from the command line with the package manager like this:

```
ppm install XML::Simple
```

The Code

This code accepts a command-line argument and builds an Amazon URL with the argument as the keyword. Create the file *amazon_http.pl* with the following code:

```
#!/usr/bin/perl
# amazon_http.pl
# A typical Amazon Web API Perl script using the XML/HTTP interface
# Usage: amazon_http.pl <keyword>

#Your Amazon developer's token
my $dev_key='insert developer token';

#Your Amazon affiliate code
my $af_tag='insert associate tag';

#Take the keyword from the command-line
my $keyword =shift @ARGV or die "Usage:perl amazon_http.pl <keyword>\n";

#Assemble the URL
my $url = "http://xml.amazon.com/onca/xml3?t=" . $af_tag .
    "&dev-t=" . $dev_key .
    "&type=lite&f=xml&mode=books&" .
    "KeywordSearch=" . $keyword;

use strict;

#Use the XML::Parser  and LWP::Simple Perl modules
```

```
use XML::Simple;
use LWP::Simple;

my $content = get($url);
die "Could not retrieve $url" unless $content;

my $xmlsimple = XML::Simple->new( );
my $response = $xmlsimple->XMLin($content);

foreach my $result (@{$response->{Details}}){
    #Print out the main bits of each result
    print
    join "\n",
    $result->{ProductName}||"no title",
    "ASIN: " . $result->{Asin} . ", " .
    $result->{OurPrice} . "\n\n";
}
```

The foreach at the end of the code loops through the results from Amazon and prints them out. By changing the variable names, you can change the information that is displayed. For example, changing OurPrice on the last line to ListPrice would display that price instead of Amazon's price.

Running the Hack

From the command line, call the script like so:

```
perl amazon_http.pl hacks
```

Be sure to enclose phrases or multiple keywords in quotes, like so:

```
perl amazon.http.pl "google hacks"
```

#81 Loop Around the 10-Result Limit

When 10 products just aren't enough, it's time to get loopy.

Amazon returns 10 results per request, but there are times you want much more data than that. Along with each response, you'll find the TotalResults and TotalPages values. By using this information and the page variable with subsequent requests, you can make several queries and combine the results.

The Code

This code builds on the previous XML/HTTP Perl example [Hack #80] but sets the URL assembly, request, and response in a loop. The page value is incremented each time through the loop until the value in TotalPages is met. Create the file *amazon_http_loopy.pl* with this code:

```
#!/usr/bin/perl
# amazon_http_loopy.pl
```

```
# A simple XML request/parse script that loops through all pages of
# a keyword search.
# Usage: perl amazon_http_loopy.pl <keyword>

#Your Amazon developer's token
my $dev_key='insert developer token';

#Your Amazon affiliate code
my $af_tag='insert associate tag';

#Take the query from the command-line
my $keyword =shift @ARGV or die "Usage:perl amazon_http_loopy.pl ↵
<keyword>\n";

use strict;

#Use the XML::Parser Perl module
use XML::Simple;
use LWP::Simple;

my $totalPages = 1;

#The loop starts here
for (my $thisPage = 1; $thisPage <= $totalPages; $thisPage++) {

    #Assemble the URL
    my $url = "http://xml.amazon.com/onca/xml3?t=" . $af_tag .
        "&dev-t=" . $dev_key .
        "&type=lite&f=xml&mode=books&" .
        "KeywordSearch=" . $keyword .
        "&page=" . $thisPage;

    my $content = get($url);
    die "Could not retrieve $url" unless $content;

    my $xmlsimple = XML::Simple->new('forcearray' => 1);
    my $response = $xmlsimple->XMLin($content);

    $totalPages = $response->{TotalPages}[0];

    foreach my $result (@{$response->{Details}}) {
      #Print out the main bits of each result
      print
      join "\n",
        $result->{ProductName}[0]||"no title",
      "ASIN: " . $result->{Asin}[0] . ", " .
      $result->{OurPrice}[0] . "\n\n";
    }

    #Wait 1 second before making another request
    sleep 1;
}
```

The sleep function at the end of the loop keeps this code compliant with the AWS terms of service. Amazon asks that you make only one request per second.

Running the Hack

Just run the script on the command line like this:

```
perl amazon_http_loopy.pl hacks
```

For this particular query, you should get around 22 pages of results returned in a continuous loop.

Hacking the Hack

You can do more than just loop through all the pages of results. If you'd rather return an arbitrary maximum number of results, set a variable somewhere outside the loop:

```
my $maxNumber = 30;
```

Then, *inside* the loop, stop the query once that maximum number has been reached. The last command provides this in Perl:

```
last unless (($thisPage * 10) <= $maxNumber);
```

We know that there are 10 results per page, so we just multiply the value of $thisPage by 10 to see how many items have been looped through. This works only for multiples of 10, but you could set a counter inside the XML loop for a more fine-grained approach.

By adding a sort variable and a line of code to exit the loop when your criteria are met, you can get just about any results you need, from a maximum sales rank to a minimum average user rating.

#82 Program XML/HTTP with VBScript

Accessing Amazon within Windows is a job for VBScript.

VBScript is a common scripting language for the Windows platform. It's very similar to Visual Basic, and in fact this hack is modified from the example VBA application included with the Amazon developer's kit. With a few slight modifications, this code could be used in a Word macro, a Visual Basic program, or an ASP web page. In this case, it's written for Windows Scripting Host, and will run just like any other program.

What You Need

This example requires a Windows machine and the Microsoft XML Parser. If Internet Explorer 4.0 or higher is installed on your machine, the parser is already there.

The Code

Create a text file called *amazon_price.vbs* with the following code:

```
' amazon_price.vbs
' This VBScript prompts for an ASIN, and returns the price.
' Usage: double-click amazon_price.vbs, enter ASIN.

Sub AmazonQuery(ASIN_In)
  Dim SelectedText
  Dim MSXML
  Dim XMLURL
  Dim Loaded

  ' Make sure that some text is selected
  If ((Len(ASIN_In) = 0) Or (ASIN_In < " ")) Then
    WScript.Echo "Please enter an ASIN."
    Exit Sub
  End If

  ' Set Associate ID and Developer Token
  AffiliateTag = "insert associate tag"
  DeveloperToken = "insert developer token"

  ' Create an instance of the MSXML Parser
  Set MSXML = CreateObject("MSXML.DOMDocument")

  ' Set MSXML Options
  MSXML.Async = False
  MSXML.preserveWhiteSpace = False
  MSXML.validateOnParse = True
  MSXML.resolveExternals = False

  ' Form the request URL
  XMLURL = "http://xml.amazon.com/onca/xml3" + _
           "?t=" + AffiliateTag + _
           "&dev-t=" + DeveloperToken + _
           "&page=1" + _
           "&f=xml" + _
           "&mode=books" + _
           "&type=lite" + _
           "&AsinSearch=" + ASIN_In

  ' Issue the request and wait for the response
  Loaded = MSXML.Load(XMLURL)
```

```
' If the request is loaded successfully, continue
If (Loaded) Then

  ' Look for the ErrorMsg tag
  Set XMLError = MSXML.SelectNodes("//ErrorMsg")

  ' If it exists, display the message and exit
  If XMLError.length > 0 Then
     WScript.Echo MSXML.SelectSingleNode("//ErrorMsg").text
     Exit Sub
  End If

  ' If there's no error, use XPath to get the product name
  ' and the price
  WScript.Echo "The price of " + _
    MSXML.SelectSingleNode("ProductInfo/Details/ProductName").text + _
    " is " + _
    MSXML.SelectSingleNode("ProductInfo/Details/OurPrice").text
Else
  WScript.Echo "The service is not available."
End If

End Sub

strASIN = InputBox("Please enter a product ASIN.")

AmazonQuery(strASIN)
```

As you can see, this script looks for two specific pieces of information in the response: the product name and the price. The XPath queries to reach those pieces of info are:

```
ProductInfo/Details/ProductName
ProductInfo/Details/OurPrice
```

By changing these paths, you can bring up any other bits of available data.

Running the Hack

To run this code, double-click the file you created. You should be prompted for an ASIN. The script will contact Amazon and return the price.

Transform AWS Results to HTML with XSLT

Amazon's XSLT service performs transformations on their servers, which can save you coding time.

If the goal of your Web Services requests is to display the information as HTML on a web site, it might be worth investigating the AWS XSLT capabilities. The extensible stylesheets language (XSL) is a way to transform XML into web-friendly HTML. The stylesheet defines how data should be placed within a design. Instead of parsing the XML document with code on your end, Amazon allows you to specify an XSL file that they then transform on their server and send back the formatted HTML. As with any method, there are advantages and drawbacks. First, the positives:

- Saves time coding.
- Easily included with existing code.
- Shifts some processing to Amazon's server.
- No need to install additional software on your server.

Alas, the drawbacks:

- You need to know XSL.
- Harder to debug.
- Can't cache the results locally.
- You can only work with the results of one request (no multi-query looping **[Hack #81]**).

The Code

XSL stylesheets look similar to HTML. Don't be fooled by the similarities, though—XSL must be valid XML, which means it's not forgiving about unclosed or mismatched tags. It's a bit more strict, but as you'll find out, it can be much more powerful.

XSL stylesheets are organized into *templates* within the document that correspond to parts of the XML document. To try out a simple XSLT example, copy the following code into a file called *list.xsl*:

```
<?xml version="1.0" encoding="UTF-8" ?>
<xsl:stylesheet xmlns:xsl="http://www.w3.org/1999/XSL/Transform" ↵
version="1.0">
<xsl:template match="/">
<html>
<head>
<title>Search Results</title>
</head>
<body>
    <h1>Search Results</h1>
    <ul>
    <xsl:apply-templates select="ProductInfo/Details"/>
    </ul>
</body>
</html>
</xsl:template>

<xsl:template match="ProductInfo/Details">
    <li><xsl:value-of select="ProductName"/> - <b><xsl:value-of ↵
```

```
select="OurPrice"/></b></li>
</xsl:template>

</xsl:stylesheet>
```

Send the file to a public web server that anyone can access. (That means there's no IP filtering or password-protection, as you need Amazon to be able to get to the file without any problem.) Including the XSL stylesheet with your request is then very straightforward. With the XML/HTTP method, simply change the value of the `f` variable from the standard `xml` to the URL of your stylesheet:

```
http://xml.amazon.com/onca/xml3?t=insert associate tag ↵
&dev-t=insert developer token&type=lite&f=http://your.server/list.xml ↵
&mode=dvd&ActorSearch=Clint%20Eastwood
```

This request should give you HTML, as in the web page shown in Figure 6-3.

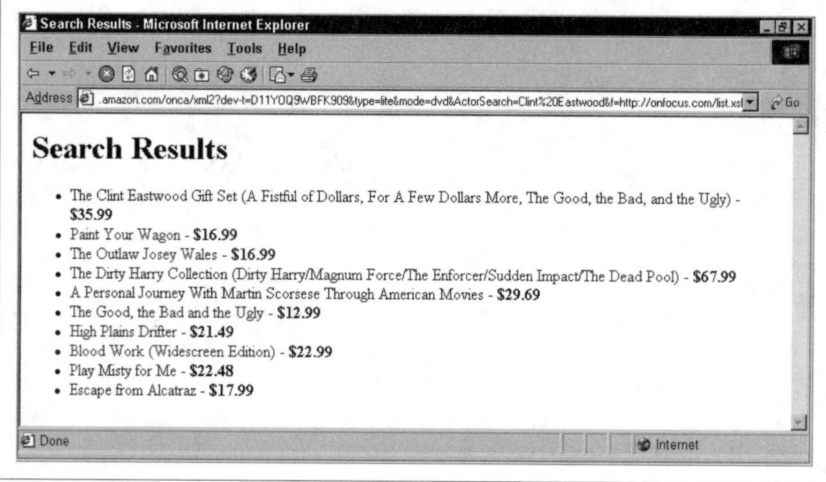

Figure 6-3. Query result with XSL URL specified

Finding problems with the stylesheet can be tricky. If something goes wrong, Amazon simply says, "We encountered an error processing your request. Please retry." It tells you something went wrong, but not exactly what. Keep in mind that XSL must also be valid XML, so running your stylesheet through an XML validator is a good place to start troubleshooting. This also means that you can bring up your stylesheet in a browser that can display XML **[Hack #76]**. If there is something wrong, you'll get a more detailed error message that should help you track down problems.

Amazon keeps a copy of your XSL file on their server for 10 minutes. If you find that your changes to the XSL file aren't reflected in the transformation, try renaming the XSL file so Amazon will grab a fresh copy.

A key advantage to working with XSL is that you can have extremely sophisticated pages in your own design with static files instead of complex server code. In fact, if you'd like to see an example of a completely designed and branded stylesheet, try replacing one of the stylesheets in this hack with *http://www.greeklandscapes.com/amazon_ws/xsl-heavy-short.xsl*. You should see your results in a completely formatted and designed store. Though you can't use the copyrighted Greek Landscapes (*http://www.greeklandscapes.com*) design, it gives an indication of just how far you can take the XSL feature.

Work Around Products Without Images

Those few items that don't have images can be pesky if your application depends on them. The key to weeding out the bad ones is byte size.

Amazon's product database contains millions of items, so it's not surprising that a few of them don't have images. The lack of images can be a problem if your application relies on them. AWS responses don't tell you if an image doesn't exist; in fact, AWS *always* returns an image URL, but in some cases the image is a single-pixel transparent GIF instead of a picture of the product. For many applications, using the invisible, single-pixel GIF won't be a problem. But if you're watching every pixel and your application works within a strict design, you'll want to find a way to work around this problem.

Although AWS responses don't directly say whether a product has an image or not, they do let you know indirectly. The image at the other end of the image URL will be considerably smaller if it's a single-pixel GIF. With a quick HTTP request, you can find the image byte size and know if it's big or small.

What You Need

The function can be used in any ASP script; these run on Windows servers running IIS. You'll also need the Microsoft XML Parser, which is usually installed by default when you install Internet Explorer.

The Code

Create a file called *hasImage.asp* with the following code:

```
Function hasImage(asin_in)

    strIURL = "http://images.amazon.com/images/P/" & asin_in
    strIURL = strIURL & ".01.THUMBZZZ.jpg"
```

```
        On Error Resume Next

        Set xmlhttp = Server.CreateObject("Msxml2.SERVERXMLHTTP")
        xmlhttp.Open "GET", strIURL, false
        xmlhttp.Send(Now)
        If Err.Number <> 0 Then
            strResponseBody = ""
            Err.Clear
        Else
            strResponseBody = xmlhttp.responseBody
        End If

        On Error GoTo 0

        Set xmlhttp = Nothing

        If Len(strResponseBody) > 403 Then
            hasImage = 1
        Else
            hasImage = 0
        End If

    End Function
```

The function requests an image, looks at the byte size, and returns true or false based on what it finds. It just so happens that the number of characters in the single-pixel GIF file is 403. This script assumes that anything greater than that must be a real product image.

Running the Hack

The hard part in testing this script is finding products without images. Only a small percentage of products don't have images, and there's no way to specifically seek them out. Still, to test it out, add the following lines to *hasImage.asp*:

```
response.write "Asin 1873176945 "
If hasImage("1873176945") Then
    response.write "has an image."
Else
    response.write "doesn't have an image!"
End If

response.write "<br>"

response.write "Asin 0596004478 "
If hasImage("0596004478") Then
    response.write "has an image."
Else
    response.write "doesn't have an image!"
End If
```

Browse to the page on your server:

```
http://example.com/hasImage.asp
```

And you should see:

```
Asin 1873176945 doesn't have an image!
Asin 0596004478 has an image.
```

Then you can confirm the results by browsing to the product detail pages.

#85 Syndicate a List of Books with RSS

Someday all data will be available as RSS. Get a head start by syndicating Amazon search results.

RSS is an XML format that's widely used to syndicate content. Depending on who you ask, it stands for *Rich Site Summary* or *Really Simple Syndication* and has become a standard way for publishers to make their content available. *News Readers* are programs that gather RSS feeds together and transform them into human-readable form. They've become a popular way to read news sites online.

With the wide audience for RSS data, just about everything is being turned into an RSS feed. This hack by Sean Nolan turns any AWS query result into an RSS feed.

What You Need

This hack uses ASP, which runs on Windows servers running IIS. The logic is straightforward, though, and could be translated to any scripting language.

The Code

Create a file called *amazon_rss.asp* and include the following code. Be sure to change the `Const` declarations to match your setup.

```
<%
'' AMAZON-RSS.ASP
'' Sean P. Nolan
'' http://www.yaywastaken.com/
''
'' This code is free for you to use as you see fit. Copy it, rewrite it,
'' run it yourself, whatever. But no warranties or guarantees either. Who
'' knows what the hell it does. Not me, that's for sure!
''
'' Generates an RSS 0.91 feed from an Amazon book query
''
''''''''''''''''''''''''''''''''''''''''''''''''''''''''''''''''''''''''''''

  Const MAX_PAGES_DEFAULT = 10
```

```
    Const DEV_TOKEN = "insert developer token"
    Const AFFILIATE_CODE = "insert associate tag"
    Const XSL_FILE = "amazon_lite.xsl" 'change to heavy for more info.

    Dim szTitle, szMaxPages, nMaxPages

    Response.ContentType = "text/xml"
    Server.ScriptTimeout = 60 * 4 ' 4-minute maximum
    Response.Expires = 0

    szMaxPages = Request.QueryString("maxpages")
    If (szMaxPages = "") Then
        nMaxPages = MAX_PAGES_DEFAULT
    Else
        nMaxPages = CLng(szMaxPages)
    End If

    szTitle = "Amazon Books: " & XMLify(Request.QueryString("keywords"))

    %><?xml version="1.0" encoding="ISO-8859-1" ?>
<rss version="0.91">
    <channel>
        <link>http://www.yaywastaken.com/amazon/</link>
        <title><%= szTitle %></title>
        <description>Create your own custom Amazon RSS feed!</description>
        <language>en-us</language>
<%
RenderItems Request.QueryString("keywords"), _
            Request.QueryString("browse") , _
            Request.QueryString("author") , _
            Request.QueryString("shortdesc"), _
            nMaxPages
%>

    </channel>
</rss>
    <%

    '''''''''''''''''''''''''''''''''''''''''''''''''''''''''''''''''''''''''''''
    ' RenderItems

    Sub RenderItems(szKeywords, szBrowseNode, szAuthor, szShortDesc, ↵
nMaxPages)
        Dim szURLFmt, szURL, xmlDoc, ipage, http, xmlErr
        Dim fParsed, xslDoc, szXSLPath, szOutput

        'On Error Resume Next

        If (szShortDesc <> "") Then
            szXSLPath = "amazon-lite.xsl"
        Else
            szXSLPath = "amazon-heavy.xsl"
        End If
```

```
Set xslDoc = Server.CreateObject("Msxml2.DOMDocument")
xslDoc.async = False
xslDoc.load(Server.MapPath(szXSLPath))

If (szBrowseNode <> "") Then
    szURLFmt = "http://xml.amazon.com/onca/xml?v=1.0&" & _
               "t=" & AFFILIATE_CODE & _
                  "&dev-t=" & DEV_TOKEN & "&BrowseNodeSearch=" & _
                  Server.URLEncode(szBrowseNode) & _
                  "&mode=books&type=heavy&page=%%%PAGE%%%&f=xml"
ElseIf (szAuthor <> "") Then
    szURLFmt = "http://xml.amazon.com/onca/xml?v=1.0&" & _
               "t=" & AFFILIATE_CODE & _
                  "&dev-t=" & DEV_TOKEN & "&AuthorSearch=" & _
                  Server.URLEncode(szAuthor) & _
                  "&mode=books&type=heavy&page=%%%PAGE%%%&f=xml"
Else
    szURLFmt = "http://xml.amazon.com/onca/xml?v=1.0&" & _
               "t=" & AFFILIATE_CODE & _
                  "&dev-t=" & DEV_TOKEN & "&KeywordSearch=" & _
                  Server.URLEncode(szKeywords) & _
                  "&mode=books&type=heavy&page=%%%PAGE%%%&f=xml"
End If

ipage = 1
Do
    szURL = Replace(szURLFmt, "%%%PAGE%%%", ipage)

    Set http = Server.CreateObject("Msxml2.ServerXMLHTTP")
    http.open "GET", szURL, False
    http.send ""

    If (http.status <> 200) Then
        Exit Do
    End If

    Set xmlDoc = Server.CreateObject("Msxml2.DOMDocument")
    xmlDoc.async = False
    xmlDoc.validateOnParse = False
    xmlDoc.resolveExternals = False
    fParsed = xmlDoc.loadXML(http.responseText)

    If (Not fParsed) Then
        Exit Do
    End If

    Set xmlErr = Nothing
    Set xmlErr = xmlDoc.selectSingleNode("ProductInfo/ErrorMsg")
    If (Not xmlErr Is Nothing) Then
        Exit Do
    End If

Set xslDoc = Nothing
```

```
            Set xslDoc = Server.CreateObject("Msxml2.DOMDocument")
            xslDoc.async = False
            xslDoc.validateOnParse = False
            xslDoc.resolveExternals = False
        xslDoc.load(Server.MapPath(XSL_FILE))

            szOutput = xmlDoc.transformNode(xslDoc)
            Response.Write szOutput

            ipage = ipage + 1
            If (ipage > nMaxPages) Then
                Exit Do
            End If
        Loop
    End Sub

    ''''''''''''''''''''''''''''''''''''''''''''''''''''''''''''''''''''''''''
    ' Helpers

    Function XMLify(sz)
        XMLify = Replace(sz, "&", "&amp;")
        XMLify = Replace(XMLify, "<", "<")
        XMLify = Replace(XMLify, ">", ">")
        XMLify = Replace(XMLify, """""", """")
        XMLify = Replace(XMLify, "'", "&apos;")
    End Function
%>
```

This file makes an Amazon Web Services XML/HTTP request based on querystring variables passed in the URL, and transforms the XML locally with an XSL stylesheet. Depending on how much detail you want in the RSS feed, there are two different stylesheets. The first, for light data, is called *amazon_lite.xsl*.

```
<?xml version='1.0'?>
<xsl:stylesheet version="1.0"
    xmlns:xsl="http://www.w3.org/1999/XSL/Transform">
<xsl:output omit-xml-declaration="yes" />
<xsl:template match="ProductInfo/Details">
    <item><link>
    <xsl:value-of select="@url" />
    </link><title>
    <xsl:value-of select="ProductName" />
    </title><description>
        <xsl:text>Author: </xsl:text>
        <xsl:value-of select="Authors/Author[1]" />
        <xsl:text>; </xsl:text>
        <xsl:value-of select="OurPrice" />
        <xsl:if test="Availability">
            <xsl:text> (</xsl:text>
            <xsl:value-of select="Availability" />
            <xsl:if test="Availability = 'Pre Order'">
```

```
                <xsl:text>: release date </xsl:text>
                <xsl:value-of select="ReleaseDate" />
            </xsl:if>
            <xsl:text>)</xsl:text>
        </xsl:if>
    </description></item>
</xsl:template>

<xsl:template match="/">
    <xsl:apply-templates select="ProductInfo/Details" />
</xsl:template>

</xsl:stylesheet>
```

Another stylesheet, appropriately titled *amazon_heavy.xsl*, provides more detailed information in the feed.

```
<?xml version='1.0'?>
<xsl:stylesheet version="1.0"
    xmlns:xsl="http://www.w3.org/1999/XSL/Transform">
<xsl:output omit-xml-declaration="yes" />
<xsl:template match="ProductInfo/Details">
    <item><link>
    <xsl:value-of select="@url" />
    </link><title>
    <xsl:value-of select="ProductName" />
    </title><description>
        <br />
        <xsl:element name="a">
            <xsl:attribute name="href">
                <xsl:value-of select="@url" />
            </xsl:attribute>
            <xsl:element name="img">
                <xsl:attribute name="src">
                    <xsl:value-of select="ImageUrlMedium" />
                </xsl:attribute>
                <xsl:attribute name="border">0</xsl:attribute>
                <xsl:attribute name="hspace">4</xsl:attribute>
                <xsl:attribute name="vspace">4</xsl:attribute>
                <xsl:attribute name="align">left</xsl:attribute>
            </xsl:element>
        </xsl:element>

        <font size="+1">
        <xsl:element name="a">
            <xsl:attribute name="href">
                <xsl:value-of select="@url" />
            </xsl:attribute>
            <xsl:value-of select="ProductName" />
        </xsl:element>
        </font>
        <br />
        <xsl:text>Author: </xsl:text>
```

```
        <xsl:value-of select="Authors/Author[1]" />
        <xsl:text>; </xsl:text>
        <xsl:value-of select="OurPrice" />
        <xsl:if test="Availability">
            <xsl:text> (</xsl:text>
            <xsl:value-of select="Availability" />
            <xsl:if test="Availability = 'Pre Order'">
                <xsl:text>, release date </xsl:text>
                <xsl:value-of select="ReleaseDate" />
            </xsl:if>
            <xsl:text>)</xsl:text>
        </xsl:if>
        <br clear="all" />

        <xsl:for-each select="Reviews/CustomerReview">
            <xsl:choose>
                <xsl:when test="Rating = 1">
                    <img src="http://g-images.amazon.com/images/G/01/↵
detail/stars-1-0.gif" border="0" hspace="2" vspace="2" />
                </xsl:when>
                <xsl:when test="Rating = 2">
                    <img src="http://g-images.amazon.com/images/G/01/↵
detail/stars-2-0.gif" border="0" hspace="2" vspace="2" />
                </xsl:when>
                <xsl:when test="Rating = 3">
                    <img src="http://g-images.amazon.com/images/G/01/↵
detail/stars-3-0.gif" border="0" hspace="2" vspace="2" />
                </xsl:when>
                <xsl:when test="Rating = 4">
                    <img src="http://g-images.amazon.com/images/G/01/↵
detail/stars-4-0.gif" border="0" hspace="2" vspace="2" />
                </xsl:when>
                <xsl:when test="Rating = 5">
                    <img src="http://g-images.amazon.com/images/G/01/↵
detail/stars-5-0.gif" border="0" hspace="2" vspace="2" />
                </xsl:when>
            </xsl:choose>
            <b><xsl:value-of select="Summary" /></b>
            <br />
            <xsl:value-of select="Comment" />
            <br /><br />
        </xsl:for-each>
    </description></item>
</xsl:template>

<xsl:template match="/">
    <xsl:apply-templates select="ProductInfo/Details" />
</xsl:template>

</xsl:stylesheet>
```

Running the Hack

The main file *amazon_rss.asp* accepts a few querystring variables. One of these is required each time you run the script.

`keywords`
: The subject of the books in the RSS feed.

`browse`
: Use this if you know the browse node code you'd like to syndicate.

`author`
: Set to the author's name to syndicate a list of their books.

Make all three files available on a web server, and then browse to *amazon_rss.asp* with a variable included. For example:

```
http://example.com/amazon_rss.asp?keywords=hacks
```

Now anyone can add this URL to their RSS news reader!

—Sean Nolan

#86 Import Data Directly into Excel

Manipulate data the old-fashioned way—with a spreadsheet.

Microsoft's Excel spreadsheet program was created to analyze and manipulate data. Using Amazon's Web Services as a source of data, you can easily integrate live information into Excel spreadsheets. This example imports sales rank data for particular books and calculates the average rank.

What You Need

This hack relies on Excel's ability to perform *web queries*, so you'll need Excel 97 or higher. Excel's Web Queries tool transforms simple HTML tables into Excel spreadsheets.

The Code

This code uses several features of both Amazon Web Services and Excel. Once you see how it's put together, building your own queries is a snap.

Getting the Data. This hack starts with a standard XML/HTTP query. We want to analyze sales ranks of O'Reilly's Hacks series, so we build a standard query to retrieve those results.

```
http://xml.amazon.com/onca/xml3?t=insert associate tag ↵
&dev-t=insert developer token&PowerSearch=publisher:O'Reilly ↵
%20and%20keywords:Hack&type=heavy&mode=books&f=xml
```

This request uses a Power Search **[Hack #9]** to specify a publisher (O'Reilly) and a keyword (Hack).

Transforming the Data. The next task is to get the Amazon response data into a form that Excel can work with. Because Excel Web Queries rely on simple HTML, Amazon's response must be transformed. As mentioned, XSL stylesheets **[Hack #83]** are a quick way to make that happen.

Put the following code into a file called *excel_SalesRank.xsl*. This file will narrow the Amazon response to the fields needed and turn it into HTML.

```
<?xml version="1.0" ?>
<xsl:stylesheet version="1.0" xmlns:xsl="http://www.w3.org/1999/XSL/
Transform">
<xsl:output method="html"/>
<xsl:template match="/">
<html xmlns:o="urn:schemas-microsoft-com:office:office"
xmlns:x="urn:schemas-microsoft-com:office:excel"
xmlns="http://www.w3.org/TR/REC-html40">
<body>
<table id="basic">
<tr>
    <th bgcolor="#cccccc" colspan="3">Sales Data</th>
</tr>
<tr>
    <th bgcolor="#999999">ASIN</th>
    <th bgcolor="#999999">Title</th>
    <th bgcolor="#999999">Sales Rank</th>
</tr>
<xsl:for-each select="ProductInfo/Details">
<tr>
    <td><xsl:value-of select="Asin" /></td>
    <td><xsl:value-of select="ProductName" /></td>
    <td><xsl:value-of select="SalesRank" /></td>
</tr>
</xsl:for-each>
<tr><td colspan="3"></td></tr>
<tr>
    <td bgcolor="#ffcc00" colspan="2" align="right">
        <b>Average Sales Rank</b>
    </td>
    <td bgcolor="#ffcc00">=ROUND(AVERAGE(C3:C<xsl:value-of
select="count(ProductInfo/Details) + 2" />),0)</td>
    </tr>
</table>
</body>
</html>
</xsl:template>
</xsl:stylesheet>
```

This file takes an AWS response and turns it into a simple HTML table. The `xsl:for-each` section loops through the `Details` node and adds a table row for each result. Once you upload this file to a publicly accessible server, you should be able to view the results of the transformation in a web browser by specifying the XSL file's URL in the request. Just modify the URL from the last step by replacing `f=xml` with `f=http://example.com/excel_SalesRank.xsl`.

```
http://xml.amazon.com/onca/xml3?t=insert associate tag↵
&dev-t=insert developer token&PowerSearch=publisher:O'Reilly↵
%20and%20keywords:Hack&type=heavy&mode=books↵
&f=http://example.com/excel_SalesRank.xsl
```

You should see a table like the one in Figure 6-4 with the data from the previous request. Note that the last cell of the table contains an Excel function. It looks like gibberish at this point, but serves an important purpose once it's inside Excel.

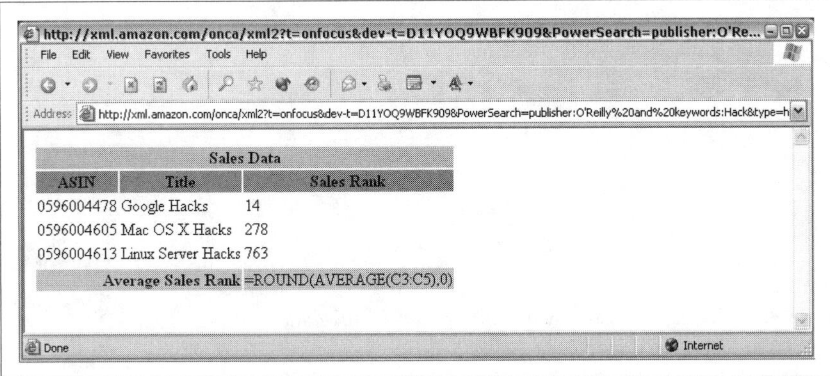

Figure 6-4. HTML table of sales data

Importing the Data. To glue the two applications together, we'll use an Excel Query (IQY) file. The file will hold all of the information about the query, including the URL that points to the data. Create a new file called *amzn_avg_sales.iqy* and add this code:

```
WEB
1
http://xml.amazon.com/onca/xml3?t=insert associate tag↵
&dev-t=insert developer token&PowerSearch=publisher:O'Reilly↵
%20and%20keywords:Hack&type=heavy&mode=books&f=http://example.com↵
/excel_SalesRank.xsl
```

The top line lets Excel know that this is a Web Query. The `1` is a Web Query version number (this will always be set to `1`) followed by the URL of the AWS query that includes the XSL file. Save the file and note its location.

Running the Hack

To run the hack, double-click the *amzn_avg_sales.iqy* file. Excel should open, contact the URL, and populate a spreadsheet resembling Figure 6-5.

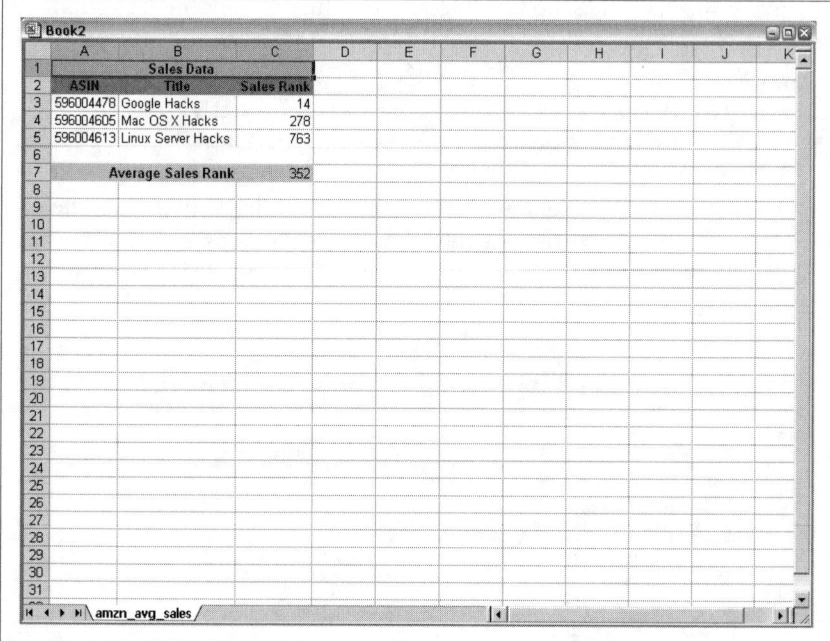

Figure 6-5. Excel spreadsheet with Amazon sales rank data

You now have some useful data—the average sales rank of the books in an application well-suited to manipulation and data analysis. You can update the data at any time by right-clicking any of the data cells in the spreadsheet and choosing "Refresh Data."

Hacking the Hack

The tough part of this hack is knowing how to get data directly from AWS into Excel. Once inside Excel the data is available to all of the features Excel offers: calculations, graphing, user input, etc. Here are a few quick ways to extend this example further.

Making the Query Dynamic. Instead of limiting the data to static information built into the query inside the IQY file, you can add a bit of interactivity. Suppose we have a list of ASINs and want to know the average sales rank, but we don't have the list when we're building the IQY file. Excel offers the ability to prompt the user for information before making the Web Query.

The only change you need to make is to place the prompt information inside the Web Query URL where you'd like the user input to go. Change the URL inside *amzn_avg_sales.iqy* to:

```
http://xml.amazon.com/onca/xml3?t=insert associate tag&dev-t=insert ↵
developer token&PowerSearch=isbn:["ASINs","Enter a list of ASINs ↵
separated by pipe symbols (|)."]&type=heavy&mode=books&f=http://↵
example.com/excel_SalesRank.xsl
```

Now, you're prompted for a list of ASINs upon opening the file, as you can see in Figure 6-6.

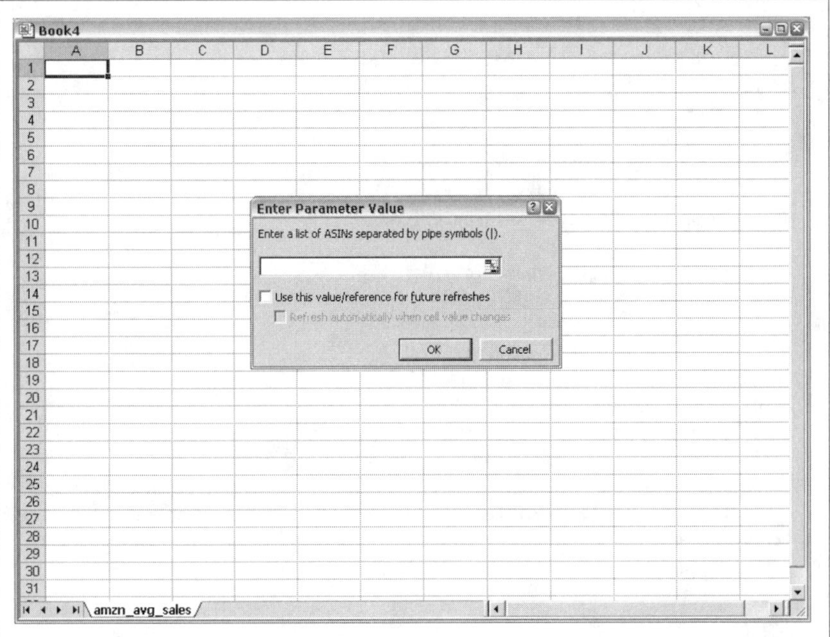

Figure 6-6. ASINs Excel dialogue

Try these if you don't have a list in mind:

```
1565927141|0596003595|0596002246|0596002505
```

This should give you the average sales rank for the ASINs you enter. It could be different every time!

Using Different Data. As in the previous example, changing the data you're working with is just a matter of changing the URL of the AWS query. But if you want to work with a different set of data (like the cost of each item rather than sales rank), you need to tweak the XSL stylesheet a bit.

To see how the stylesheet makes all the difference, create a new file called *excel_PriceDiff.xsl* and add the following code:

```
<?xml version="1.0" ?>
<xsl:stylesheet version="1.0" xmlns:xsl="http://www.w3.org/1999/XSL/
Transform">
<xsl:output method="html"/>
<xsl:template match="/">
<html xmlns:o="urn:schemas-microsoft-com:office:office"
xmlns:x="urn:schemas-microsoft-com:office:excel"
xmlns="http://www.w3.org/TR/REC-html40">
<body>
<table id="basic">
<tr>
    <th bgcolor="#cccccc" colspan="4">Sales Data</th>
</tr>
<tr>
    <th bgcolor="#999999">ASIN</th>
    <th bgcolor="#999999">Title</th>
    <th bgcolor="#999999">List Price</th>
    <th bgcolor="#999999">Amazon Price</th>
</tr>
<xsl:for-each select="ProductInfo/Details">
<tr>
<td>
  <xsl:value-of select="Asin" />
</td>
<td>
  <xsl:value-of select="ProductName" />
</td>
<td>
  <xsl:value-of select="ListPrice" />
</td>
<td>
  <xsl:value-of select="OurPrice" />
</td>
</tr>
</xsl:for-each>
<tr><td colspan="3"></td></tr>
<tr>
    <td bgcolor="#ffcc00" colspan="3" align="right">
        <b>Average List Price</b>
    </td>
    <td bgcolor="#ffcc00">=ROUND(AVERAGE(C3:C<xsl:value-of
select="count(ProductInfo/Details) + 2" />),2)
    </td>
</tr>
<tr>
    <td bgcolor="#ffcc00" colspan="3" align="right">
        <b>Average Amazon Price</b>
    </td>
    <td bgcolor="#ffcc00">=ROUND(AVERAGE(D3:D<xsl:value-of
select="count(ProductInfo/Details) + 2" />),2)
    </td>
```

```
</tr>
</table>
</body>
</html>
</xsl:template>
</xsl:stylesheet>
```

Upload this XSL file to a public server and note the URL. Create a new query file called *amzn_price_diff.iqy* and use the same code as in previous examples, but change the `f=` variable to the URL of the new stylesheet. Open the file and you should see a new spreadsheet with the list price and the Amazon price, as shown in Figure 6-7.

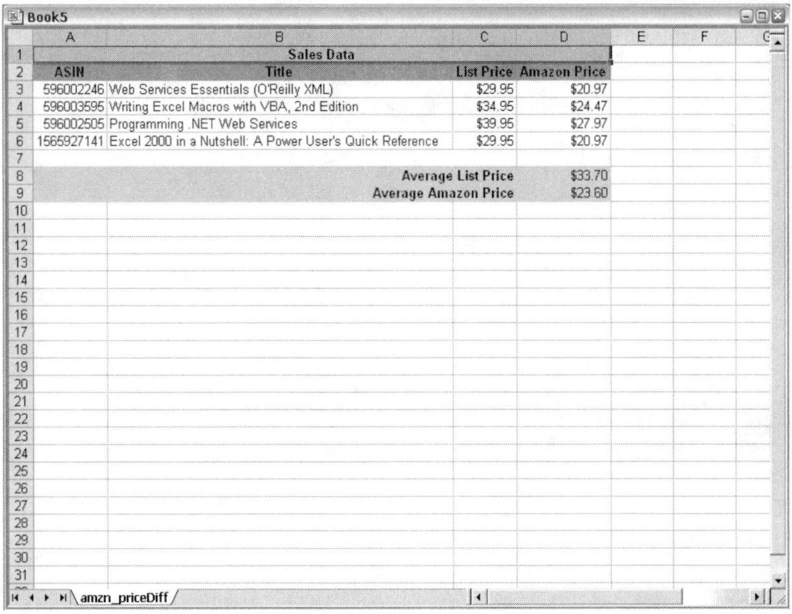

Book5

	A	B	C	D
1	Sales Data			
2	ASIN	Title	List Price	Amazon Price
3	596002246	Web Services Essentials (O'Reilly XML)	$29.95	$20.97
4	596003595	Writing Excel Macros with VBA, 2nd Edition	$34.95	$24.47
5	596002505	Programming .NET Web Services	$39.95	$27.97
6	1565927141	Excel 2000 in a Nutshell: A Power User's Quick Reference	$29.95	$20.97
7				
8			Average List Price	$33.70
9			Average Amazon Price	$23.60

amzn_priceDiff

Figure 6-7. Excel spreadsheet with price data

Graphing Results. Once the data is in Excel, it's easy to create graphs to get a sense of what the data means at a glance. Here's how to add a graph to the spreadsheet:

1. Building on the last example, run the *amzn_price_diff.iqy* file. You should see data that includes a list of books along with the list price and Amazon price.
2. Highlight all of the Title, List Price, and Amazon Price cells.
3. Choose Insert → Chart from the menu. This will start the chart wizard.
4. Click "Finish."

You should now have a nice graphic representation of the data (Figure 6-8).

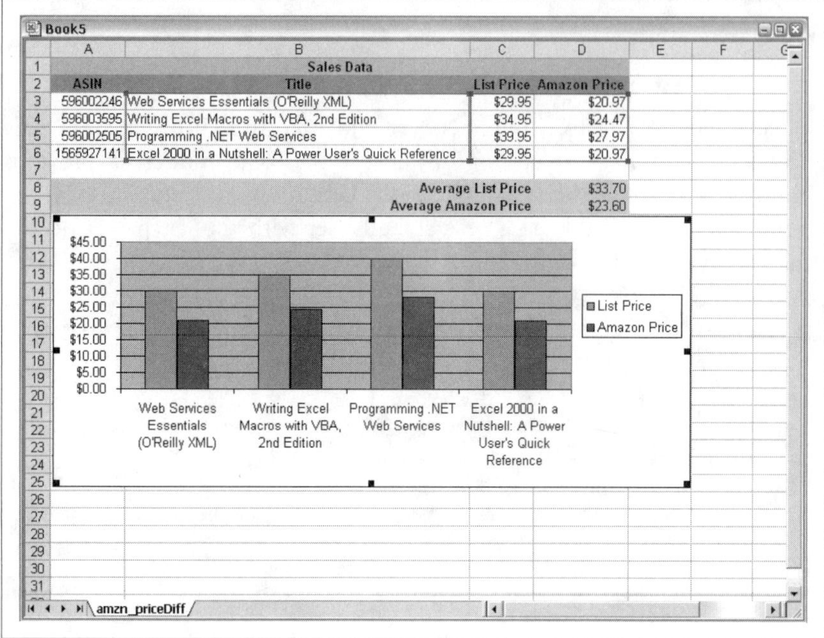

Book5

ASIN	Title	List Price	Amazon Price
596002246	Web Services Essentials (O'Reilly XML)	$29.95	$20.97
596003595	Writing Excel Macros with VBA, 2nd Edition	$34.95	$24.47
596002505	Programming .NET Web Services	$39.95	$27.97
1565927141	Excel 2000 in a Nutshell: A Power User's Quick Reference	$29.95	$20.97
	Average List Price		$33.70
	Average Amazon Price		$23.60

Figure 6-8. Graph of price data

Program AWS with SOAP and VB.NET

VB.NET was made for Web Services. With some WSDL magic, much of the code is generated for you.

This little application isn't particularly fascinating, but the code here can be used as a foundation for more complex VB.NET applications that use Amazon Web Services. The basic methods of creating a SOAP proxy and the syntax for making the request can be used no matter how simple or complex the application.

WSDL (Web Service Description Language) files can allow Web Services to describe what features and functions are available. Software can examine the WSDL file and automatically generate the code necessary to access it. This is exactly what the .NET framework can do. By supplying the Amazon Web Services WSDL file, much of the work is done for you!

What You Need

First, make sure you have the .NET framework and the .NET SDK, both freely available at *http://msdn.microsoft.com/library/default.asp?url=/*

downloads/list/netdevframework.asp. You could also create the program in Visual Studio if you have it available, but it's not necessary.

Next, create the SOAP client proxy. The *wsdl.exe* program examines a WSDL file and generates the code to create the class. You run it on the command line like this, providing the latest WSDL file:

```
wsdl.exe /l:vb http://soap.amazon.com/schemas2/AmazonWebServices.wsdl
```

This creates the file *AmazonWebServices.vb*.

To get a sense of what this program is working with, bring up the WSDL file in a browser. You'll see definitions for all of the possible SOAP requests and the parameters they accept. It's surprisingly easy to understand once you spend some time working with them; in fact, it's often easier to check the WSDL file instead of the documentation when you want to find which parameters you need to send for a specific request.

The Code

Create a text file called *Amazon.vb* and include the following code:

```
Imports System
Module Amazon
Sub Main(ByVal args As String())
    'Your AWS developer's token
    Dim devToken As String ="insert developer token"

    'Your Affiliate Code
    Dim afTag As String ="insert associate tag"

    'Take the query from the command-line
    If args.Length <>1 Then
        Console.WriteLine("Usage:amazon.exe <keyword>")
        Return
    End If
    Dim kword As String = args(0)

    Dim amazonSearch As AmazonSearchService = New AmazonSearchService()

    Dim KeywordReq as new KeywordRequest()
    KeywordReq.keyword = kword
    KeywordReq.type = "lite"
    KeywordReq.tag= afTag
    KeywordReq.devtag = devToken
    KeywordReq.mode = "books"

'Query Amazon
Dim results As ProductInfo = amazonSearch.KeywordSearchRequest(KeywordReq)
```

```
        'results?
        If results.Details Is Nothing Then Return

        'Loop through results
        Dim result As Details
        For Each result In results.Details
            Console.WriteLine( )
            Console.WriteLine(result.ProductName)
            Console.WriteLine("ASIN: " & result.ASIN)
            Console.WriteLine( )
        Next
    End Sub
    End Module
```

Once both the proxy code (*AmazonWebServices.vb*) and the search code (*Amazon.vb*) are ready to go, you can compile the program. It's a good idea to explicitly include references to the files (assemblies) that contain code that the program needs. You can specify these with the `/r:[file name]` switch.

```
vbc /out:amazon.exe /r:System.dll /r:System.Web.Services.dll ↵
/r:System.xml.dll *.vb
```

Running the Hack

The program is called from the command line, followed by the keyword you'd like to look for:

```
amazon.exe hacks
```

You should see several lines returned that look something like this:

```
Google Hacks
ASIN: 0596004478

Mac OS X Hacks
ASIN: 0596004605
```

To search for a phrase instead of a single word, enclose it in quotes.

#88 Program AWS with SOAP::Lite and Perl

Use a standard Perl SOAP module to make requests and work with the responses.

Though SOAP requests and responses are more complex than those of XML/HTTP, they're just as easy to work with if you have the right tools.

What You Need

SOAP::Lite has become the standard way for Perl developers to work with SOAP services. Many ISPs have SOAP::Lite installed, but it's not yet ubiquitous. A quick request via email could save you hours of straining with the manual installation process. If you're on a Windows server, you can install it fairly painlessly with the package manager at a command prompt:

```
ppm install SOAP::Lite
```

The Code

Instead of assembling URLs, making an Amazon request with SOAP requires assembling a collection of variables and their values. Create a file called *amazon.pl* with the following code:

```
#!/usr/bin/perl
# amazon.pl
# A typical Amazon Web API Perl script that uses the SOAP::Lite Module.
# Usage: perl amazon.pl <keyword>

#Your Amazon developer's token
my $dev_token='insert developer token';

#Your Amazon affiliate code
my $af_tag='insert associate tag';

#Location of the Amazon WSDL file
my $amazon_wdsl = "http://soap.amazon.com/schemas2/AmazonWebServices.wsdl";

use strict;

#Use the SOAP::Lite Perl module
use SOAP::Lite;

#Take the query from the command-line
my $keyword =shift @ARGV or die "Usage:perl amazon.pl <keyword>\n";

#Create a new SOAP::Lite instance, feeding it Amazon's WSDL
my $amazon_search = SOAP::Lite->service("$amazon_wdsl");

#Query Amazon
my $results = $amazon_search ->
    KeywordSearchRequest(SOAP::Data->name("KeywordSearchRequest")
        ->type("KeywordRequest")
           ->value(\SOAP::Data->value(
        SOAP::Data->name("keyword" => $keyword),
        SOAP::Data->name("page" => "1"),
        SOAP::Data->name("mode" => "books"),
        SOAP::Data->name("tag" => $af_tag),
        SOAP::Data->name("type" => "lite"),
        SOAP::Data->name("devtag" => $dev_token)
        ))
    );

foreach my $result (@{$results->{Details}}){
    #Print out the main bits of each result
```

```
        print
            $result->{ProductName}|| "no title",
            "\nby ",
            join (', ', @{$result->{Authors}}),
            "\n$result->{OurPrice}",
            "\nASIN: $result->{Asin}",
            "\n\n";
}
```

Running the Hack

Just call the script from the command line, with the keyword as an argument:

```
perl amazon.pl "hacks"
```

#89 Program AWS with NuSOAP and PHP

PHP's standard SOAP module NuSOAP makes SOAP simple.

Like Perl, PHP has its emerging standard method of working with SOAP applications. NuSOAP is a single PHP script (with over 4,000 lines of code!) that handles all of the SOAP heavy lifting for you. Get your copy from *http://dietrich.ganx4.com/nusoap/* and include the file in the same directory as your scripts.

The Code

The script, *amazon_soap.php*, is meant to be run as a web page. It accepts a variable, `keyword`, in the URL. With this, it creates the proper SOAP request and returns the results as an array.

```
<html>
<head>
<title>Amazon Keyword Search</title>
</head>
<body>
<?
#Use the NuSOAP php library
require_once('nusoap.php');

#Set parameters
$parameters = array('keyword' => $HTTP_GET_VARS['keyword'],
    'type' => 'lite',
    'page' => '1',
    'mode' => 'books',
    'tag' => 'insert associate tag',
    'devtag' => 'insert developer token');

#Create a new SOAP client with Amazon's WSDL
```

```
$soapclient = new soapclient('http://soap.amazon.com/schemas2/↵
AmazonWebServices.wsdl','wsdl');
$proxy = $soapclient->getproxy( );

#query Amazon
$results = $proxy->KeywordSearchRequest($parameters);

//echo 'Request: <xmp>'.$proxy->request.'</xmp>';
//echo 'Response: <xmp>'.$proxy->response.'</xmp>';

#Results?
if (is_array($results['Details'])) {
    print "<p>Search for <b>" . $HTTP_GET_VARS['keyword'] . "</b>" .
          " found " . $results['TotalResults'] . " results." .
          " <br>Here are the first " . count($results['Details']).".".
          " </p><ol>";
    foreach ($results['Details'] as $result) {
    print
        "<li><b>" . $result['ProductName'] . "</b>" .
        "<br /> by " . $result['Authors'][0] .
" <a href='" . $result['Url'] . "'>" . $result['OurPrice']. "</a><br><br>";
    }
    print "</ol>";
}

#No Results
else {
    print "Your Amazon query for '" . $HTTP_GET_VARS['keyword'] .
    "' returned no results";
}
?>
</body>
</html>
```

Running the Hack

To run the code, place the file on a web server, and browse to:

```
http://example.com/amazon_soap.php?keyword=hacks
```

If you run into problems or are curious about what's being sent between the servers, uncomment the //echo statement by removing the slashes. This will print out the entire SOAP request and Amazon's SOAP response. It's a good way to get a sense of the formatting work being done behind the scenes.

Create a Wireless Wish List

Take your Wish List wherever you go with AWS, XSLT, and WAP!

How many times have you been browsing at a bookstore or video store and you can't remember which books or movies you wanted to pick up? Sure, you could write them all down on a piece of paper and take it with you, but what fun would that be? Instead, you can use powerful cell networks and web applications to do the work for you. If you track wanted books and movies with your Amazon Wish List and have a WAP-enabled cell phone, you can always have your list handy.

WAP stands for Wireless Access Protocol, and it's used for delivering information to cell phones and other handheld devices. The information itself is formatted with WML (Wireless Markup Language), an XML format.

Just as HTML pages have `<body>` elements that contain the bulk of the page, WML pages have `<card>` elements. Each WML page can contain several cards, but only one card is displayed at a time. Also, links work much the same way as in HTML. Instead of `<a href>` tags, WML relies on `<anchor>` and `<go href>` tags. This example creates one card with a list of items. Each item links to the Amazon WAP product detail page for that item.

The Code

Making AWS responses available to a cell phone is just a matter of converting one XML format (AWS response) to another (WML). Once again, Amazon's XSLT service makes this quick work.

Create an XSL file called *wap_wishlist.xsl* with the following code:

```
<?xml version="1.0" encoding="ISO-8859-1"?>
<xsl:stylesheet version="1.0" xmlns:xsl="http://www.w3.org/1999/XSL/↵
Transform">
<xsl:output method="wml" doctype-public="-//WAPFORUM//DTD WML 1.1//EN" ↵
doctype-system="http://www.wapforum.org/DTD/wml_1.1.xml"/>
<xsl:template match="/">
    <wml>
    <card id="Menu" title="Wishlist">
    <p><b>My Wishlist</b><br/><br/>
    <xsl:for-each select="ProductInfo/Details">
            <b><xsl:value-of select="Catalog" />:</b>
            <br/><xsl:value-of select="ProductName" />
            <xsl:if test="Artists">
                <br/>by
                <xsl:value-of select="Artists/Artist" />
            </xsl:if>
            <xsl:if test="Authors">
                <br/>by
                <xsl:value-of select="Authors/Author" />
            </xsl:if>
            <br/><xsl:value-of select="OurPrice" />
            <br/><anchor>Details<go><xsl:attribute name="href">http://↵
www.amazon.com/exec/obidos/redirect?tag=insert associate tag%26creative=↵
insert developer token%26camp=2025%26link_code=xm2%26path=ct/text/↵
vnd.wap.wml/-/tg/aa/xml/glance-xml/-/<xsl:value-of select="Asin" />↵
```

```
</xsl:attribute></go></anchor>
            <br/><br/>
    </xsl:for-each>
    </p>
    </card>
    </wml>
</xsl:template>
</xsl:stylesheet>
```

There are a few important things to note in this code. First, the output type has been set to WML with the `<xsl:output>` tag. Without this, the required `<!DOCTYPE` tag would not be included in the transformed page. Also notice the link to WAP Amazon detail pages. The URL format is the same (see "Deep Linking to Amazon's Mobile Device Pages" **[Hack #72]**), but the ampersands have all been changed to the encoded `%26`. Ampersands aren't valid when used in URLs inside a WML file, and phones can't display the page if they aren't escaped.

Running the Hack

The code is just an Amazon query, so we need to get the right URL. Find your Wish List ID **[Hack #18]** and include it in a wish list search like this:

```
http://xml.amazon.com/onca/xml3?t=insert associate tag ↵
&dev-t=insert developer token&WishlistSearch=[your wishlist]&type=lite&f=xml
```

Upload *wap_wishlist.xsl* to a publicly accessible server and change the value of `f=` to the URL for the file:

```
http://xml.amazon.com/onca/xml3?t=insert associate tag ↵
&dev-t=insert developer token&WishlistSearch=[your wishlist]&type=lite ↵
&f=http://example.com/wap_wishlist.xsl
```

There's just one more change that needs to be made. WAP browsers are looking for a certain content type. Content types are specified as HTTP headers, and there's no way to include those in our XSL file. Luckily, Amazon provides a way to specify an alternate content type header with the query itself. Add the ct= variable and set the content type to `text/vnd.wap.wml`.

```
http://xml.amazon.com/onca/xml3?t=insert associate tag ↵
&dev-t=insert developer token&WishlistSearch=[your wishlist]&type=lite ↵
&f=http://example.com/wap_wishlist.xsl&ct=text/vnd.wap.wml
```

That's all there is to it. Unfortunately this URL is a bit long to type into your phone with your keypad, but there are a couple of ways to work around this. First, see if your cell provider has a web interface for adding bookmarks to your phone's WAP browser. If so, you could copy and paste this monster into your cell provider's site, and then have 1-click (ahem) access through your phone's bookmarks. Another method is to upload a WML file to your site that contains a link to your wish list via this URL. Then you'd just need to browse to your own WAP page first and follow the link. If you go this route, try giving your WAP page a short name, like *a.wml*; this will save some keying.

#91 Make Product Titles Shorter

There are tools for cutting and slicing strings in every programming environment. Here are some quick examples of cutting book titles down to size.

The `ProductName` that Amazon returns is always the full name of the product. It's good to be accurate, but sometimes you need only part of the title. For example, O'Reilly has a book called *Malicious Mobile Code: Virus Protection for Windows* (O'Reilly Computer Security), and this is exactly what Amazon sends as the `ProductName` value. Weighing in at 80 characters, it's a bit long when *Malicious Mobile Code* could work just as well.

The Code

By looking at book titles as a template, code can automate shortening the titles. In many cases they follow this pattern:

```
[short title]:[sub title]([series title])
```

Using string-dicing functions built into most languages for trimming is easy work.

JavaScript

```
var title = "Malicious Mobile Code: Virus Protection for Windows";
shortTitle = title.split(":")
alert(shortTitle[0]);
```

Perl

```
my $title = "Malicious Mobile Code: Virus Protection for Windows";
@shortTitle = split /:/, $title;
print $shortTitle[0];
```

VBScript

```
strTitle = "Malicious Mobile Code: Virus Protection for Windows"
shortTitle = Split(strTitle,":")
Wscript.Echo shortTitle(0)
```

PHP

```
$title = "Malicious Mobile Code: Virus Protection for Windows";
$shortTitle = split(":",$title);
echo $shortTitle[0];
```

Python

```
import string
title = "Malicious Mobile Code: Virus Protection for Windows";
shortTitle = string.split(title,":");
print shortTitle[0];
```

Each of these bits of code splits the string at the colon (:) and prints everything before it (i.e., *Malicious Mobile Code)*. These code snippets would work with books that don't have colons as well by returning the entire title.

#92 Encode Text for URLs

Make sure the text in XML/HTTP queries is valid for URLs.

One thing to keep in mind when making XML/HTTP requests is that they behave exactly like URLs for web pages. This means that spaces and symbols need to be *encoded*. Spaces aren't allowed in URLs, so anything after a space could be disregarded by the server. Also, characters like ampersands (&), question marks (?), and number signs (#) give directions to the server about how the URL should be processed. So if you're doing an XML/HTTP Amazon `ArtistSearch` for a band like *Kruder & Dorfmeister*, you've got trouble—the spaces and ampersand will break the request. But you can translate the characters into a URL-friendly format.

Technically, you can encode these characters by using the percent sign (%) followed by their hexadecimal numeric values. The numeric value for a space is `20`, so a space is represented as `%20` in a URL. Spaces can also be escaped as plus signs (+) for many systems, including Amazon's. Here are some commonly escaped characters and their encoded values:

Ampersand (&)	`%26`
Question mark (?)	`%3F`
Number sign (#)	`%23`
Comma (,)	`%2C`
Colon (:)	`%3A`

The `ArtistSearch` mentioned will only work if the band name is encoded as `Kruder%20%26%20Dorfmeister`. Doing this by hand each time you make a request is out of the question. Luckily, this is such a common task that most programming environments have built-in functions to handle this for you.

The Code

Here are few common ways to escape text for URLs in various scripting languages.

JavaScript

```
var artist = "Kruder & Dorfmeister";
artist = escape(artist);
```

Perl

```
use URI::Escape;
my $artist = "Kruder & Dorfmeister";
$artist = uri_escape($artist);
```

VBScript

```
strArtist = "Kruder & Dorfmeister"
strArtist = Server.URLEncode(strArtist)
```

PHP

```
$artist = "Kruder & Dorfmeister";
$artist = urlencode(strArtist);
```

Python

Unlike the previous examples, Python's `urlencode` takes variable/value pairs and creates a properly escaped querystring:

```
import sys
from urllib import urlencode
artist = "Kruder & Dorfmeister"
artist = urlencode({'ArtistSearch':artist})
```

This sets the variable artist equal to:

```
ArtistSearch=Kruder+%26+Dorfmeister
```

Encoding strings for URLs is an easy problem to solve, and it's something to look at if your XML/HTTP requests aren't working quite right.

Cache Amazon Images Locally

Caching product images locally can save your users several trips to the Amazon server and speed up your applications.

The easiest way to save an image locally is to visit the product detail page, right-click on the image, and choose "Save Picture As…". Of course, "easy" is relative. If you have to do this for hundreds of products, suddenly it's the hard way.

Luckily, every programming environment has methods for retrieving an image from a remote server and saving it as a local file.

The Code

Each of these examples takes an ASIN, builds the proper URL [Hack #5], grabs the image, and saves it locally as *[ASIN].jpg*.

Perl

This uses the `getstore( )` function of LWP::Simple to request and save the file. `$rp` is the return code, and to shore this function up you could take additional action if it's equal to 404.

```
use LWP::Simple;
$Asin = "0596004478";
$rp = getstore(
      "http://images.amazon.com/images/P/$Asin.01.MZZZZZZZ.jpg",↵
      "$Asin.jpg");
```

VBScript

Writing binary files like images isn't quite as straightforward with VBScript, so you have to turn to some unusual components. The Server-XMLHTTP component makes the request, which is written to an ADODB stream. The ADODB component has the ability to write binary files.

```
strASIN = "0596004478"
strURL = "http://images.amazon.com/images/P/" & strASIN & _
         ".01.MZZZZZZZ.jpg"
strFile = strASIN & ".jpg"

'Get the Image
Set xmlhttp = CreateObject("Msxml2.SERVERXMLHTTP")
xmlhttp.Open "GET", strURL, false
xmlhttp.Send(Now)

'Create a Stream
Set adodbStream = CreateObject("ADODB.Stream")

'Open the stream
adodbStream.Open
adodbStream.Type = 1 'adTypeBinary
adodbStream.Write xmlhttp.responseBody
adodbStream.SaveToFile strFile, 2 'adSaveCreateOverWrite
adodbStream.Close

Set adodbStream = Nothing
Set xmlhttp = Nothing
```

This code will run as a WSH file. Simply add `Server.` before the `CreateObject` commands to use this code in an ASP file.

PHP

The key to this PHP code is setting the `fopen( )` function to read and write binary files. Note the `rb` (read binary) and `wb` (write binary) options.

```
$asin = "0596004478";
$url = "http://images.amazon.com/images/P/".$asin.".01.MZZZZZZZ.jpg";
$filedata = "";
$remoteimage = fopen($url, 'rb');
if ($remoteimage) {
    while(!feof($remoteimage)) {
           $filedata.= fread($remoteimage,1024);
    }
}
fclose($remoteimage);
$localimage = fopen($asin.".jpg", 'wb');
fwrite($localimage,$filedata);
fclose($localimage);
```

Python

As with PHP, be sure to set the file open command to `wb` (write binary) so it can save the file properly.

```
import urllib
asin = "0596004478"
url = 'http://images.amazon.com/images/P/' + asin + ".01.MZZZZZZZ.jpg"
filedata = urllib.urlopen(url).read( )
f = open(asin + '.jpg', 'wb')
f.write(filedata)
f.close( )
```

Amazon's license asks that you update any information you've cached from its servers every 24 hours. Check the Last Saved property of your local copy of the file before running any of these snippets; if it's longer than 24 hours, rerun the code to stay in compliance. (See *http://www.amazon.com/gp/aws/license_agree.html*.)

#94 Cache AWS Responses Locally

You can improve application performance by saving Amazon data locally and updating it on a regular schedule.

If you find your application requesting the same data from Amazon over and over again, you may be able to speed things up by caching the data locally. Why make the same request for live data again and again if you're getting the same data each time? A local version will always be faster. Also, if Amazon's server happens to be down for maintenance, you can rely on your local cache to make up for it.

As mentioned in the previous hack, Amazon requires that the data you display on your site be up to date. The Web Services Licensing Agreement says that data must be updated every 24 hours. If you want to cache data for longer periods of time, you'll need a written agreement from Amazon.

Adding a data cache requires just a few lines of extra code and can make your applications much more efficient. There are many approaches to caching data; the code here shows two different ways to go about it.

Cache in Memory with ASP

This ASP code stores the Amazon XML response as an `Application` variable, which means the code is available to the entire application in memory. Storing data in memory makes it available for quick access, but memory is a limited commodity. This is a great solution if you're storing only a few responses locally.

Along with the cached XML, this code sets a DateCached application variable that stores when the data was last saved. A check at the top of the file against the current time (Now( )) plus 24 hours determines whether new data should be cached.

```
<%
strURL = "http://xml.amazon.com/onca/xml3?t=insert associate tag"
strURL = strURL & "&dev-t=insert developer token"
strURL = strURL & "&type=lite&f=xml&AsinSearch=0596005423"

'If cached XML doesn't exist or is old, make a request for new XML.
If Application(strURL) = "" OR DatePart("h",Application("DateCached")) <
DateAdd("h",24,Now( )) Then

    'Make XML/HTTP request
    Set xmlhttp = Server.CreateObject("Msxml2.SERVERXMLHTTP")
    xmlhttp.Open "GET", strURL, false
    xmlhttp.Send( )
    Set AllXML = xmlhttp.responseXML

    'If the XML looks good...
    If AllXML.parseError.ErrorCode = 0 Then

        'Set the XML to an application variable
        Application(strURL) = AllXML.xml

        'And set the time it was cached
        Application("DateCached") = Now( )

    End If

   Set AllXML = Nothing
   Set xmlhttp = Nothing
End If
response.write "<xmp>" & Application(strURL) & "</xmp>"
%>
```

This code can be incorporated into any existing ASP file, and the Application variable that holds the XML can be used as if it were a fresh response from Amazon.

Cache to Disk with Perl

This bit of Perl code by Jeff Barr saves XML responses as a local text file. Before making a request, it checks to see if the cached version has been saved within the last 24 hours. If not, it writes the data to the cache file. Using local text files as your cache is more scalable than saving the responses in memory, especially if you have more than a handful of responses you'd like to cache.

Be sure to set the value of $cache_dir to the local directory you want to store the cache files in.

```
use LWP;
use Digest::MD5 qw/md5_base64/;

my $LWP_request;
my $LWP = new LWP::UserAgent;

my $cache_dir = "C:\\";
my $URL = "http://xml.amazon.com/onca/xml3?t=insert associate tag ↵
&dev-t=insert developer token&type=lite&f=xml&AsinSearch=0596005423";

# Check for cached data (URL is cache key)
  my $used_cache = 0;
  my $cache_file = $cache_dir . "\\" . md5_base64($URL);
  print $cache_file . "\n\n";
  if (-e $cache_file && (-M $cache_file <= 1.0/24.0))
  {
    # Use the cached data
    if (open(CACHE_FILE, $cache_file))
    {
      my @all_xml = <CACHE_FILE>;
      close CACHE_FILE;

      $xml_text   = join "\n", @all_xml;
      $used_cache = 1;
    }
  }

# If the cache doesn't exist, make the request
  if (!$used_cache)
  {
    # Request the data & process the response
    $LWP_request = new HTTP::Request(GET => $URL);
    my $result = $LWP->request($LWP_request);
    if (!$result->is_success)
    {
      # Handle error. Could use stale cached data if desired.
    }
    else
    {
      $xml_text = $result->content;
    }
  }

  # Update the cache
  if (!$used_cache)
  {
    if (open(CACHE_FILE, ">$cache_file"))
```

```
      {
        print CACHE_FILE $xml_text;
      }

      close CACHE_FILE;
    }

  print $xml_text;
```

This code just prints out the XML, cached or not. But you could easily incorporate this caching method into your existing AWS applications.

Create an Amazon AIM Bot

Chat with some Perl code to get book prices via AOL Instant Messenger.

AOL Instant Messenger isn't the most likely place you'll need Amazon book data, but that doesn't mean the applications aren't fun to connect. With Perl and the Net::AIM module, you can have your own chattering book-bot requesting Amazon information for you.

What You Need

First you'll need the Net::AIM library, which provides all the functions for logging into AIM and sending or receiving messages. You can find it at activestate.com (*http://aspn.activestate.com/ASPN/CodeDoc/Net-AIM/AIM.html*). To get a jumpstart on coding, check out the tutorials at Wired Bots (*http://www.wiredbots.com/tutorial.html*). They have some fully functional sample bots and lots of example code for working with Net::AIM.

You'll also need an AIM screen name and password for your new virtual assistant, along with a screen name for yourself if you don't have one; sign up at *http://www.aim.com*.

The Code

Create a file called *asin_bot.pl* and include the following code. The code that communicates with Amazon is based on a previous hack ("Program AWS with Perl" [Hack #80]), though the AWS request is made inside the `on_im` subroutine, when a message comes in. Instead of printing out to the console, it saves the results in a variable, `$detail`, and sends it as an instant message back to the person sending the message.

```
#!/usr/bin/perl
# asin_bot.pl
#
# An AIM bot that given an ASIN will
# return the product title and price.
```

```
# Usage: perl asin_bot.pl

use warnings;
use strict;
use Net::AIM;
use LWP::Simple;
use XML::Simple;

# fill in your relevants.
my $aim_un = 'insert AIM username';
my $aim_pw = 'insert AIM password';
my $dev_key = 'insert developer token';
my $af_code = 'insert affiliate tag';

# create an AIM connection
# and return it for usage.
my $aim = new Net::AIM;
$aim->newconn(Screenname=>$aim_un,Password=>$aim_pw)
                or die "Cannot connect to AIM.";
my $conn = $aim->getconn();

# Set up a handler for messages.
$conn->set_handler('im_in', on_im);
$conn->set_handler('error', on_error);
print "Logged on to AIM!\n\n";
$aim->start;

# incoming.
sub on_im {

    my ($aim, $evt, $from, $to) = @_;
    my $args = $evt->args();
    ($from, my $friend, my $msg) = @$args;

    # cheaply remote html.
    $msg =~ s/<(.|\n)+?>//g;

    # if this isn't an ASIN sized string,
    # send back an error message stating such.
    $aim->send_im($from, "I only accept ASINs.") unless length($msg) eq 10;

    # create our final URL.
    my $url = "http://xml.amazon.com/onca/xml3?t=$af_code".
              "&dev-t=$dev_key&type=lite&f=xml&".
              "AsinSearch=$msg";

    my $content = get($url);
    my $response = XMLin($content);
    my $detail = $response->{Details}->{ProductName}||"no title";
    $detail   .= " $response->{Details}->{OurPrice}";
    $aim->send_im($from, $detail);
}
```

```
    # oops!
    sub on_error {
        my ($self, $evt) = @_;
        my ($error, @stuff) = @{$evt->args()};

        # Translate error number into English.
        # then filter and print to STDERR.
        my $errstr = $evt->trans($error);
        $errstr =~ s/\$(\d+)/$stuff[$1]/ge;
        print "ERROR: $errstr\n";
    }
```

Notice that inside the on_im subroutine, the script checks to make sure the incoming message is exactly 10 characters, the length of an ASIN. Otherwise it sends back the message, "I only accept ASINs." It's a good idea to set up rules like this for any kind of queries you allow. Bots should always send a message about success or failure.

Running the Hack

Start up AOL Instant Messenger and add the virtual screen name you gave your bot to your buddy list. When you run *asin_bot.pl*, you should see the bot appear among your online buddies. Send a message consisting of only an ASIN, and you should get the book title and Amazon price back. This conversation is shown in Figure 6-9.

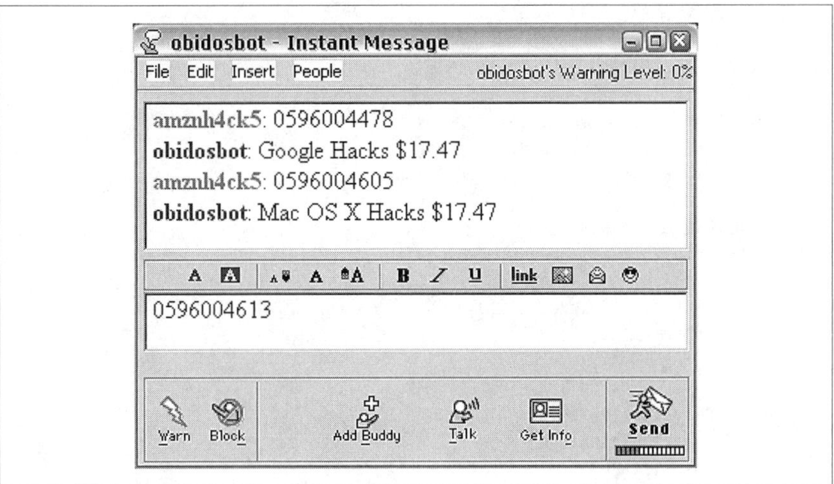

Figure 6-9. Talking ASINs with an AIM bot

Not exactly stimulating conversation, but expanding its vocabulary is simply a matter of adding Amazon requests and responses to the script.

Compare International Sales

Find out what products are hot on either side of the pond with Amazon locale-based queries.

Why are some albums more popular in the U.K. than in the U.S.? This hack can't answer that question, but it can point out what the differences are. It uses two features of AWS requests, sort and locale, to generate parallel lists of bestsellers by artist.

The Code

This ASP code makes two ArtistSearch requests. Both are sorted by sales rank, and the only difference between the two is the setting for the locale. In the first query, locale is left blank, for the default Amazon.com store. The other query sets the locale to uk, searching Amazon.co.uk. Create a file called *us_vs_uk.asp* with the following code:

```
<html>
<head>
    <title>International Sales</title>
</head>

<body>
<%
Dim arUSResults(10,4)
Dim arUKResults(10,4)

Sub AmazonTopArtist(artist,locale)

' Set Associate ID and Developer Token
AssociatesID = "insert associate tag"
DeveloperToken = "insert developer token"

  ' Form the request URL
XMLURL = "http://xml.amazon.com/onca/xml3" & _
       "?t=" & AssociateID & _
       "&dev-t=" & DeveloperToken & _
       "&page=1" & _
       "&f=xml" & _
       "&mode=music" & _
       "&type=lite" & _
       "&sort=+salesrank" & _
       "&ArtistSearch=" & Server.URLEncode(artist)
       If locale = "uk" Then
           XMLURL = XMLURL & "&locale=uk"
       End If

Set xmlhttp = Server.CreateObject("Msxml2.SERVERXMLHTTP")
xmlhttp.Open "GET", XMLURL, false
```

```
xmlhttp.Send(Now)

' Issue the request and wait for the response
Set ProductInfo = xmlhttp.ResponseXML

Set Details = ProductInfo.SelectNodes("//Details")
For x = 0 to (Details.length-1)
    If locale = "uk" Then
      arUKResults(x,1) = Details(x).selectSingleNode("ProductName").text
      arUKResults(x,2) = Details(x).selectSingleNode("Asin").text
      arUKResults(x,3) = Details(x).selectSingleNode("ImageUrlSmall").text
      arUKResults(x,4) = Details(x).getAttribute("url")
    Else
      arUSResults(x,1) = Details(x).selectSingleNode("ProductName").text
      arUSResults(x,2) = Details(x).selectSingleNode("Asin").text
      arUSResults(x,3) = Details(x).selectSingleNode("ImageUrlSmall").text
      arUSResults(x,4) = Details(x).getAttribute("url")
    End If
Next
Set Details = Nothing
Set ProductInfo = Nothing
Set xmlhttp = Nothing

End Sub

strArtist = request("artist")

Call AmazonTopArtist(strArtist,"us")
Call AmazonTopArtist(strArtist,"uk")

response.write "<table border=""1"" cellpadding=""5"">"
response.write "<tr><th>UK Top Sales</th><th>US Top Sales</th></tr>"
response.write "<tr>"
For y = 0 To 9
    response.write "<tr>"
    response.write "<td align=""center"" valign=""top"">"
    response.write "<a href=""" & arUKResults(y,4) & """>"
    response.write arUKResults(y,1)
    response.write "</a><br><br>"
    response.write "<img border=""0"" src=""" & arUKResults(y,3) & """>"
    response.write "</td>" & vbCrLf
    response.write "<td align=""center"" valign=""top"">"
    response.write "<a href=""" & arUSResults(y,4) & """>"
    response.write arUSResults(y,1)
    response.write "</a><br><br>"
    response.write "<img border=""0"" src=""" & arUSResults(y,3) & """>"
    response.write "</td>" & vbCrLf
    response.write "</tr>"
Next
response.write "</table>"
%>
</body>
</html>
```

The results are saved in arrays, `arUKResults` and `arUSResults`. Once both queries are set, they're used to print out a table with the results.

> Though you can use your associate tag to make alternate locale requests, you'll need to be a member of the specific locale's associates program to get affiliate fees from the links. For example, if you're a U.S. Amazon associate pointing to Amazon.co.uk, you won't receive affiliate fees from those sales. To do so, you would need to create a separate affiliate tag with the U.K. associates program.

Running the Hack

To run this code, put *us_vs_uk.asp* on a server and request it from your browser, passing the `artist` variable in the querystring, like so:

```
http://example.com/us_vs_uk.asp?artist=Dylan
```

Figure 6-10 shows the differing results for Bob Dylan's sales.

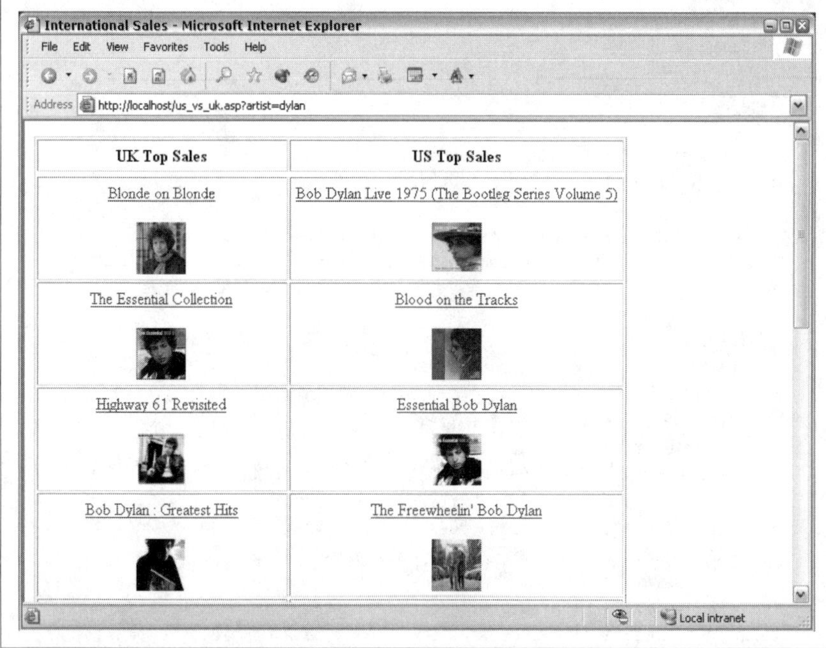

Figure 6-10. International sales differences of Bob Dylan CDs

This code is also using the `SmallImageURL` value to display an image. The images come from their respective servers, so half are from the *images-eu.amazon.com* server, while the rest are from *images.amazon.com*.

Program AWS with Mozilla

Mozilla provides all the tools you need to build applications that integrate with Amazon's Web Services.

Mozilla is more than an alternative web browser—it's also a platform for building applications. It has a built-in XML-based format for defining application interfaces called XUL (XML-based User-interface Language). When you combine the tag-based XUL with JavaScript and Mozilla's built-in components, you have a cross-platform development environment perfect for building web applications.

This hack provides an interface for searching Amazon. The XUL defines a simple search form, a space for search results (called a *tree*), and an HTML iframe for viewing the product detail pages of search results.

The Code

The first part of the application is the XUL file itself. Beyond defining the interface, it holds the code that contacts Amazon to perform the search. When you click the Search button, the `doSearch( )` function is triggered. This fetches the search results from Amazon and puts them in the search results tree. The other function, `displayItem( )`, runs when an individual item in the search results is clicked. It sets the HTML iframe location URL to the product detail page for that item (formatted with your associate tag, of course).

Save this code in a file called *hack.xul*.

```
<?xml version="1.0" encoding="UTF-8"?>

<!-- ***** BEGIN LICENSE BLOCK *****
- Version: MPL 1.1/GPL 2.0/LGPL 2.1
-
- The contents of this file are subject to the Mozilla Public License
- Version 1.1 (the "License"); you may not use this file except in
- compliance with the License. You may obtain a copy of the License at
- http://www.mozilla.org/MPL/
-
- Software distributed under the License is distributed on an "AS IS"
- basis, WITHOUT WARRANTY OF ANY KIND, either express or implied. See the
- License for the specific language governing rights and limitations under
- the License.
-
- The Original Code is Mozilla XUL Amazon Hack.
-
- The Initial Developer of the Original Code is America Online, Inc.
- Portions created by the Initial Developer are Copyright (C) 2003
- the Initial Developer. All Rights Reserved.
-
- Contributor(s): Myk Melez <myk@mozilla.org>
```

```
-                   Paul Bausch <pb@onfocus.com>
-
- Alternatively, the contents of this file may be used under the terms of
- either the GNU General Public License Version 2 or later (the "GPL"), or
- the GNU Lesser General Public License Version 2.1 or later (the "LGPL"),
- in which case the provisions of the GPL or the LGPL are applicable
- instead of those above. If you wish to allow use of your version of this
- file only under the terms of either the GPL or the LGPL, and not to
- allow others to use your version of this file under the terms of the
- MPL, indicate your decision by deleting the provisions above and replace
- them with the notice and other provisions required by the LGPL or the
- GPL. If you do not delete the provisions above, a recipient may use your
- version of this file under the terms of any one of the MPL, the GPL or
- the LGPL.
-
- ***** END LICENSE BLOCK ***** -->

<?xml-stylesheet href="chrome://global/skin/" type="text/css"?>

<window xmlns="http://www.mozilla.org/keymaster/gatekeeper/there.is.↵
only.xul">

  <script type="application/x-javascript">
  <![CDATA[
    const ASSOC_ID = "insert associate tag";
    const DEV_TOKEN = "insert developer token";

  // The base URL for all searches done by this application.
  // http://.../rdf.xsl is an XSLT stylesheet that converts Amazon results
  // into RDF for consumption by this application's XUL tree template.
  // "ct=application/xml" specifies that Amazon should return the results
  // with that content type, which is necessary for Mozilla to recognize
  // them as RDF.
  const AWS_URL_BASE = "http://xml.amazon.com/onca/xml3?t=" + ASSOC_ID +
                       "&dev-t=" + DEV_TOKEN +
                       "&type=lite&ct=application/xml&locale=us" +
                       "&f=http://www.melez.com/mozilla/amazon/rdf.xsl";

  function doSearch( ) {
    // Construct a REST (XML over HTTP) URL for executing the search
    // and retrieving the results.
    var cat = document.getElementById('search-catalog').value;
    var fld = document.getElementById('search-field').value;
    var str = document.getElementById('search-string').value;
    var url = AWS_URL_BASE + "&mode=" + cat + "&" + fld + "Search=" + str;

 // Request access to Mozilla's component architecture so we can do things
 // that would normally be restricted.

netscape.security.PrivilegeManager.enablePrivilege("UniversalXPConnect");

 // Use Mozilla's REST API to execute the search and retrieve the results.
```

```
// Afterwards we'll use the RDF parser to parse them into a data source.
// We should be able to use Mozilla's RDF loader to do both retrieval
// and parsing in a single call, but the loader requires the server
// to return data as text/xml or application/xml, and a bug in Amazon's
// web services API causes data to be returned as type "$ctype"
// when you override the default "text/html" using the "ct" parameter,
// so we work around the problem by doing the retrieval ourselves.
     var request = new XMLHttpRequest( );
     request.open("GET", url, false);
     request.send(null);
     var results = request.responseText;

// Create an RDF/XML data source into which the results will be parsed.
     var ds = Components
            .classes["@mozilla.org/rdf/datasource;1?name=xml-datasource"]
            .createInstance(Components.interfaces.nsIRDFDataSource);

// Create a URI object representing the base URI of the RDF data source.
// This URI gets used by the parser when parsing relative URIs
// in the search results.
     var ioService = Components
                       .classes["@mozilla.org/network/io-service;1"]
                         .getService(Components.interfaces.nsIIOService);
     var uri = ioService.newURI(url, null, null);

// Create an RDF/XML parser.
     var parser = Components
                 .classes["@mozilla.org/rdf/xml-parser;1"]
                 .createInstance(Components.interfaces.nsIRDFXMLParser);

// Parse the results, adding them to the data source.
     parser.parseString(ds, uri, results);

// Add the data source to the tree's database (collection of data sources)
// and rebuild the tree, which populates it with the items in the data
// source.
     var tree = document.getElementById('results-tree');
     tree.database.AddDataSource(ds);
     tree.builder.rebuild( );
   }

    function displayItem( ) {
   // Get the URL (on the Amazon web site) of the currently selected item.
     var tree = document.getElementById('results-tree');
     var items = tree.getElementsByTagName('treeitem');
     var selectedItem = tree.currentIndex+1;
     var selectedItemURL = items[selectedItem].id;

     // Load the URL in the iframe widget.
     var browser = document.getElementById('item-browser');
     browser.setAttribute('src', selectedItemURL);
   }
  ]]>
```

```
  </script>

  <toolbar align="center">
    <label control="search-catalog" value="Find"/>
    <menulist id="search-catalog" persist="value">
      <menupopup>
        <menuitem label="Apparel" value="apparel" />
        <menuitem label="Baby" value="baby" />
        <menuitem label="Books" value="books" />
        <menuitem label="Classical Music" value="classical" />
        <menuitem label="DVD" value="dvd" />
        <menuitem label="Electronics" value="electronics" />
        <menuitem label="Outdoor Living" value="garden" />
        <menuitem label="Kitchen &amp; Housewares" value="kitchen" />
        <menuitem label="Magazines" value="magazines" />
        <menuitem label="Popular Music" value="music" />
        <menuitem label="Computers" value="pc-hardware" />
        <menuitem label="Camera &amp; Photo" value="photo" />
        <menuitem label="Software" value="software" />
        <menuitem label="Toys &amp; Games" value="toys" />
        <menuitem label="Tools &amp; Hardware" value="universal" />
        <menuitem label="Video" value="vhs" />
        <menuitem label="Computer &amp; Video Games" value="videogames" />
      </menupopup>
    </menulist>
    <label control="search-field" value="whose"/>
    <menulist id="search-field" persist="value">
      <menupopup>
        <menuitem label="Keyword" value="Keyword" />
        <menuitem label="Author" value="Author" />
        <menuitem label="Artist" value="Artist" />
        <menuitem label="Actor" value="Actor" />
        <menuitem label="Director" value="Director" />
        <menuitem label="Manufacturer" value="Manufacturer" />
        <menuitem label="UPC Code" value="Upc" />
      </menupopup>
    </menulist>
    <label control="search-string" value="is like"/>
    <textbox id="search-string" type="text" size="30" persist="value"
      onkeypress="if (event.keyCode == KeyEvent.DOM_VK_ENTER || ↵
event.keyCode == KeyEvent.DOM_VK_RETURN) doSearch();" />
    <button id="search-button" label="Search" oncommand="doSearch();" />
  </toolbar>

  <tree id="results-tree" flex="1" enableColumnDrag="true" ↵
onselect="displayItem();"
        datasources="rdf:null" ref="urn:amazon:ProductInfo" >↵
    <treecols>
      <treecol id="ProductName_column" label="Product" primary="true"
flex="6" persist="width hidden ordinal" />
      <splitter class="tree-splitter"/>
      <treecol id="Authors_column" label="Authors" flex="3"
        persist="width hidden ordinal" />
```

```
      <splitter class="tree-splitter"/>
      <treecol id="ReleaseDate_column" label="Release Date" flex="1"
persist="width hidden ordinal" />
      <splitter class="tree-splitter"/>
      <treecol id="Manufacturer_column" label="Manufacturer" flex="1"
persist="width hidden ordinal" />
      <splitter class="tree-splitter"/>
      <treecol id="ListPrice_column" label="List Price" flex="1"
persist="width hidden ordinal" />
      <splitter class="tree-splitter"/>
      <treecol id="OurPrice_column" label="Our Price" flex="1"
persist="width hidden ordinal" />
      <splitter class="tree-splitter"/>
      <treecol id="UsedPrice_column" label="Used Price" flex="1"
persist="width hidden ordinal" />
      <splitter class="tree-splitter"/>
      <treecol id="Catalog_column" label="Catalog" flex="1"
        persist="width hidden ordinal" />
      <splitter class="tree-splitter"/>
      <treecol id="Asin_column" label="Asin" flex="1"
persist="width hidden ordinal" />
    </treecols>
    <template>
      <rule>
        <conditions>
          <content uri="?uri" />
          <triple subject="?uri" predicate="http://xml.amazon.com/schemas2/
dev-lite.xsdDetails" object="?Details" />
          <member container="?Details" child="?item" />
        </conditions>
        <bindings>
          <binding subject="?item" predicate="http://xml.amazon.com/↵
schemas2/dev-lite.xsdProductName" object="?ProductName" />
          <binding subject="?item" predicate="http://xml.amazon.com/↵
schemas2/dev-lite.xsdAuthors" object="?Authors" />
          <binding subject="?item" predicate="http://xml.amazon.com/↵
schemas2/dev-lite.xsdReleaseDate" object="?ReleaseDate" />
          <binding subject="?item" predicate="http://xml.amazon.com/↵
schemas2/dev-lite.xsdManufacturer" object="?Manufacturer" />
          <binding subject="?item" predicate="http://xml.amazon.com/↵
schemas2/dev-lite.xsdListPrice" object="?ListPrice" />
          <binding subject="?item" predicate="http://xml.amazon.com/↵
schemas2/dev-lite.xsdOurPrice" object="?OurPrice" />
          <binding subject="?item" predicate="http://xml.amazon.com/↵
schemas2/dev-lite.xsdUsedPrice" object="?UsedPrice" />
          <binding subject="?item" predicate="http://xml.amazon.com/↵
schemas2/dev-lite.xsdCatalog" object="?Catalog" />
          <binding subject="?item" predicate="http://xml.amazon.com/↵
schemas2/dev-lite.xsdAsin" object="?Asin" />
        </bindings>
        <action>
          <treechildren>
            <treeitem uri="?item">
```

```
                <treerow>
                <treecell ref="ProductName_column" label="?ProductName" />
                <treecell ref="Authors_column" label="?Authors" />
                <treecell ref="ReleaseDate_column" label="?ReleaseDate" />
                <treecell ref="Manufacturer_column" label="?Manufacturer" />
                <treecell ref="ListPrice_column" label="?ListPrice" />
                <treecell ref="OurPrice_column" label="?OurPrice" />
                <treecell ref="UsedPrice_column" label="?UsedPrice" />
                <treecell ref="Catalog_column" label="?Catalog" />
                <treecell ref="Asin_column" label="?Asin" />
                </treerow>
              </treeitem>
            </treechildren>
          </action>

        </rule>
      </template>
    </tree>

    <splitter collapse="after" state="open" persist="state">
       <grippy/>
    </splitter>

    <iframe id="item-browser" src="about:blank" flex="2" persist="height" />

  </window>
```

Because the doSearch( ) function is expecting the XML in RDF (Resource Description Framework) format, the other piece of this application is an XSL stylesheet to transform Amazon's XML into RDF. Create a file called *rdf.xsl* with the following code:

```
<?xml version="1.0" encoding="UTF-8" ?>
<xsl:stylesheet xmlns:xsl="http://www.w3.org/1999/XSL/Transform"
  version="1.0" xmlns:rdf="http://www.w3.org/1999/02/22-rdf-syntax-ns#"
  xmlns="http://xml.amazon.com/schemas2/dev-lite.xsd">
  <xsl:strip-space elements="*" />
  <xsl:output indent="yes" media-type="application/xml" />
<xsl:template match="/">
<rdf:RDF xmlns:rdf="http://www.w3.org/1999/02/22-rdf-syntax-ns#"
xmlns="http://xml.amazon.com/schemas2/dev-lite.xsd">
  <xsl:apply-templates />
</rdf:RDF>
</xsl:template>

<xsl:template match="ProductInfo">
<ProductInfo rdf:about="urn:amazon:ProductInfo">
 <Details>
 <rdf:Seq>
  <xsl:apply-templates />
 </rdf:Seq>
 </Details>
</ProductInfo>
```

```
</xsl:template>

<xsl:template match="Details">
<rdf:li>
  <rdf:Description rdf:about="{@url}">
   <xsl:for-each select="./*">
    <xsl:element name="{name( )}">
      <xsl:value-of select="." />
    </xsl:element>
   </xsl:for-each>
  </rdf:Description>
</rdf:li>
</xsl:template>

<xsl:template match="TotalResults" />
<xsl:template match="TotalPages" />

</xsl:stylesheet>
```

This stylesheet transforms the standard Amazon lite XML results into RDF, which allows the code in *hack.xul* to use Mozilla's built-in RDF parser to work with the results. Amazon's XSLT service makes the transformation an easy process. The reference to the stylesheet is set when the search is made at Amazon with the `f=` variable.

If the thought of typing all this is leaving you cold, it's all available along with the rest of this book's code at *http://www.oreilly.com/catalog/amazonhks/*.

Running the Hack

Once you've saved *hack.xul*, you can run it by double-clicking the file. It will open Mozilla and bring up the search interface, as you see in Figure 6-11.

If you want to run this application on a remote server instead of locally, you'll need to set your web server to send the proper content type for XUL files. Add a MIME type entry for XUL files that sends `application/vnd.mozilla.xul+xml` as the content type to get it working.

—*Myk Melez*

#98 Search or Browse Amazon with Watson

You can use Watson's interface to find items at Amazon or integrate Amazon's data into other Mac applications.

An alternative way to access Amazon.com if you're a Mac user is to use Watson, from Karelia Software. Watson is a "Swiss army knife" of over 20 tools that access the most useful web services. Along with movie and TV list-

Figure 6-11. Mozilla search application

ings, package tracking, telephone lookup, weather forecasts, online recipes, searching, translation, and more, Watson also features a tool for browsing and searching Amazon.com through their API.

Watson's Amazon.com tool is divided into four sections, organized vertically (see Figure 6-12). At the top of the window (below the optional toolbar for easy access to other tools) is the search field. The user selects which "store" to search within, or a particular aspect of the selected store (such as searching by ASIN or UPC number, actor or director, etc.), enters a search term, and clicks the Find button.

The second section is the browser, which allows the user to browse the store hierarchically. The main stores appear in the leftmost column, and as the user selects an item, the columns to the right populate with lists of subcategories.

The third section is the result list, displaying either the search results or the featured items for a selected category. Only 10 items are loaded at a time; pressing the down arrow below the list will append another "page" to the list. Select an item in the list and press the "Buy selected items from Amazon.com" button to add it to your shopping cart.

Finally, the "drawer" below displays details about the item currently selected in the results list. On the left, a thumbnail of the item is displayed;

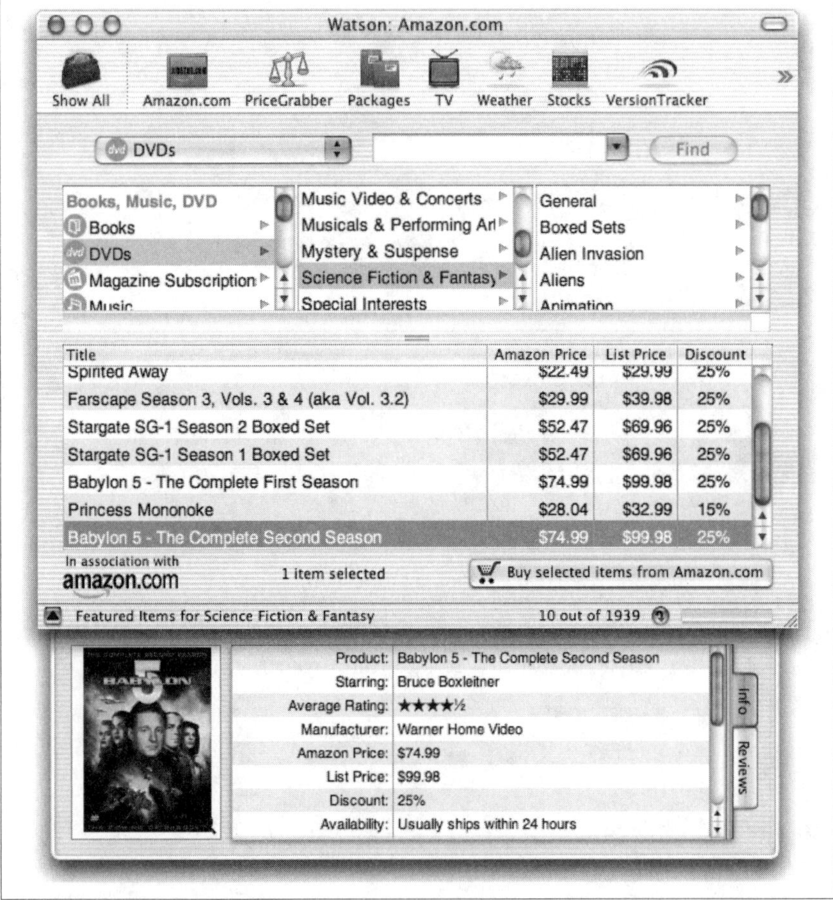

Figure 6-12. Amazon and Watson integration

click the little magnifying glass icon to pop up a larger version of the image. A list of details about the selected item alternates with a list of reviews for the product.

Integrate with Other Tools

Watson's Amazon.com tool provides a number of ways to export data. Details about the selected item can be copied to the clipboard and pasted as text. The user can also drag out from the thumbnail image to export additional textual details (if dragged onto a text editor) or the large version of the image (if dragged onto the Mac's desktop or a graphics program, or even onto iTunes 4 to fill in the album cover art as you see in Figure 6-13).

Figure 6-13. Amazon data from Watson integrating with iTunes

Similarly, Figure 6-14 shows dragging the image into Spring from UserCreations to instantiate a "Spring Object" of that project.

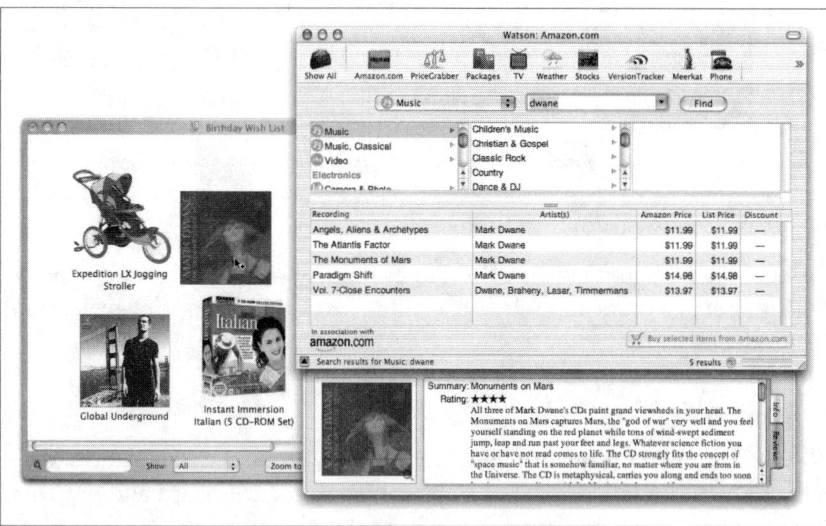

Figure 6-14. Amazon data from Watson integrating with Spring

How It Works

The Amazon.com tool on Watson depends mostly on Amazon Web Services. Mac OS X Version 10.2 and up contains built-in support for Web Services through SOAP, since it was built under (and is still compatible with) earlier versions of Mac OS X. However, Watson instead uses the simple XML/HTTP interface to get the XML data, and then parses the XML to populate the user interface.

One major aspect of the tool that doesn't use Web Services is the category-browsing capability. The Browse IDs **[Hack #8]** for the subcategories of a given category are obtained by scraping Amazon's site. When the user clicks on a category in the browser to load up the subcategories, an HTML page that contains the list of subcategories is loaded. The list of subcategories is parsed, and the list of Browse IDs is cached for two weeks.

—*Dan Wood*

#99 Add Cover Art to Your Digital Music Collection

Add cover art back into your music experience with MP3 Piranha.

If you've moved from listening to CDs to listening to MP3 files on your computer, you're probably missing some of the fun of CDs. MP3 files don't provide the original album cover art or release date information. Using Amazon's Web Services, a tool from CapeScience (*http://www.capescience.com*) can add some extra information while you're browsing your MP3 files.

MP3 Piranha (*http://www.capescience.com/piranha/*) is a Java application that queries Amazon for information about your digital music files. MP3s store metadata in *ID3 tags* (at the end of the MP3 file) that contain a file's title, artist, album name, release date, genre, track number, and so on. This is the way that many MP3 players automatically know the track name, artist name, and other information about the song.

The first step in developing Piranha was to generate a Java client from the Amazon WSDL file using Cape Clear Studio. WSDL files are machine-readable XML files that describe all of the SOAP methods available at a particular service. This provided the skeleton code, which was then modified to incorporate a graphical user interface. The client uses Amazon's SOAP interface to invoke Web Service methods.

In addition to AWS, MP3 Piranha relies on an open source Java library called *Java MP3Info*. MP3Info is a set of Java classes that can read from and write ID3 tags. More information on this library can be found at *http://sourceforge.net/projects/mp3info/*.

The Cape Clear–generated clients create a proxy object, which makes it easy to call Web Service methods exposed by Amazon:

```
//create a client proxy
AmazonSearchBindingClient client = AmazonSearchBindingClientFactory.↵
create( );
```

Using Piranha, you can browse to an MP3 file using the client provided. Piranha reads ID3 metadata from the file and queries Amazon for the artist information found in the tag, supplying the other parameters required by Amazon's `ArtistSearch` method:

```
//perform an ArtistSearch
ArtistInfo artistInfo = client.ArtistSearchRequest(new ArtistRequest↵
(artist, page, "", associateId, "lite", devToken, ""));
```

Alternatively, you can search for an artist by typing the artist's name into a text box.

Each album that the artist has recorded is downloaded at once and stored in a Java list. Storing all the information on the client side from the outset eliminates the need for sending further queries to Amazon about that artist. The list contains information such as the album title, release date, and URL to the album cover art on Amazon's site. All this data is used to build a table that can be sorted in various ways. For example, you could view an artist's albums in alphabetical order (as in Figure 6-15) or chronological order by release date.

In addition, when you select an item in the table, Piranha fetches the cover art for the album and displays it. The cover art image also acts as a link to the purchase page for the item. Clicking on it will open the purchase page in your default browser so that you can get more information on the title or buy it directly from Amazon.

Also, when you select an album in the table and click the "view albums similar to" button, Piranha performs a similarity search based on the ASIN for that product:

```
//perform SimilaritySearch
SimilarInfo similarInfo = client.SimilaritySearchRequest(new ↵
SimilarityRequest(asin, "", associateId, "lite", devToken, ""));
```

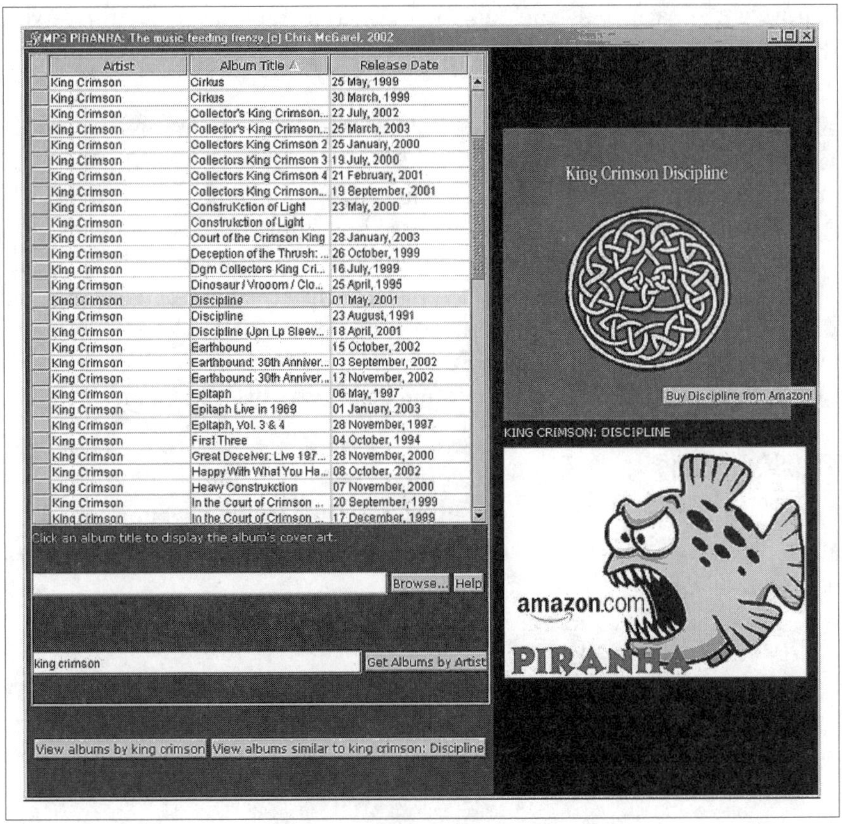

Figure 6-15. MP3 Piranha list sorted by album title

By joining together media file metadata with Amazon's Web Services, MP3 Piranha has added a new way to browse your music files and potentially find new music in the process.

—Chris McGarel

#100 Using All Consuming's SOAP and REST Interfaces

You can retrieve a list of the most-mentioned books in the weblog community, as well as personal book lists and recommendations, through either of All Consuming's two Web Service APIs.

This hack could represent the future of web applications. It glues together pieces of several Web Service APIs, and then in turn offers an API to its features. If someone were to create a derivative application with this API, it would represent a third layer of abstraction from Amazon's service. Entire lightweight services may someday be built layer upon layer like this—with dozens of interconnected applications exchanging data freely behind the scenes.

All Consuming **[Hack #47]** is a fairly small application built on top of a mountain of information that has been made freely available through Web Services. Amazon's Web Services fuel the invaluable book information, Google's API allows me to get related web sites for book titles, and weblogs.com has an XML file that lets me know which web sites have been updated each hour. Combining these three services, I can create lists of books that are being talked about on the Web. It only makes sense for me to give back to this generous community by opening up SOAP and REST interfaces to All Consuming's information, to be used for free and in any way that can be invented.

The SOAP Code

Here's an example of how you can access All Consuming information on your own using SOAP and Perl **[Hack #88]**. Create a file called *display_weekly_list_with_soap.cgi*:

```
#!/usr/bin/perl -w
# display_weekly_list_with_soap.cgi

use strict;
my ($hour,$day,$month,$year) = qw( 12 05 28 2003 );

use SOAP::Lite +autodispatch =>
    uri => 'http://www.allconsuming.net/AllConsumngAPI',
    proxy => 'http://www.allconsuming.net/soap.cgi';

my $AllConsumingObject =
AllConsumingAPI->new(
                   $hour,  # optional
                   $day,   # optional
                   $month, # optional
                   $year   # optional
                  );
```

This creates a new object, `$AllConsumingObject`, which you can then use to retrieve the following types of data.

Most Mentioned Lists. Every hour, All Consuming crawls recently updated weblogs to see if any new books were mentioned for the first time on any given weblog. It combines this information with Amazon.com's Web Services, aggregates frequently mentioned books into hourly and weekly lists, and archives them all the way back to August 2002. `GetHourlyList` will send you the most recent hour's list information, `GetWeeklyList` will send you the most recent aggregation of all activity during the last week, and

GetArchiveList will send you the hourly or weekly list that corresponds with the date that you specified when creating the object (the $hour, $day, $month, and $year variables). For example:

```
my $HourlyData = $AllConsumingObject->GetHourlyList;
my $WeeklyData = $AllConsumingObject->GetWeeklyList;
my $ArchivedData = $AllConsumingObject->GetArchiveList;
```

Personal Book Lists. People have created their own book lists directly through All Consuming, assigning them to categories like "Currently Reading" **[Hack #48]**, "Favorite Books," and "Completed Books." Although some of these lists are available for use on other sites through other methods like JavaScript includes, if you wanted to completely integrate the "Favorite Books" list with your site, you'd have to use the SOAP or REST interfaces to do so.

```
my $CurrentlyReadingList = $AllConsumingObject->↵
GetCurrentlyReadingList('insert name');

my $FavoriteBooksList = ↵
$AllConsumingObject->GetFavoriteBooksList('insert name');

my $PurchasedBooksList = ↵
$AllConsumingObject->GetPurchasedBooksList('insert name');

my $CompletedBooksList = ↵
$AllConsumingObject->GetCompletedBooksList('insert name');
```

Book Metadata and Weblog Mentions. Some users have added valuable metadata about books, like first lines and number of pages. This is mostly for fun, and allows me to have an hourly "first line trivia" question on my home page to see if people can guess the book that a given first line comes from. In any case, if you want to retrieve book metadata for a given book, you can do so with the following method:

```
My $MetadataForBook = $AllConsumingObject->GetMetadataForBook('insert ↵
ASIN');
```

The argument passed in is the ISBN for the book you'd like to retrieve metadata from. For a list of metadata that's currently available for use, you can check out the metadata scorecard at All Consuming at *http://www.allconsuming.net/scorecard.html.*

Alternatively, if you'd like to receive a list of all the weblogs that have mentioned a particular book, you can do so using the following method:

```
My $WeblogMentionsForBook = $AllConsumingObject-> ↵
  GetWeblogMentionsForBook('insert ASIN');
```

Friends and Recommendations. All Consuming also tracks "friend relationships" between people who have marked their favorite web sites so they can keep track of what they're reading, as well as book recommendations based on the network of all those relationships. You can get a list of web sites that you or someone else has marked as a favorite, or "friend," by including your weblog URL:

```
my $Friends = $AllConsumingObject->GetFriends('insert URL');
```

And to get a list of books that all of your friends are currently reading, sorted by those that are mentioned recently and the most times, you can do this:

```
my $Recommendations = $AllConsumingObject->GetRecommendations('insert URL');
```

To iterate through the results that these methods return, you can do something like this:

```
# The array here may differ depending on the type of data
# being returned
print "Content-type: text/html\n\n";
if (ref($WeeklyData->{'asins'}) eq 'ARRAY') {
    foreach my $item (@{$WeeklyData->{'asins'}}) {
        print "<p>TITLE: $item->{'title'}<br />",
              "AUTHOR: $item->{'author'}</p>";
    }
}
```

Of course, in either of the above examples, you can change the URL passed through to any other URL. For a full list of methods that you can invoke on this object, visit the instructions (*http://allconsuming.net/news/000012.html*) and code samples (*http://allconsuming.net/soap-code-example.txt*).

The REST Code

For those who think using SOAP is overkill for simple applications like this, you can get the exact same information REST-style. Add this code to a file called *display_weekly_list_with_rest.cgi*:

```
#!/usr/bin/perl -w
# display_weekly_list_with_rest.cgi

use strict;
use LWP::Simple;
use XML::Simple;

# Any of the URLs mentioned below can replace this one
my $URLToGet = 'http://allconsuming.net/rest.cgi?weekly=1';

my $XML = get($URLToGet);
my $ParsedXML = XMLin($XML, suppressempty => 1);
print "Content-type: text/html\n\n";
```

```
# The array here may differ depending on the type of data
# being returned
if (ref($ParsedXML->{'asins'}) eq 'ARRAY') {
  foreach my $item (@{$ParsedXML->{'asins'}}) {
     print "<p>TITLE: $item->{'title'}<br />", "AUTHOR: ↵
$item->{'author'}</p>";
  }
}
```

Here's a list of the URL formats you can access via HTTP to return XML data directly.

Most-Mentioned Lists. Here's the REST interface for requesting the hourly and weekly most mentioned lists:

```
http://allconsuming.net/rest.cgi?hourly=1
http://allconsuming.net/rest.cgi?weekly=1
```

If you'd like to retrieve an archived list of most-mentioned books, you can specify the date like so:

```
http://allconsuming.net/rest.cgi?archive=1&hour=12&day=12&month=5&year=2003
```

Personal Book Lists. To retrieve any of your categorized books in an XML format, add your username to any of the following URLs (note the category names):

```
http://allconsuming.net/rest.cgi?currently_reading=1&username=insert name
http://allconsuming.net/rest.cgi?favorite_books=1&username=insert name
http://allconsuming.net/rest.cgi?purchased_books=1&username=insert name
http://allconsuming.net/rest.cgi?completed_books=1&username=insert name
```

Book Metadata and Weblog Mentions. To get XML data about specific items, include the ASIN in these URLs. You can get either the item's metadata or weblog mentions:

```
http://allconsuming.net/rest.cgi?metadata=1&isbn=insert ASIN
http://allconsuming.net/rest.cgi?weblog_mentions_for_book=1&isbn=insert ASIN
```

Friends and Recommendations. To find XML data that includes friends or recommendations for a given weblog, you can include the weblog's URL in the appropriate format:

```
http://allconsuming.net/rest.cgi?friends=1&url=insert weblog URL
http://allconsuming.net/rest.cgi?recommendations=1&url=insert weblog URL
```

Running the Hack

Both of these example CGI scripts should be uploaded to your web server and called from your browser. They should display a list of titles and authors.

The returned output of both the SOAP and REST interfaces will be XML that looks something like this:

```
<opt>
  <header
    lastBuildDate="Sat May 28 13:30:02 2003"
    title="All Consuming"
    language="en-us"
    description="Most recent books being talked about by webloggers."
    link="http://allconsuming.net/"
    number_updated="172"
  />
  <asins
    asin="0465045669"
    title="Metamagical Themas"
    author="Douglas R. Hofstadter"
    url="http://www.erikbenson.com/"
    image="http://images.amazon.com/images/P/0465045669.01.THUMBZZZ.jpg"
    excerpt="Douglas Hoftstadter's lesser-known book, Metamagical Themas,
has a great chapter or two on self-referential sentences like 'This sentence
was in the past tense.'."
    amazon_url="http://amazon.com/exec/obidos/ASIN/0465045669/"
    allconsuming_url="http://allconsuming.net/item.cgi?id=0465045669"
  />
</opt>
```

If multiple items are returned, there will be multiple `<asins />` elements.

Hacking the Hack

Although All Consuming currently surfaces only book trends, it also stores information about other types of items available at Amazon like CDs, DVDs, and electronics. You can't find this information anywhere on All Consuming's site, but if you use either of the APIs to retrieve weblog mentions for an ASIN that belongs to another product category, All Consuming will faithfully return any weblog data that it has for that item.

—Erik Benson

Index

Numbers

A

B

J

K

L

M

N

P

Q

R

S

T

U

V

W

X

Y

Z

Colophon

Our look is the result of reader comments, our own experimentation, and feedback from distribution channels. Distinctive covers complement our distinctive approach to technical topics, breathing personality and life into potentially dry subjects.

The tool on the cover of *Amazon Hacks* is a machete. The machete is a cleaver-like knife that is normally used to clear land or cut a path through thick vegetation. Unfortunately, it can also be used as a weapon.

Emily Quill was the production editor and copyeditor for *Amazon Hacks*. Melanie Wang was the proofreader. Colleen Gorman, Sarah Sherman, and Claire Cloutier provided quality control. Jamie Peppard and Mary Agner provided production assistance. Tom Dinse and Johnna VanHoose Dinse wrote the index.

Hanna Dyer designed the cover of this book, based on a series design by Edie Freedman. The cover image is an original photograph by Ellie Volckhausen. Emma Colby produced the cover layout with QuarkXPress 4.1 using Adobe's Helvetica Neue and ITC Garamond fonts.

David Futato designed the interior layout. This book was converted by Andrew Savikas to FrameMaker 5.5.6 with a format conversion tool created by Erik Ray, Jason McIntosh, Neil Walls, and Mike Sierra that uses Perl and XML technologies. The text font is Linotype Birka; the heading font is Adobe Helvetica Neue Condensed; and the code font is LucasFont's TheSans Mono Condensed. The illustrations that appear in the book were produced by Robert Romano and Jessamyn Read using Macromedia FreeHand 9 and Adobe Photoshop 6. This colophon was written by Emily Quill.

How to stay in touch with O'Reilly

1. Visit our award-winning web site

http://www.oreilly.com/

★ "Top 100 Sites on the Web"—PC Magazine
★ CIO Magazine's Web Business 50 Awards

Our web site contains a library of comprehensive product information (including book excerpts and tables of contents), downloadable software, background articles, interviews with technology leaders, links to relevant sites, book cover art, and more. File us in your bookmarks or favorites!

2. Join our email mailing lists

Sign up to get email announcements of new books and conferences, special offers, and O'Reilly Network technology newsletters at:

http://elists.oreilly.com

It's easy to customize your free elists subscription so you'll get exactly the O'Reilly news you want.

3. Get examples from our books

To find example files for a book, go to:

http://www.oreilly.com/catalog

select the book, and follow the "Examples" link.

4. Work with us

Check out our web site for current employment opportunites:

http://jobs.oreilly.com/

5. Register your book

Register your book at:

http://register.oreilly.com

6. Contact us

O'Reilly & Associates, Inc.
1005 Gravenstein Hwy North
Sebastopol, CA 95472 USA
TEL: 707-827-7000 or 800-998-9938
(6am to 5pm PST)
FAX: 707-829-0104

order@oreilly.com
For answers to problems regarding your order or our products. To place a book order online visit:

http://www.oreilly.com/order_new/

catalog@oreilly.com
To request a copy of our latest catalog.

booktech@oreilly.com
For book content technical questions or corrections.

corporate@oreilly.com
For educational, library, government, and corporate sales.

proposals@oreilly.com
To submit new book proposals to our editors and product managers.

international@oreilly.com
For information about our international distributors or translation queries. For a list of our distributors outside of North America check out:

http://international.oreilly.com/distributors.html

adoption@oreilly.com
For information about academic use of O'Reilly books, visit:

http://academic.oreilly.com